T0367200

LUBITSCH CAN'T WAIT

Lubitsch Can't Wait

A Theoretical Examination

EDITED BY IVANA NOVAK, JELA KREČIČ,
AND MLADEN DOLAR

SLOVENIAN CINEMATHEQUE, LJUBLJANA

Slovenian Cinematheque, Miklošičeva cesta 28, 1000 Ljubljana, Slovenia

info@kinoteka.si

Slovenian Cinematheque is the national museum with responsibility to research, conserve and present film heritage in the public interest. The Cinematheque and its publications are supported by the Ministry of Culture of the Republic of Slovenia.

All rights reserved.

Moral rights of the authors have been asserted.

Distributed by Columbia University Press

Design, cover, and layout: Maja Rebov

Printed in Ljubljana by Mat-Format

The illustration appearing on the inside cover was captured from *Als ich tot war* (Ernst Lubitsch, 1915), Slovenian Cinematheque Archive.

CIP - Cataloguing-In-Publication

National and University Library, Ljubljana

791.633-051(73):929Lubitsch E.(082)

   LUBITSCH can't wait : a theoretical examination / edited by Ivana Novak, Jela Krečič, and Mladen Dolar. - 1st English ed. - Ljubljana : Slovenian Cinematheque, 2014

   ISBN 978-961-6417-84-6

1. Lubitsch, Ernst 2. Novak, Ivana

268975104

Contents

vii   **Preface**

1   **Ivana Novak and Jela Krečič**
Introduction: The Importance of Being Ernst

19   **Aaron Schuster**
Comedy in Times of Austerity

39   **Russell Grigg**
The Joyful Art of Ernst Lubitsch: *Trouble in Paradise*

65   **Robert Pfaller**
What is so Funny About Multiple Love? The Polygamous Lubitsch Touch

83   **Tatjana Jukić**
Garbo Laughs: Revolution and Melancholia in Lubitsch's *Ninotchka*

111   **Mladen Dolar**
To Be or Not to Be? No, Thank You

131   **Elisabeth Bronfen**
Lubitsch's War: Comedy as Political Ploy in *To Be or Not to Be*

151   **Gregor Moder**
The Beard, the Bust, and the Plumed Helmet

165   **Alenka Zupančič**
Squirrels to the Nuts, or, How Many Does it Take to Not Give up on Your Desire?

181   **Slavoj Žižek**
Lubitsch, The Poet of Cynical Wisdom?

206   Contributors
208   Index

Ernst Lubitsch, 1920

PREFACE

In his time, during the 1930s and '40s, Ernst Lubitsch was one of the biggest shots in Hollywood, instantly recognizable as a figurehead by his verve and inimitable style. A master of cinema direction and narrative, a lively mentor and driving force, he was reputedly the founder of vintage genres such as the "romantic comedy" and the musical. His influence on the development of cinema was immense.

So what happened since? There is an enigma attached to his fate and the fate of his work. How come there are dozens upon dozens of volumes on all the major Hollywood figures—Hitchcock or Chaplin, say—but so little literature on Lubitsch? How come Lubitsch is highly appreciated only by cinema aficionados, while his name remains largely unknown to the general public? How come even educated cinema audiences are nowadays so surprised and shocked when they see a Lubitsch movie for the first time, that it comes to them as a revelation?

The point of this collected volume is not to set the historical record straight and do justice to a forgotten genius—let the film historians take care of that. None of the contributors to this volume is a film historian; they all come from philosophy, the humanities, or the social sciences, and they take Lubitsch as a privileged interlocutor for the pressing concerns of their fields. The ambition of this collection is far beyond the scope of film theory or history. *Lubitsch Can't Wait*—the title is calqued on that of one of his most successful comedies, *Heaven Can Wait* (1943). Lubitsch *can't* wait because his oeuvre addresses the pressing issues of his time in ways that are directly relevant to ours, and that touch upon large questions about the nature of art, politics, love, and the elementary driving forces of the psychic and the social.

No doubt the disregard for Lubitsch's work is due to the general disregard for the particular genre in which he excelled, that of comedy, which is still largely frowned upon as a lower kind of art, a pastime or mere entertainment. Hegel, alone among philosophers, considered comedy the highest form of art, and the new theoretical approaches aiming to rehabilitate the tradition of comedy and show the profound seriousness of the comical, its critical subversive potential, will have to pass through Lubitsch—its lucid and sublime grandmaster. Comedy, properly practiced, is never intended merely to provide comic relief. Here one can do no better than quote Lubitsch himself: "I was tired of the two established, recognized recipes, drama with comedy relief, and comedy with dramatic relief. I made up my mind to make a picture with no attempt to relieve anybody from anything, at any time."[1] When the true spirit of comedy is at work, there is no relief from relief—it is a relentless relief that goes straight to the core of the subject and the social.

The cinematography of Ernst Lubitsch is not intended to serve simply as an example—as empirical material through which philosophers might test their claims and illustrate their theoretical propositions known in advance. Rather, it is approached as a body of work that opens up an entirely new field of reflection on the subject of comedy and the concepts it implicates. Lubitsch's opus is also treated here as raising a series of critical questions concerning cinematic form and practice, and although the present volume has no ambition to cover his entire oeuvre or provide a systematic account of his art (it focuses in particular on his Hollywood comedies), we can nevertheless describe its trajectory as a sorely needed attempt at a "return to Lubitsch." Indeed, it would be no exaggeration to say that all the contributors to this volume share the premise that Lubitsch is the author of one of the most important and foundational comic opuses that we have at our disposal. Perhaps the sharpened articulation of Lubitsch's masterpieces provided by the texts in this collection is especially welcome in our time, when traces of comic spirit in cinema have become increasingly rare, despite the vast quantity of short-lived comic reliefs.

This volume includes revised and expanded versions of lectures presented at a symposium on Ernst Lubitsch entitled "First as Comedy, Then as Farce," held

---

1   Quoted in Peter Barnes, *To Be or Not to Be* (London: BFI, 2002), 55.

at Slovenian Cinematheque in October 2012. The Cinematheque has since its foundation been very closely connected to Lubitsch. By sheer coincidence, the sole existing copy of Lubitsch's early movie, *When I Was Dead* (*Als ich tot war*, 1915) was found and identified in the early 1990s in Slovenia and presented in 1994 at the foundation of the new Cinematheque (after the disintegration of Yugoslavia). This silent German comedy, which had for a long time been presumed lost, is the oldest preserved film we have by Lubitsch. We hope that the present volume may be true to the spirit of this lost and found "origin," and that it may instigate a new field of "Lubitsch studies."

The editors would like to thank the Slovenian Cinematheque for making this event possible, in particular Ivan Nedoh, its director, and Jurij Meden, who also gave us great support and guidance in the preparation of the English edition. We would like to express special gratitude to Tim Clark for his effective and reliable copy-editing.

The Editors

IVANA NOVAK AND JELA KREČIČ

Introduction:
The Importance of Being Ernst

The Lubitsch affair first appears as a problem of translation. The famous Lubitsch touch (the motto under which his films were publicized and which cinema theory gladly appropriated) is a kind of original cypher which cannot be properly translated into other languages. *Touch* refers to the author's signature or mark, but also connotes the lightness and elegance that are the most basic thematic and stylistic features of Lubitsch's work. "Cypher" indicates that Lubitsch did something that very few other directors were capable of doing: he avoided the standard ("spontaneous," clichéd) approach to his topics and thus already at a formal-structural level undermined naturalism. We may not know exactly what Lubitsch is, but we know very well what he isn't: a naturalist. Aaron Schuster, whose contribution to this volume considers Lubitsch's work in the light of Lacan's notion of style, makes this point beautifully: "Never say anything directly when a good metaphor will do." He thereby reverses the standard perspective according to which simplicity and immediacy are considered the best ways to convey something. *Where's the fun in that?*, we might ask. And, above all, is there such a thing as pure immediacy at all? Thus we begin with Lubitsch's first lesson: that language is not to be taken as a medium for expressing inner psychic states—rather, language holds in its grasp both its content and its speakers.

No wonder, then, that Lubitsch was a great lover of jokes: jokes bear witness to our inextricable entanglement in language, in the symbolic order, since the technique of the joke consists precisely in transforming words and their established meanings. We could say that Lubitsch enforced this principle of transformation at the level of cinematic representation: he did not show things directly.

In his musical *Monte Carlo* (1930), Lubitsch pushed this rejection of immediacy so far that he based the entire plot on the form of a riddle. Even if this form is not what Lubitsch is best known for, the example calls for comment. The story tells of a young girl who for the third time abandons her fiancé in front of the altar and leaves for Monte Carlo. On the train there, she is surprised by the conductor and, what makes the scene even funnier, she in her turn surprises him, to such an extent that he makes a riddle out of the encounter to share with the other passengers in the corridor—here is his line:

> Here's a puzzle and believe me, it's hot. She comes from a wedding, she has nothing on, she's left her husband behind, she has no ticket, she has no idea where she wants to go, and she goes to Monte Carlo. How *old* is her husband?—*Too* old.

The circumstances of the riddle are in a way inessential. The riddle accounts for the girl's story and for her "psychic economy" through condensations and displacements much more efficiently than would a standard narrative recapitulation: "I left my husband because he is boring and too old for me. / So what will you do now? / I'm on my way to Monte Carlo in search for my luck." We learn about this plot from a second-hand source: a complete stranger, the conductor, who appears in the film once only, to pass on the enigma further. Later in the film, the riddle reverberates once more when the too-old fiancé travels by train to Monte Carlo to find his runaway bride. This time, the fiancé himself naively passes on the riddle to his travel companion—initially happy to share the joke with a third party, he suddenly freezes when he realizes that the riddle is about him, that it has returned to its source, that he is himself the answer to it—the sucker both of the riddle and of the film's plot. When we first hear it, the riddle functions as a joke designed to repeat the film's basic story in an amusing way; but through its own repetition it becomes a true comic riddle. In coming back to find its addressee, it provides a purely material answer to its own question: the *too-old fiancé* who is now able to recognize himself in the riddle's otherwise universal comic truth.

The way Lubitsch operates within this minimal frame of the riddle has at least three features. First, there is definitely something naughty and farcical in the shift of narrative focus: the serious impasse faced by the woman is presented in a frivolously cynical way. The detour through the riddle functions here as a condensed principle of comedy and reflects one of its fundamental techniques: presenting the central plot as it would appear to a naive observer, ignoring information inaccessible to the latter. It elevates the fate of a woman—which might have been unique, while her life course could have been tragic—into a type or a model, one which provides the generic formula for a whole series of stories: *damsel in distress and a husband who is too old*. In whatever direction we look, comedy searches for affinities, geometric similarities, abstractions, repetitions and redoublings.[1] The texts of Mladen Dolar and Elisabeth Bronfen in this volume discuss in detail the meaning of this comedic redoubling and repetition.

The second feature that can be deduced from the scene is that, with the non-negligible help of the conductor, Lubitsch characterizes, in passing as it were, not only one but two figures: the runaway bride and her fiancé. The seemingly minor narrative mechanism thereby displays a great narrative power—sometimes "a good metaphor will do" for the articulation of a key point.

The third feature concerns the content, which turns on Lubitsch's favorite topic: love relationships both within and outside marriage, adultery, secret cravings, desire and passion. The first part of the present volume is dedicated to this most obviously Lubitschean theme: his treatment of sexuality in the wide sense of the word. Throughout his opus, Lubitsch approached sexuality in a very funny and witty way—his earliest Berlin comedies are in this respect outrightly farcical—but Lubitsch always offers something more, representing these sensitive motifs in a non-standard and often unique way.

Already with this example of the riddle we can see how Lubitsch is concerned not with the view a person has of his own situation, but with the comedic principle according to which the way a person is caught up in the field of appearances will play a crucial role in the story.

The Director of Appearance

In this respect, a scene from the comedy *One Hour With You* (1932), with one of Lubitsch's first Hollywood actors, Maurice Chevalier, is indicative. A woman and

---

[1] Another redoubling of the story occurs in the same film: the heroine realizes her fundamental deadlock while watching a performance of the operetta *Monsieur Beaucaire*, a tragic story about a princess who abandons her lover upon learning that he is a mere hairdresser, although by the end of the story we discover that he is actually a member of the aristocracy. We should mention here one of the fundamental texts on the techniques of comedy, Henri Bergson's *Laughter. An Essay On the Meaning of the Comic* (Rockville: Arc Manor Publishers, 2008). Mladen Dolar notes apropos Bergson that redoubling solicits its own multiplication: when we encounter twin brothers the situation seems to call for the appearance of another similar couple, such as twin sisters. See Mladen Dolar, "Comedy and Its Double," in Robert Pfaller (ed.), *Stop That Comedy! On the Subtle Hegemony of the Tragic in Our Culture* (Vienna: Sonderzahl, 2005), 181–209.

a man, Mitzi and Andre, both married but not to each other, accidentally find themselves in the same taxi. Their affair is set in motion by the fact that, to an imagined external observer, it seems *as if* they are lovers, although they are just sitting in the privacy of a cab. Mitzi says: "Now, do you see anything wrong with that? Two strange people of opposite sex, riding in a cab, sitting side by side ... The gentleman reading a newspaper ..." Andre laughs naively. She points her finger at him: "Explain THAT to your wife!" Andre is shocked: "She wouldn't believe it. Would you believe it?" Mitzi is sure: "Never!"

Andre cannot resist the power of appearance. Although he clearly loves his wife, the appearance of his sharing the cab with another woman is incriminating and its effects, which are quite real, cannot be erased. Mitzi does not refer here primarily to an instance which is physically present, in the sense of "if someone actually sees us now, he will automatically conclude we are having an affair." What she has in mind is more complex and calls for a notion deployed by, among others, Robert Pfaller—that of a naive observer who judges a situation not with regard to a subject's true intentions but exclusively in terms of how things appear.[2] There is more truth in the appearance than in the subject's intention; or, to put it even more pointedly, appearance is true precisely in the sense that it lies: it offers a way in which to lie with the truth. Lubitsch fully exploited this complex functioning of appearances. In a scene from the same film, for example, Mitzi's husband and the detective he has hired to prove his wife's adultery are listening to what's going on in the next room, occupied by Mitzi. When they hear her voice calling "Darling!", the husband gravely concludes: "She is lying again." The detective whispers to him: "Lie back." So the husband shouts: "Yes, dear?" Many authors in the present volume propose a more detailed analysis of Lubitsch's commitment to appearances, discerning in it the philosophical implications of his (directorial) style. What counts in his films, what pushes the stories forward, is of a distinctly comical character: while drama locates the tragic truth in the subject's intimate desire and its discrepancy with external reality, in Lubitsch's opus the unsurpassable truth appears as an intersection of appearances. Lubitsch integrates this intersection into the comic plot better than most other directors who resorted to metaphor (for example, Hitchcock, in a slightly different genre).

This naive consideration of appearances is only one of the dimensions of appearance in Lubitsch's work: we can also include in this field the particular style

---

2   See Robert Pfaller, *Das schmutzige Heilige und die reine Vernunft* (Frankfurt am Main: Fischer, 2012).

of acting in his films. A Lubitsch actor is aware that he is acting and thus enacts acting itself (thereby in a way constantly deceiving himself); this redoubled acting is sustained by the director's compliance with the meaning of tiny objects and metaphors. The first part of the present volume is dedicated to this field. In Russell Grigg's text, appearance plays a central role in relations of love and sex: he shows how *Trouble in Paradise* (1932) is proof that pretence or 'keeping up appearances' should in no way be dismissed as a deceitful or malicious pursuit—in love, the moment of pretence is necessary and brings joy. Aaron Schuster links this element to Lubitsch's narrative style of ellipses, indications, and suggestions. No wonder it was around the time that *Trouble in Paradise* was made that the expression "the Lubitsch touch" first appeared: the film provides an exemplary case of this stylistic feature, by which the most sensitive aspects of the plot are not directly revealed but rather inscribed into the world of objects. For example, Lubitsch will present the love entanglement of a couple by showing their shared breakfast, the passage of time (a clock), the closed doors of a bedroom, and so on.

The contributors to this volume advocate the idea that, by proceeding in this way, Lubitsch was not merely smuggling into the cinematic narrative prohibited ticklish motifs in the epoch of the Production Code (better known as Hays Code), which severely restricted the explicit showing of sensitive images and topics. In fact, Lubitsch's "elliptic" and "metaphoric" project had begun well before the imposition of the Code, and his emphasis upon actions which are not seen or shown was not only a naughty way of arousing the viewer's imagination but also attests to the meaning Lubitsch conferred on appearances and external manifestations. In a Lubitsch film, closed doors do not conceal some ticklish (indecent, prohibited) object, but rather suggest it: something more is taking place in the very way it appears. The style—how something appears and how it is shown—becomes the object we are looking at and, put simply, is what is most amusing in watching a Lubitsch film. This style is thus arguably the key feature of Lubitsch's approach—both the way he shows something and the way he shows it instead of something else. In some cases we are dealing merely with a witticism; in others an actual political project is implied (we will address this aspect later).

We thus touch on the ticklish subject of cinematic representation, which can perhaps best be introduced with an anecdote: Once, when sitting in a movie theater watching a graphic scene showing the operation of removing a bullet from a man's body, Lubitsch exploded: "Doesn't he know that he shouldn't show this?" We should not understand this as revealing Lubitsch as an old conservative expressing moral indignation at the direct depiction of a traumatic event, but rather in an exactly opposite sense which concerns cinematic (or, in a slightly different way, any artistic) representation. The conviction that the power of a film resides in the explicit and immediate character of what it gives us to see, or in its providing a naked view of reality, is at odds with the logic of representation. If there is something like the "film's power" it resides elsewhere, in its construction of a gaze, i.e., of what we see and what we cannot see, and, furthermore, in the mode of representation it applies when something cannot be represented. The starting point for Elisabeth Bronfen's contribution is the impossibility of representing the Real of War (war as such), a point she elaborates apropos *To Be or Not to Be* (1942). In this comedy Lubitsch deals with the topic of war but does so by intermixing two kinds of representation, theatrical and cinematic, to produce the effect of the real through this very accent on the act of representation. In the context of playing with the logic of representation and its dialectical essence, a special role is played by the comedic strategy of manipulating the phallic supplement (say, the putting on and off of the fake beard)—a feature which Gregor Moder discusses in detail in his text included here.

The Comic Equation of Love

Among other things, what makes a return to Lubitsch necessary is the fact that today's cinematography has failed to learn Lubitsch's basic lesson (in contrast to his contemporaries—Lubitsch was the master for a series of highly respected authors such as Billy Wilder, or Otto Preminger). While Lubitsch was a philosopher of appearances who took representation very seriously, contemporary cinema—and contemporary culture as such—naively believes in the thing itself beyond appearances, and, following a hidden necessity, what it finds there, at the heart of the thing, is tragedy. In his chapter in this volume—as throughout his entire work—Robert Pfaller locates a cultural paradigm shift that concerns a whole series of human practices: what predominates in today's culture is a tragic perspective which, to summarize it in a very rough way, is repelled by all the cultural levers of enjoyment: smoking, say, or socializing without benefits, or games, humor, sex, care for appearances, politeness even; all our activities are regulated by a tendency to find forms of individual and allegedly more authentic pleasure or enjoyment. What is at stake here is not only the fact that the subject, left to himself in the quest for his own authentic joys, tends to sink into sadness; such a quest also leads to a loss of the social dimension and thereby to a loss of the source of political activity. Cinematic representation has also shifted accordingly: the films which are most highly appreciated by critics are also the most tragic and dull, with no sense of humor (nor even of irony); they are indifferent towards appearances and renounce charismatic objects as well as forbidden passions, suspecting that they contain a deceptive evil component which doesn't fit the "true" state of man.

These features stand out most prominently in the domain of sex, couples, and love—Lubitsch's most popular "troika." As we have already pointed out apropos the riddle from *Monte Carlo*, Lubitsch consistently deals with sexual relations within the frame of comedy. If there is a Lubitschean principle which applies here, it is that there is no prescribed formula or mould for love: love is an equation which never turns out according to our expectations since its key ingredient is surprise. For Lubitsch, a permanent couple is mostly impossible, while love is an experience that derails, not an ideal which allocates to all its elements their proper place. Lovers are polygamous in their passion and are not committed to the search for the ultimate solution in the guise of the ideal partner; marriage (the marital link) is not the highest act of love (as is the case in today's "rom-coms"), adultery is not the greatest betrayal, and children (who are practically absent from Lubitsch's films) are not the ultimate goal of the love relationship. Lubitsch creates models which differ radically from those of today, and although they are very diverse with regard to their content, they display a structural affinity: they all extend the scope of what love is. *Design for Living* (1933) begins and ends with love in a threesome, two men and a woman. In his early comedy *I Don't Want to be a Man* (*Ich möchte kein Mann sein*, 1918), shot almost a century ago, a man falls in love with a woman when she is masked as a man, and even if we ignore the film's plot, the key scene is truly extraordinary in being totally free of all tragic or perverse connotations—it is simply a scene of two people falling in love. Love stands for a surprise, which is why we shouldn't be surprised or politically correct when we see how this formula encompasses love in both its traditional and non-traditional forms.

The models offered by Lubitsch are thus revolutionary in a structural way: the ideal of the sexual relationship is not the fusion into a harmonious One presumably embodied in the monogamous heterosexual couple, but—even when we are dealing with the couple of a man and a woman—the field of an impossible encounter. It is easy for comedy to appropriate this field, in which it can function smoothly, since it is only the comical element—the object which introduces imbalance into love—which in a way renders love possible. All that is connected with sex and love is thus for Lubitsch a riddle which never finds its "correct" answer: perhaps the only answer lies in a comic appropriation of the specified themes, in permutations and triangulations, in alternations and surprising discoveries. In other words, for Lubitsch, love is structurally a comical relationship, not a tragic one.[3]

Today, this riddle of love has become so problematic it can no longer be treated as the stuff of comedy—with some rare and precious exceptions. When dealing with sex and sexual relationships, contemporary film appears utterly grave and lacking in wit, and for this very reason putatively closer to the final intimate truth about sex and passion. Rare are the directors who deal with passion without automatically depicting its bearer as a broken subject, a victim of his own psychological splits, or a morally compromised sinner. The obvious corollary of such an approach implies something even more problematic and worthy of criticism, namely that the subject is better than his (sometimes bizarre) terrestrial passions, or that he can bring them—if, of course, he is able to control them—into a state of reconciliation, balance and harmony. Such a solution deserves a resolute "no thanks" and one can argue that there is no better model for such a rejection in the entire history of cinema than Lubitsch's opus.

This is what Slavoj Žižek considers the most valuable part of Lubitsch's legacy. Although in the majority of Lubitsch's films about the amorous couple, adultery, and marriage Žižek identifies traces of conservative transgression which serve to stabilize the normative structure of the existing order, he also discerns in some of Lubitsch's masterpieces a strategy of love for our time.

The Politics of Comedy
In contrast to the common-sense perception, a true comedy does not cushion the trouble or trauma; rather it succeeds in displacing it through its mechanisms, providing the trauma with new coordinates within which its problems acquire new meaning. Such a procedure opens up a new field of understanding of political reality, outlining the possibility of political action. Even if the topics of love, sex, couples, and gender prevail in Lubitsch's work, the contributions to this volume demonstrate that some of his masterpieces—perhaps even the greatest ones—explicitly address the political problems and crucial political deadlocks of his and also of our time. Schuster, for example, locates Lubitsch's political project along

---

3   See Alenka Zupančič, *The Odd One In: On Comedy* (Cambridge MA: MIT Press, 2008).

the axis of *Trouble in Paradise*, *Ninotchka* (1939), and *To Be or Not to Be*. Politically the most explicit as well as most engaged of these three films is *To Be or Not to Be*, a comedy about the Nazi occupation of Poland and the attempt of a Warsaw theater group to prevent the German crackdown on the resistance movement. Mladen Dolar shows apropos this film how it is possible to discern multiple levels of political gesture in Lubitsch's universe. To put it in an extremely concise way, the very fact that Lubitsch decided to shoot a comedy about the Nazis—generally perceived as a pure diabolical evil, as an invincible killing machine—is already a political gesture. In this comedy, he mercilessly makes fun of both sides, the Poles and the Nazis. The effect of this strategy is to undermine the aura of omnipotence of the allegedly strongest army in the world, and to make it appear vulnerable and weak—so weak that it can be defeated even by a clumsy group of theater people. The resort to comedy when dealing with a traumatic political situation can thus be very efficient—it can give hope, provide a momentum for resistance, and enable us to find strength in a seemingly hopeless situation.

Lubitsch's political stance is discernible already at the level of his comic strategies of redoubling and repetition. What happens when we redouble Hitler and the Gestapo officers, as Lubitsch does in *To Be or Not to Be*? As pointed out by Dolar, the original loses its power through its redoubling. Even more, redoubling blurs the boundary between the original and its imitation, so that the original starts to function as its own caricature. The copy suspends in advance the hypnotic power of the original. By means of such redoubling, Nazism appears as a pale copy of itself. Comedy puts forward repetition, réplique, which is only later followed by the original, so that when the latter appears it can only function as its own farce.

Lubitsch's political stance is most obvious in *To Be or Not to Be*, where the political struggle (against Nazism) directly occupies the narrative. In *Trouble in Paradise* as well as in *Ninotchka*, the political gesture or comment is not so obvious, since it is interlaced with the love relationship in the story's foreground. It is nonetheless impossible to ignore the fact that the historical context of the narrative of *Trouble in Paradise* is economic: the story takes place at the time of the Great Depression, amid massive unemployment and poverty. Lubitsch thus appears as a peculiar critic of political economy.

The film's two heroes, Lily and Gaston, are experienced and cunning thieves. We soon learn that Gaston is the legendary robber who entered the Bank of Constantinople and came out with the Bank of Constantinople. We could read this description as Lubitsch's comic paraphrase of Brecht's famous motto "What is the robbing of a bank compared to the founding of a new bank?" In other words, there is something daring in the very fact that two thieves figure as the film's two heroes, and thereby as the two main figures for the spectator's identification, all the more so if we take into account the fact that the film was shot at the time of the imposition of the so-called Hays Code and of the Great Depression.

The context of deep economic crisis associated with poverty, shortages, and injustice is crucial for this film. But Lubitsch's point is not simply that in times of crisis small people are justified in being resourceful and making the best of things in whatever ways they can, legal or illegal. He also deftly avoids the temptation to demonize the rich, such as the third principal character, the affluent heiress Madame Colet. Lubitsch shows how, as a rule, the greatest financial crimes are perpetrated at the very top of the social pyramid, by the wealthiest, and also how, due to the way the system works, these super-criminals will never be punished for their wrongdoings. If the presentation of systemic injustice in *Trouble in Paradise* obviously belongs to another era (in comparison to the operations of the financial sector today, the financial crimes of Lubitsch's era cannot but appear amateur), Aaron Schuster shows how the measures proposed by those in power to fight the crisis of the 1930s are fully flush with the measures advocated by companies and governments today in relation to our own crisis, and especially with the discourse used by official politics in confronting that crisis. The film plays deftly with the phrase "in times like these". During a meeting of the board of trustees of Madame Colet's company, the board members employ the phrase to justify a reduction of workers' salaries; when Madame Colet buys a wickedly expensive purse, an angry young communist berates her using the same phrase. This type of discourse, that of crisis-reaction, forcefully recalls the justification of today's austerity measures in the exact same terms.

Yet another comic effect is generated by the fact that the phrase "in times like these," intended to emphasize a period of crisis, leaves the three main characters completely indifferent, even though they also on occasion use it themselves. Each of them is simply dedicated to her or his own cause—Madame Colet, for example, to the dreamy naivety of her pleasurable life of wealth, from which the vulgar realm of economic exchange is either absent or ignored as irrelevant. She is so affluent that she can afford not to know anything about the origin and rise of her fortune, which, of course, she does not want to know anything about. When the board of trustees requires her finally to lower the wages of her workers, "in times like these," she refuses to yield to their pressure—not out of a sense of justice, but simply because these are matters she doesn't care for and doesn't want to burden herself with. In a similar way, things and their prices—the price, say, of her wickedly expensive purse—are of no concern for her, at least not in a material sense. Her indifference becomes especially palpable when, without giving the matter any deep consideration, she leaves the management of her fortune to Gaston. The comedy here draws its efficiency from this discrepancy between a rich woman indifferent towards her wealth and the actual economic predicament of the society around her.

If Madame Colet is thoroughly indifferent towards the world of things and their values, and their imbrication in the economic circuit, the two thieves (the couple Lily and Gaston) are completely drawn into this circulation—implicated in it to such an extent that they lose all distance from it. Taking possession of things by robbery impregnates their entire life: it is their professional passion; but, as noted by several authors, it is also their mode of functioning in love.

Wherein, then, lies the subversive character of Lubitsch's confrontation with capitalism? Already at the level of its mechanism, comedy is an appropriate genre for the elaboration of the critique of political economy. That is to say, the basic premise of Lubitsch's comedy, like that of Marx's critique of political economy, is that the problem of the crisis indicated by the phrase "in times like these" is a systemic one: an economic crisis does not occur simply because of the actions of greedy, evil, megalomaniac, or self-deluded individuals—it stands for the moment of truth of the entire system. The crisis signifies not merely an accidental "trouble in paradise" but the fact that paradise itself is the trouble.

This is why the analysis of capitalism requires a comical approach. In a tragedy, the hero is a victim of his own actions, he is ultimately responsible for his own downfall—the moment of tragic recognition occurs when the appalled hero discovers that his fate is a consequence of his own previous deeds (Oedipus is forced to realize that he really killed his father and married his own mother, and consequently blinds himself). In capitalism, however, even in the most terrifying accidents that accompany it, the hero's downfall is never a tragedy of character. When a capitalist goes bankrupt as a consequence of his unsuccessful market speculation, his fall is the result of an impenetrable play of external contingencies, and in no way reveals a profound truth about his character.

In the universe of modern capitalism, subjects are contingent and ignorant hostages of the situation in which they find themselves. The classic example of a subject getting caught up in the wheels of a system is Charlie Chaplin as the worker in *Modern Times* (1936), where he becomes the disturbing element in the functioning of the complex machinery—an element which quite literally becomes entangled in the machine's activity. In a similar way, the crisis in *Trouble in Paradise* is not the sign of a fate confronting the hero with his own existential truth, but rather a contingent, cold, neutral mechanism that exploits and misuses subjects for its own ends—which are not even evil but simply systemic. In *Trouble in Paradise*, the "victims" of this process are Madame Colet, who accidentally finds herself occupying the place of a disinterested wealthy woman, and the two principal thieves, who try to get their slice of cake from this general constellation. The latter two are thus "glitches" in the system who nonetheless know how to turn it to their own advantage, acting in a way like a more elegant and cunning Chaplin.

The love story in *Ninotchka* analyzed in the present volume by Tatjana Jukić takes place in a different territory: the heroine of the film's title is a Stalinist political functionary who while in the West meets the love of her life, Leon, a wealthy Paris *bon vivant*. In their confrontation, the comic arrow targets primarily the anomalies of Stalinism.

In the encounter of the two heroes, two wholly different logics stumble upon each other— so no wonder that the film begins in a comic mood. The heroine functions as a bizarre product of Stalinism, a kind of cold rational-pragmatic robotic subject totally immersed in and identified with the great social project. It is precisely for this reason that the figure of Ninotchka arouses such interest: she seems to harbor no doubts whatsoever about the Stalinist regime.

This is precisely why the famous scene in which Greta Garbo bursts into laughter deserves a closer look. Previously, Leon has used all his charm in attempting to seduce her, but she remained cold and unimpressed. Eventually, he follows her into a working-class restaurant and tries to soften her up by telling jokes—here is his last desperate effort: "A man comes into a restaurant. He sits down at the table and says, 'Waiter! Bring me a cup of coffee without cream.' Five minutes later the waiter comes back and says, 'I'm sorry, sir, we have no cream, can it be without milk?'" A group of workmen listening in all burst into laughter, but Ninotchka continues to eat her soup with no trace of a smile. Furious, Leon says: "Not funny, huh?" "No." "Well it is funny! Everybody else thought it was funny! Maybe you didn't get the point … I'll tell it to you again … A man comes into a restaurant. Did you get that?" "Yes." "He sits down at the table and says to the waiter … Did you get that?" "Yes." "It isn't funny so far, but wait a minute. He says

Ninotchka (Greta Garbo) and Leon (Melvyn Douglas) before the fall. *Ninotchka*

to the waiter, 'Waiter! Bring me a cup of coffee,' and five minutes later the waiter comes back and says, 'I'm sorry, sir, we're all out of coffee.'" (He realizes he has made a mistake.) "Oh no, no, you've got me all mixed up now…" (He starts over again.) "That's it … he says 'Waiter, bring me a cup of coffee without cream,' and five minutes later the waiter comes back and says, 'I'm sorry, sir, we have no cream, can it be a glass of milk!'" When Ninotchka still doesn't react, Leon leans back in his chair exclaiming angrily: "Oh! You have no sense of humor! None whatsoever!" In his excitement he leans back too far onto the table behind. It topples over and he crashes to the floor, the contents of the table strewn all around him. A terrific roar of laughter arises; the whole restaurant is rocking with mirth. For a split second Ninotchka tries to control the irresistible impulse to laugh, but loses the battle and starts to roar with laughter. Leon snaps back indignantly: "What's so funny about this?" As Jukić emphasizes, Ninotchka's laughter here is not a soft feminine laughter, but uncontrollable and spasmic.

Wherein lies the trick of this scene? It is well known that *Ninotchka* was publicized with the slogan "Garbo Laughs"—the star who until then had always played melancholic heroines, finally bursts into laughter. Her melancholy, as Tatjana Jukić points out, provides the key for understanding the film.

What is the result of her falling into laughter, if we may use this term in analogy with falling into tears? The first thing that strikes us is that Ninotchka does not burst out laughing earlier, when Leon tells her a truly great joke—a fine example of how jokes draw on and function against the background of language, of the symbolic order and the differentiality that is its basic characteristic (the joke mobilizes the basic dialectical fact that the absence of a feature also defines the identity of an object[4]). What, then, can follow such an excellent joke? Only a *fall*, a collapse into mere vulgarity—which, of course, is not merely that, since it complicates the signifying dialectic even further, adding another turn of the screw: the fall out of the signifying chain. Indeed, what follows is a whole series of falls. First, there is a fall in the immediate physical sense: Leon falls on his ass in the most embarrassing and clumsy way. But this also signals a fall from his symbolic status as a sophisticated charmer, a fact directly registered by his expression of anger ("What's so funny about this?")—he no longer controls the game of seduction and is momentarily lost. And, as befits true love, Ninotchka does not react to this

---

4   Alenka Zupančič provides a detailed analysis. See Zupančič, "Not-Mother: On Freud's Verneinung", *e-flux journal* 33 (March 2012).

fall with condescending grace ("don't worry, when you stumble, I love you even more"), but with *her own fall*—the two falls overlap. At the immediate level, she *falls into uncontrollable laughter*—loses control of herself in exactly the same way one loses control when one falls into tears. Her fall, however, goes much deeper, providing an exemplary instance of what Lacan calls "subjective destitution."

In what has Ninotchka's identity consisted up to this point? She is not a stubborn communist lacking any sense of bodily pleasure (she has already confessed to Leon a previous encounter with a Polish lancer, whom she later killed). Her key characteristic is that she maintains a distance towards her pleasures, as if using a meta-language to talk about them. When, prior to her fall, Leon kisses her twice, she happily admits that she finds it pleasant, and that she likes him, but she simultaneously characterizes these feelings as the effects of chemical processes in her body, i.e., as matters that do not concern the core of her subjectivity. (Ninotchka's distance exactly mirrors Leon's own: up to his fall, he also maintains the distance of a sophisticated seducer who knows how to manipulate his conquests.) When she falls into laughter, she falls precisely into the situation towards which she had until then been maintaining a safe distance: after her fall, a kiss is no longer merely an interesting feeling to be analyzed objectively, but something that seizes her in the very heart of her subjectivity.

Leon and Ninotchka's respective falls can be linked to what follows them—the third and shared fall clearly expressed by the English phrase *to fall in love* (see also the French expression *tomber amoureux*). This fall designates love as an event, as a traumatic encounter which throws both participants off the rails of their habitual existence and through which they are both reborn as new subjects. Lubitsch here points towards the thesis, elaborated by Alenka Zupančič, about the comical character of love: both subjects have to fall in the sense of falling out of their symbolically defined subjectivity—there is no love without a mutual fall, that is, without comedy.

Wherein, then, resides the political character of this series of falls? After her return to the Soviet Union, Ninotchka is not happy, she is melancholic, bemoaning the end of her Paris adventure, and dreaming about a different life outside of Soviet misery and anxiety. The fall into laughter is thus not without political consequences. What kind of laughter is it into which Ninotchka falls? According to the standard view of how laughter relates to a political system and the ideology that sustains it, laughter cushions the horrors of political power: it allows for the maintenance of a minimal distance towards ideology and thus transforms individuals into its ideal subjects. In the case of Ninotchka and her fall into laughter, we see the opposite process at work: jokes which usually bring a little light relief to our difficult lives don't strike a nerve with her, don't shake her Stalinist firmness. Jokes are an integral part of the functioning of ideology, but what eventually undermines the stability of Ninotchka's ideological edifice, of her dedication to the Stalinist cause, is a fall into laughter which coincides with her falling in love. Only such a fall enables her to gain an insight into where she stands. In other words, her fall into laughter is not of the kind that carries a jesting cynical distance towards ideology, a distance which helps us to endure its hold more easily; on the contrary, paradoxically it makes the distance disappear and compels the subject to face up to the horror of her situation. Such a fall prevents us precisely from finding a bearable way to continue with our everyday lives, and enables us to confront a trauma.

The key to *Ninotchka* is thus provided by Lubitsch's politics of laughter, which unfolds against the background of comical love and its presentation—a laughter which does not rock us into ideological sleep, but on the contrary demands its pound of flesh in the guise of the political emancipation of a subject who has to confront the horror of a political regime.

To sum up our introduction to Lubitsch's politics of comedy, the three films discussed in this volume offer three efficient and uncompromising comic approaches to a specific political deadlock: in *To Be or Not to Be*, redoubling is mobilized as a weapon against the original; *Trouble in Paradise* provides a comic re-appropriation of the subject of political economy; and in *Ninotchka* the fall into laughter awakens us from an ideological dream.

***

It may appear that we have unduly neglected some of Lubitsch's key films which, on account of their peculiarity or their commercial success, deserve a much greater attention—such as *The Shop Around the Corner* (1940), or *That Uncertain Feeling* (1941), in which Lubitsch returns to the chamber orientation of his earlier comedies and again deals in a lighter mode with the temptations that pose a threat to the marriage link. Although the texts collected here deal in less detail with these films than with those of his political trilogy from the same period, it goes without saying that, like all of Lubitsch's works, these films also abound with brilliant moments.

In lieu of a detailed analysis of these notable works, the present volume—
and the text by Alenka Zupančič in particular—focuses on the overlooked (in
the field of the cinema theory at least) *Cluny Brown* (1946), Lubitsch's final film,
and an absolute masterpiece. In contrast to the predominant tendency of comedy authors to conclude their career on a more somber note (Chaplin being the
exemplary case), Ernst Lubitsch here again reveals himself as one of the most
unusual directors of Hollywood comedy. This last film is unique in his opus and,
as Zupančič argues, marks a crucial leap. The film tells the story of Cluny who,
thanks to her bizarre love for pipes, tubes, and plumbing, cannot find her place in
English society shortly before World War II. Lubitsch boldly focuses on Cluny's
bizarre passion, but rather than simply celebrating it, he treats it as indicative of
the heroine's peculiarity and, in a broader sense, of the peculiarity of an object
of enjoyment which resists appropriation in any social context or standard romantic scenario. Lubitsch's final and—up to a point—anti-humanist position is
unique even for a comedy; it offers a radical answer to a no less radical question:
What is it in a human being that is worth saving at all?

AARON SCHUSTER

Comedy in Times of Austerity

The Style is the Film Itself

How to summarize the plot of a Lubitsch film? As François Truffaut rightly pointed out, it's a hopeless task. "There is no Lubitsch plot on paper, nor does the movie
make any sense after we've seen it. Everything happens *while* we are looking at the
film. An hour later, or even if you've just seen it for the sixth time, I defy you to
tell me the plot of *To Be or Not to Be*. It's absolutely impossible."[1] From where does
this impossibility stem? First of all, the storylines of the films tend to be madden-
ingly complicated, with so many twists and turns and dialectical reversals as to
frustrate any attempt to clearly spell out the sequence of events. Yet the difficulty
comes not only from the convoluted plots, but more fundamentally concerns the
very form of their telling. Any summary, no matter how good, inevitably misses
the point since it is not the story itself that matters but *how* it is told. Lubitsch is
all about style, which often appears as an explicit theme within his films, but is
always involved in the way he constructs individual scenes as well as the totality
of the work. For Lubitsch, style is not simply a vehicle for storytelling but the very
point of the film. Or put otherwise, instead of style serving the story, the story is
there to serve the style. The particular way that Lubitsch pulls this off is what has
become known as the Lubitsch touch.

Lubitsch is a director who works by indirection, he is a master of the oblique,
the allusive, and the suggestive; his basic principle might be stated, "Never say

---

1   François Truffaut, *The Films in My Life*, trans. Leonard Mayhew (New York: Simon & Schuster, 1978), 52.

anything directly when a good metaphor will do." Among the many attempts to distill his technique, there are two formulations that I find especially helpful. Gerald Mast characterizes Lubitsch's art as one of "omission," an "art of the 'not'."[2] Lubitsch excels at *not* showing things, at leaving things unsaid, at absences and ellipses. But this showing less at the same time goes together with its opposite, a showing more: the corollary of the gaps in Lubitsch's films is his investment of ordinary objects and details, like buttons, canes, swords, wallets, hats, handbags, etc., with an unusual charge or significance—in his first American film, its star Mary Pickford complained that Lubitsch was a director of doors. There is a link between a big missing "something" and a proliferation of details or seemingly banal objects that take on a special resonance. Raymond Durgnat adds that

> The famous "Lubitsch touch" is … not so much a something added to a story as a method of telling a story through ellipse and emphasis. Omitting the obvious presentation, Lubitsch substitutes allusive detail, and then emphasizes that detail … in such a way that the sweet nothing becomes an ornamental equivalent of the dramatic sense.[3]

This dialectic of lack and surplus, with its unexpected displacement of emphasis and crafty correlation between the absence of the thing itself and the presence of a curious detail, may be seen as the hallmark of Lubitsch's style, and is our first attempt to discern the "sublime object" of Lubitsch's comedy.

Trouble in Paradise, which will be the focus of this essay, arguably presents the greatest accomplishment of the director's technique. The film has been widely praised for its elegant construction, where the "touch" is at its lightest and most deft. "As for pure style," Lubitsch reminisced in 1947 looking back on his career, "I think I have done nothing better or as good."[4] The film was made in 1932, with longtime collaborator Samson Raphaelson writing the screenplay, one of his finest, based (as is typical for Lubitsch) on an obscure Hungarian play. To risk the impossible and provide a short summary of the plot: *Trouble in Paradise* is essentially a love triangle involving two high-society thieves and a wealthy heiress, the owner of the perfume conglomerate Colet & Co., set against the backdrop of the Great

2   Gerald Mast, *The Comic Mind: Comedy and the Movies* (Chicago: University of Chicago Press, 1979), 207.
3   Raymond Durgnat, *The Crazy Mirror: Hollywood Comedy and the American Image* (London: Faber and Faber Limited, 1969), 110.
4   Cited in James Harvey, *Romantic Comedy in Hollywood from Lubitsch to Sturges* (New York: Da Capo Press, 1998), 47.

Depression (which, again, is almost never directly present, but frequently alluded to). A clever variation on the "gentleman crook" genre, Lubitsch's film is a rarefied and suave comedy of manners, where appearances are almost always deceiving and the best laid plans turn against their conspirators and then turn back again. The action starts off in Venice, where famed thief Gaston Monescu, the man who "walked into the Bank of Constantinople and walked out with the Bank of Constantinople," has just robbed a certain Monsieur Filiba while disguised as a doctor. A few doors down, now posing as "the Baron," he is dining with the beautiful "Countess," in reality the high-class crook Lily—"It must be the most marvelous supper," he instructs the waiter. "We may not eat it, but it must be marvelous." The two quickly discover that they are both impostors and career thieves and fall madly in love. We now shift to Paris: the happy couple has fallen on hard times. To procure needed funds, Gaston steals the jeweled handbag of Madame Colet (Mariette) one night at the opera; upon discovering that she is offering a substantial reward for its recovery, he decides to return it to its owner instead of fencing it. The meeting between Gaston and Mariette goes even better than hoped; she is charmed by his polished and confident manners, and hires him as her personal secretary. A new plan is hatched: Gaston and Lily, now posing as "Monsieur Laval" and his assistant "Mademoiselle Gautier," will take Colet for as much as they can. A terrific scheme, but the trouble is that Gaston is falling in love with his mark. Meanwhile Filiba, who happens to be one of Madame Colet's suitors, bumps into Gaston at a cocktail party at Madame's house; while he doesn't immediately recognize his robber-doctor, Gaston knows he does not have long—and adding to the difficulties is the CEO of Colet & Co., Monsieur Giron, who detests Gaston's influence and starts to suspect him of foul play (Giron himself, as it is later revealed, is far from innocent: he has been embezzling cash from the company). Gaston and Lily prudently decide to take the money and run, foregoing a larger sum being delivered to the house safe only a couple days later. But when Gaston changes their departure date at the last minute, Lily knows she has been betrayed. There follows a series of confrontations at Madame Colet's house: first between Giron and Gaston, then Gaston and Lily, Gaston and Mariette, Mariette and Lily, and finally all three lovers. The result is that the truth of Gaston's identity is revealed and Lily storms out with the money, leaving him to his new life and his new lover. After a poignant romantic exchange, Gaston in turn leaves Mariette—"It could have been glorious." "Lovely." "Divine ... But that terrible policeman!"—and the film ends in the back of a taxicab, with the original thieving couple happily reunited and on the run.

Style, money, and love: these are the three major themes of the film, which we shall have to consider in turn. This truncated outline, however, tells us little about the film's impact and charm, so before continuing our analysis let us look at a few specific examples of Lubitsch's technique.

The opening credits. Already there is something special in the title sequence. Right after the Paramount logo, the phrase "Trouble in" appears onscreen, but what immediately follows is the image of a fancy double bed. Wait a few seconds, and the word "Paradise" fades in to complete the title. Then the credits roll out, with the names of the two female stars, "Miriam Hopkins" and "Kay Francis," appearing just above "Herbert Marshall" to form a triangle right on top of the bed. The graphic design alone is a triumph of sly obscenity. Meanwhile the soundtrack sings, "Most any place can seem to be a paradise / While you embrace just the one that you adore..." Trouble in bed? Will this be a sex farce? Is bed the paradise? Or is it the source of the trouble?

The opening scene. Lubitsch liked to begin with trash—literally. It's nighttime. We see a portly man pick up a trash can, carry it a little ways and then dump it into a big pile of rubbish. He starts singing an aria in Italian. The rubbish dump turns out to be a garbage gondola, which the man starts navigating down a canal. Probably the city of Venice has never been introduced in a more de-sublimated way. Lubitsch foregoes the standard establishing shot of romantic canals and beautiful palazzo architecture while setting up one of the central metaphors of the film: from the outset it's announced that we're going to see the rot beneath the polished surfaces of high society. But note that garbage is not simply an object of disgust but also lovingly serenaded. A similarly trashy opening is employed in *Cluny Brown* (1946), this time in the form of a clogged sink full of peelings and floating bits. "Is there anything more interesting than a sink out of order?," asks the Czech professor, again neatly encapsulating the film's look into the nether regions. The philosophical analogue of these scenes may be found in one of the oddest and most intriguing passages in Plato's corpus: At one point in the *Parmenides* the question arises as to whether "vile and paltry" things like "hair, mud and dirt" have their complements in the realm of the Forms (130c). While a young Socrates suggests that there's nothing of interest in such leftover objects—trash is "in fact just what we see"—he is admonished by the older and wiser Parmenides for his non-philosophical attitude: there is nothing too lowly for philosophical contemplation. Likewise for Lubitsch, for whom comedy is not only about revealing the ugly muck behind idealized appearances, but also about showing that there is something sublime in the trash.

In bed with the Lubitsch touch.
Trouble in Paradise

The Venetian epiphany. Filiba happens upon Gaston, now masquerading as Monsieur Laval, Madame Colet's private secretary, at a cocktail party and has the funny feeling of having met him before. "If I like a man, I remember him, and if I don't like a man I never forget him." How does Lubitsch stage Filiba's dawning recognition of his Venice hotel suite assailant? Instead of directly showing us the "aha" moment, through a flashback or sudden revelation in the middle of the night, the director takes a roundabout route via a lucky object. We see that Filiba is thinking hard, he stares at his cigarette then stubs it out in the ashtray ... which just happens to be in the shape of a silver gondola. Back to Filiba. A close-up of the ashtray. Filiba again. It's starting to come together. My God! Venice![5]

The eternal embrace. The bed, as we have seen, is a central object in the film, and nowhere is it more strikingly used as a setting and a metaphor than in this scene. Gaston has professed his love for Mariette, and implores her to cancel her engagement and spend the night with him. "We have a long time ahead of us Gaston," she promises. And then with drawn-out sensuality whispers, "Weeks. Months. Years." With each word there is presented a frozen tableau of the two lovers, first in the mirror over the bed ("Weeks"), then in the circular mirror on the dressing table ("Months"), and finally as ghostly shadows fallen on the white bedsheets, the two silhouettes slowly bending towards each other and embracing ("Years"). A sexuality in the shadows, passion suspended in the void: we see nothing but

---

5   This scene was one of Truffaut's favorite examples of the Lubitsch touch; I borrow from his description.

outlines and reflections, but this tells us everything about the slow burning intensity of their desire, so different from the kinky kinetics of Gaston and Lily. The montage works both to arrest the passage of time and to impossibly accelerate it. Like Fénelon said, "In this divine ravishing the centuries pass by more rapidly than the hours."[6]

What's the Trouble in Paradise?

While the Lubitsch touch is often viewed as a clever way of evading censorship, it cannot be reduced solely to vehicle for smuggling in illicit content. The touch is not just an efficient means to overcome sexual or political taboos but is itself the message it wants to convey. If there is a veritable connection between Lubitsch and psychoanalysis, it lies not so much in any shared themes (sexuality, love, "it takes more than two to make a couple," etc.) but in this distinct formal sensibility. (Incidentally, there is a marvelous exchange about psychoanalysis in *That Uncertain Feeling* (1941), the one film of Lubitsch's that deals directly with the topic. "Wouldn't you like to meet you?," asks the analyst to his new patient. "No," she replies, "you see I'm a little shy." Is this not a most graceful, "well-spoken" expression of reticence towards the unconscious, the desire to leave the unconscious precisely for what it is, viz. unconscious? On the other hand, *That Uncertain Feeling* is also one of Lubitsch's less successful films. There is something of a curse hanging over movies that take psychoanalysis as their object: they almost always end up flat.) Lubitsch, like Freud, is less concerned with the hidden meaning of things than with *how* these hidden meanings are expressed on the surface; what fascinates him is not so much the buried contents of the unconscious as the displacements and condensations, short-circuits and reversals by which these contents manifest themselves. And, who knows?, perhaps deep down there is nothing but the same filthy banalities endlessly repeated—what really singularizes people is their unique distortions and tics, the creative ciphering which gives style to one's symptom. As Deleuze liked to say, the charm of a person stems from that point where he or she is a little unhinged, a little mad, an eccentric point that intimately belongs to and yet undoes a person's identity. With Lubitsch there is a passion not for the real behind appearances but for the kinks within the appearances themselves.[7]

---

6   François Fénelon, *Les aventures de Télémaque* (Paris: Librairie Hachette, 1920), 350.
7   On comedy's passion for appearances as opposed to the passion for the real, see Mladen Dolar, "Comedy and Its Double," in Robert Pfaller (ed.), *Stop That Comedy! On the Subtle Hegemony of the Tragic in Our*

The style is the film itself, to paraphrase the well-known line from Buffon. Georges-Louis Leclerc, later Comte de Buffon, delivered his famous "Discours sur le style" (Discourse on style) upon his election to the Académie Française in 1753. In it he distinguishes between writers who merely transmit knowledge and thus are inherently replaceable and those who, through the ingenuity of their personal style, become truly singular figures, the "Immortals." This text is the very first reference that figures in Lacan's collected writings. The preface to the *Écrits*, titled "Overture to This Collection," starts with a meditation on the phrase of Buffon,[8] and a brief passage through the Lacanian problematic of style can help us to specify further what is at stake in the Lubitsch touch. The opening sentence of the *Écrits* reads "'The style is the man himself,' people repeat without seeing any harm in it, and without worrying about the fact that man is no longer so sure a reference point."[9] Lacan will introduce two modifications to Buffon's formula, which preserve his praise of style while subverting its accompanying humanism. In effect, Lacan's question is, what happens to the notion of style after our image of man has been radically decentered by the Freudian unconscious? How to conceive of personal style when the notion of the unity of the person is no longer sustainable? Lacan first adapts Buffon's phrase by writing that "the style is the man *whom one addresses*." This alteration makes clear that rather than being an inner possession, style is something that it is bound up with and exposed to the outside, it must pass through the Other. Style implies a splitting, a cut between the speaker and what is said by him (the address of his speech), and concerns the way that the subject relates himself to this cut. Another passage from the *Écrits* neatly sums this up: "It is not a question of knowing whether I speak of myself in a way that conforms to what I am, but rather of knowing whether I am the same as that of which I speak."[10] What is striking here is the way that Lacan reverses the standard psychological perspective: instead of the outer expression being dominated by the inner intention, it is the inside which is dominated by the outside. In this inverted world, it's not me who means things with words, but rather the words that create meanings in which I am implicated, and towards which I can adopt different attitudes (of resistance, denial, identification, uncertainty, etc.).

Culture (Vienna: Sonderzahl, 2005), 181–209.

8   We may also note that the essay "The Problem of Style" was one of Lacan's earliest publications, for the surrealist journal *Minotaur*.

9   Jacques Lacan, "Overture to This Collection," *Écrits*, trans. Bruce Fink (New York: W.W. Norton & Co., 2006), 3.

10   Lacan, "The Instance of the Letter in the Unconscious, or Reason Since Freud," *Écrits*, 165.

Normally we don't take language all that seriously, but subordinate the material word to the amorphous realm of personal intentions, the endless game of shifts and clarifications, revisions and equivocations, of "what I wanted to say" and "what I really meant," that constitutes everyday discourse. Psychoanalysis is a strange practice precisely because it takes language (not the speaker) very seriously—even, and especially, when it's a matter of jokes.

Style may be defined in two ways. On an imaginary level, it designates a certain ideal of behavior and appearance. What counts as stylish is, of course, contingent and changes according to time and place; *Trouble in Paradise* embodies a pastiche-European ideal of elegance and manners, whose conventions it exploits for comic effect (there is a nice side-joke on the film's target audience when Lily flatters Gaston by having mistaken him for an American, "someone from another world, so entirely different"). On a symbolic level style refers not to any particular content but to the way the actor (the subject) relates to his or her performance. What is typical of Lubitsch films is that the actors not only act but act at acting; his comedies exploit the phenomenon of theatricalization, of theatrical splitting and doubling. This is most clearly the case in *To Be or Not to Be* (1942), but also figures in an interesting way in *Trouble in Paradise*, where the characters appear to be in perfect, even too-perfect, possession of their roles. The coolness and imperturbability of the consummately polished performances is no doubt one of the main reasons why Lubitsch considered the film his best for pure style. Consider the first meeting between Gaston and Lily. Everything in Gaston's chic Venetian suite is there for show, including the moon in champagne and the dinner which must be marvelous though it may not be eaten. The scene is staged as a kind of play within a play. Gaston and Lily are playing the Baron and the Countess, but at the same time they are both aware that the other is acting; she knows he is the thief who robbed "the wallet of the gentleman in two fifty-three, five, seven, and nine" because she lifted it off his person, and he knows that she too is a crook because she "tickled" him when she did so. In maintaining the charade, the actors show a supreme self-control and elegance, a comically exaggerated adherence to appearances. The sublime moment comes when the Countess "confesses" to the Baron that he "is a crook" then politely asks him to pass the salt; totally undisturbed by the accusation, he calmly responds by offering her the pepper too. Style here is more than a matter of conformity to an imaginary ideal; it also involves an affirmation of acting as such, an attitude of fully assuming and sticking to one's role. It is as if nothing could break the polished surface of the outward appearances, the smooth functioning of the performance-machine. To paraphrase the previous citation from Lacan: if the unstylish question is, Does the role I am playing correspond to who I am?, the properly stylish one is, Am I up to or worthy of the role that I am playing? Can I perform at the level demanded by the masquerade?

But there is yet another twist; neither Lubitsch nor Lacan has said his final word.

Towards the end of the "Overture" Lacan writes that "It is the object that corresponds to the question about style that I am raising," and further adds that the term "man" in Buffon should be replaced by the notion of the "fall of the object."[11] In another of his writings, Lacan condenses this to the pithy formula "the style is the object."[12] Style, then, cannot be conceived solely in terms of imaginary ideals and symbolic norms, but also has to do with the object of desire, the famous *objet petit a*. It is ultimately the object which stylizes and which poses the problem of style, precisely as that which, we might say, "troubles" the workings of the performance-machine. There is a whole series of linked notions in Lacan, *bien-dire* (the "well spoken"), *mi-dire* (the "half said"), sublimation (the elevation of an ordinary object to dignity of the Thing), and style ("the style is the object"), that bear on this issue, and whose complicated interrelations deserve a full study. But here I wish to make an abrupt turn and raise another question: Why is Lubitsch specifically known for his "touch" as opposed to other great cinema *auteurs*? Why not multiply the touches? There is a Scorsese touch (think of his pioneering use of long traveling shots leading from the off-stage to the main setting), a Tarkovsky touch ("sculpting in time"), a Leone touch (the face as landscape), a Hitchcock touch (which with its fetishistic sensitivity for ordinary objects and penchant for indirection is very close to the Lubitsch touch), and so on. This is no doubt true: for every author, his or her unique signature. What is perhaps different about Lubitsch, and at the risk of overstating the case, is that his style is not just one among many but stands in the cinematic lexicon for style as such. That any event worthy of the name should find its truth in just the right gesture, a "sweet nothing," or the stray lucky object, is with Lubitsch practically an ethical imperative—or rather the question of style itself.

If "the style is the object," then what object are we dealing with in that consummately stylish film *Trouble in Paradise*? What is the nature of the Lubitschean comic object? One hint may be discerned from an aphorism by Emil Cioran: "I ponder C., for whom drinking in a café was the sole reason to exist. One day

---

11   Lacan, "Overture to This Collection," *Écrits*, 4–5.
12   Lacan, "The Youth of Gide, or the Letter and Desire," *Écrits*, 624.

when I was eloquently vaunting Buddhism to him, he replied, 'Well, yes, nirvana, all right, but not without a café.'"[13] For Cioran's colleague, the café is the "troublesome object" which both disturbs the peacefulness of paradise and, through this very disturbance, renders it bearable. One could reiterate, "Well, yes, paradise is wonderful, but only on one condition: the odd detail that messes it up." This would also seem to be Lubitsch's underlying message, that the trouble *in* paradise is also the trouble *with* paradise: imbalance and disharmony are the very soul of desire, so that the object of desire is what embodies this turbulence rather than putting a "happy end" to it. "I want to make it tough for you," Mariette seductively challenges Gaston, and is not Lubitsch's method one of making the simple task of storytelling a lot tougher than it has to be, of actively searching for clever ways of "not telling the story,"[14] so that the obstacle to the task becomes its very goal? But we can also read the title of the film in another way. As the opening credits reveal, the trouble in paradise is a trouble in bed, and thus a sexual commotion. But the bed in the film is above all the bed of Madame Colet, upon which the shadow of the lovers fatefully fall. Could it be that paradise is actually the scandalous love affair of Gaston and Lily, two chic thieves fending for themselves, and trouble is the sublimely statuesque Mariette? That, in a tantalizing irony, Mariette is the snake luring Gaston from his blissfully sinful Garden of Eden? At least one thing is certain: the determination of the object will have to pass through an analysis of the dynamic between the two couples.

"In Times Like These..."

A gentleman entered a pastry-cook's shop and ordered a cake; but he soon brought it back and asked for a glass of liqueur instead. He drank it and began to leave without having paid. The proprietor detained him. "What do you want?" asked the customer.—"You've not paid for the liqueur."—"But I gave you the cake in exchange for it."—"You didn't pay for that either."—"But I hadn't eaten it."[15]

This wonderful joke is cited by Freud in *Jokes and Their Relation to the Unconscious* as an example of the nonsense technique: the appearance of logic hides a faulty reasoning, the joke is really a sophistry. As Freud explains, the trick is that the

---

13   Emil Cioran, *Anathemas and Admirations*, trans. Richard Howard (London: Quartet Encounters, 1992), 112.
14   Truffaut, *The Films In My Life*, 51.
15   Sigmund Freud, *Jokes and Their Relation to the Unconscious*, SE VIII, 60.

word "exchange" is used in two different and incompatible ways. But what if there were a deeper truth in the defective reason? In fact, this ridiculous barter provides a nice illustration of the violence underlying so-called primitive accumulation: first one steals (expropriates resources), then one trades the plunder one didn't pay for back to its original owners in order to extract extra profit. Property is theft, or as the famous line from *The Threepenny Opera* goes, "What is the crime of robbing a bank compared with the crime of founding a bank?" These reversals capture well the dexterous comic dialectics of *Trouble in Paradise*, which admits no bright line between law and transgression, honesty and villainy—in Lubitsch's universe there are but degrees of theft and not only the "self-made" criminals but everyone seems to be a crook. As in the pastry-shop joke, at the center of the film lies what will prove to be a very fateful "false exchange." Gaston steals Madame Colet's handbag, and then gives it back to her, first for a check ("Make it out to cash" he purrs), and then, as it turns out, something else. The crooked maxim of the film could thus be articulated as follows: Return to the owner what you have seized from her in order to exchange it for other goods.

As I mentioned before, *Trouble in Paradise* was made in 1932, at a time when the world economy was in full decline, and even though it is only glimpsed awry— we encounter but a single revolutionary, who is himself ridiculed, and catch a brief glance at workers during a perfume ad—the social and historical context is very much a part of the film. If *Ninotchka* (1939) is a film about communism and *To Be or Not to Be* about fascism, *Trouble in Paradise* is a comic treatment of the worst economic crisis the world has seen, the Great Depression. These three films, the most socially conscious in Lubitsch's oeuvre, form a kind of trilogy which deals with the crisis of capitalism and its two historic solutions: fascism and communism. And "in times like these," of budget cuts, bank busts, and Euro-zone bailouts, the film's study of capitalist manners has only gained in relevance. Indeed, *Trouble in Paradise* is perhaps the ultimate comedy for times of austerity: for that reason alone it should be required viewing today. This does not mean, however, that one should expect any kind of straightforward critique or moral sermon from Lubitsch; the point is not that beneath all the entertaining banter and funny reversals there lies a serious message—again, the serious message is already there in the comedy itself. (It is no coincidence that the authors who have best captured the bafflingly complex dealings behind the financial crisis, like John Lanchester and Michael Lewis, have a flair for the comical). One of the best running gags of the film consists in the repeated use of the line "In times like these…," a catchphrase meant to convey an air of resigned worldly wisdom on its speaker; equally invoked by the CEO, the Bolshevik, the crook, and the society lady, in Lubitsch's hands it becomes the vehicle of a biting social satire. Let us cite each of the six instances:

GIRON: I'm sure, Madame Colet, if your husband were alive, the first thing he would do *in times like these*—cut salaries.
MARIETTE: Unfortunately, M'sieur Giron, business bores me to distraction—and besides I have a luncheon engagement. So I think we'd better leave the salaries just where they are.

***

BOLSHEVIK: But let me tell you—any woman who spends a fortune *in times like these* for a handbag—phooey, phooey, phooey!

***

GASTON: But, madame, you keep a hundred thousand francs—in your safe—at home?
MARIETTE: You think that's too much?
GASTON: No! Not enough! *In times like these*, when everything is uncertain, every conservative person should have a substantial part of his fortune within arm's reach.

***

GIRON: Speaking for the board of directors as well as myself, if you insist, *in times like these*, on cutting the fees of the board of directors, then we resign.
GASTON: Speaking for Madame Colet as well as myself—resign!
CLOSE-UP GIRON
GIRON: Very well! (He hesitates.) We'll think it over, M'sieur Laval!

***

LILY: And her jewelry is worth a fortune!
GASTON: No jewelry! Hands off jewelry! If we're broke—all right. I might pick up a million-franc necklace. But *in times like these* when we're doing a cash business—why take a chance on jewelry?

***

MARIETTE: How much is your salary?
LILY: Three hundred francs.

MARIETTE: Well, *in times like these* most people are cutting salaries, but suppose we say, in your case, three hundred and fifty?
LILY: Oh, madame, you're just too sweet for words!

The first case presents a truly novel answer to the politics of austerity: Sorry, but business is too boring to be bothered with cuts, and besides I have a luncheon date. Such whimsical disdain is hardly a Marxist response, but it is an intriguing tactic. Mariette's reply may be seen as a clever counter to the board's condescending *diktat*, playing into their stereotype of feminine triviality while using it against them. Next, the board's expert advice is thrown back at them when Gaston, acting in Madame Colet's name, decides to cut not the workers' but the executives' salaries. Now the refrain takes on a completely different meaning: difficult times call for high (not low) wages presumably in order to retain the best talent. We see how slippery this "in times like these" is! But the real focus of the scene is on Gaston's cool reply, his refusal to yield to the corporate blackmail: resign if you wish, he tells them, the world will not end, an utterly sensible position which is even less imaginable today than when the film was made (picture Gaston as a financial regulator). Elsewhere he uses the same line to warn Mariette against confidence in the banking system: in troubled times it's best to keep a substantial part of your fortune in the safety of your home. Of course "safe" is a relative term and Gaston is setting up a more lucrative robbery, but you can't exactly blame him since crooks have fallen on hard times too—he's a member of the "nouveau poor." And anyway, who is the real thief here? Is it the man who walked into the Bank of Constantinople and walked out with the Bank of Constantinople? Is it his pickpocketing partner with her eye on the jewels? Is it the opulent society lady who has the audacity to spend 125,000 francs on a handbag "in times like these" while around her the economy craters? Or is it Monsieur Adolph J. "I have enjoyed the confidence of this family for more than forty years" Giron, the respected chairman of the board, who has been embezzling untold sums from Colet and Co. while covering his tracks with fraudulent bookkeeping? No one in the film is spared, the satire cuts in all directions, but Lubitsch's sympathy is clearly for the classy "self-made" criminals over the hypocrite institutional crooks. In this radical comedy, "the thieves not only get away with the loot but actually go on to a charmed life of more thievery"[16]—an astonishing ending for a Hollywood picture of that era.

---

16 William Paul, *Ernst Lubitsch's American Comedy* (New York: Columbia University Press, 1983), 51.

But we should add that the other thieves will presumably have a happy end too: Giron will be safe (a hushed-up scandal, a golden parachute), Madame will go on with her shopping sprees, and the board will have its way. Everyone is stealing, and no one is punished—that, in a nutshell, is Lubitsch's portrait of the times.

Trouble in Paradise is a film of illicit exchanges, and one of the qualities of objects in the film is that they tend to be missing from their place—so much so, in fact, that one begins to wonder whether they have a "proper" place at all. To start with, the first meeting between Gaston and Lily (as Baron and Countess) turns on a doubly stolen article. He steals back from her the wallet he had previously stolen from Filiba, and the seduction scene plays out as a competitive contest between virtuoso pickpockets. Items appear and disappear into pockets, folds and pouches, a remarkable circulation of goods. The stakes escalate as each produces a more improbable prize: her pin, then his pocket watch, which in the meantime she has regulated, and finally, the *coup de grâce*, the Countess's garter. After that we have the mendacious return of Madame Colet's stolen handbag, *the* pivotal object of the film, whose errant paths we shall have to examine soon. And finally there is the whole loaded question of money and sex, the very model of illicit exchange, which Lubitsch mines for great comic effect. "So far as I'm concerned, her whole sex appeal is in that safe!" Gaston assures a jealous Lily, but she, quite rightly, is not so sure. There is an incredibly sophisticated joke about prostitution running though the film, which is worth taking the time to dissect. Scheming to seduce Gaston, Mariette plies Lily ("Mademoiselle Gautier") for information one morning while eating breakfast in bed. In a rather transparent attempt to buy her loyalty, Mariette offers to raise Mademoiselle Gautier's salary, by a measly 50 francs—"in times like these" when salaries are being slashed (suddenly she recalls the expert advice of Giron and the members of the board), this token of generosity should go a long way. Lily takes the offer for what it is, a naked bribe. The game is up, now she know what Mariette really wants. "You!," she tells Gaston. "And she's willing to pay as high as fifty francs." This indecent proposal then returns in what, in my opinion, is the most well written scene of the film, as well as a terrific lesson in how to break up (incidentally, a study of all of Lubitsch's break-up scenes would be a highly worthwhile endeavor). We are in Madame Colet's house, with all three lovers. Lily has stolen the 100,000 francs out of the safe, but Gaston covers for her, taking the blame himself. Supremely disappointed that Gaston chose the money over her, Mariette goes into the next room where she stumbles onto Lily, who has overheard their conversation and confesses the whole caper.

Lily (Miriam Hopkins) and Mariette (Kay Francis) bargaining under false pretences (above).
Lily and Gaston (Herbert Marshall) reunited (below).
Trouble in Paradise

It was she who took the cash, Gaston, for once, is not the crook, the two are free to love. But not only does Lily relinquish Gaston, she also gives up the money, ceremoniously tossing it (where else?) on the bed. The sexual commerce could not be clearer. "You wanted to buy him for fifty francs. Well, you can have him for nothing!" By means of this double renunciation, Lily extracts herself from the obscene exchange that Mariette proposed earlier; though she may be in thrall to money, she shows that she cannot be bought, not for 50 francs nor even 100,000. Yet immediately afterwards—and therein lies the genius of the scene—she retakes the cash in order to demonstrate exactly the same point. She cannot be bought, but Gaston *can*. His *not stealing* the money means that he has *sold out* (he has prostituted himself, become a gigolo), and as proof of his corruption she'll accept the 100,000 in exchange for him, a sum which—the final insult!—is less than what Madame paid for her precious handbag. Lily has her cake and eats it too: first she rejects the cash to prove she cannot be bought, then she accepts it to prove the other can be sold. In psychoanalytic terms, one could say that Lily deftly cheats castration: she doesn't have to choose between her money and her life. In comedy you can have it both ways.[17]

Venus's Missing Handbag

Yet the film ends not with a break-up but with a reconciliation, even a 'remarriage' of sorts. Lubitsch again reverses the standard logic. Instead of the respectable couple who break up over an adulterous affair and then, after many trials and tribulations, rediscover their true love for one another, we have a disreputable criminal couple where the man cheats by going straight and then afterwards returns to his faithfully lying, cheating, stealing spouse. Paradise, the good life, is the life of crime full of glamour and risks, and evil temptation comes in the form of Madame Colet, whose wealth holds the promise of an easy-going *dolce vita* without real criminal daring or subterfuge, only the humdrum hypocrisy of the respectable classes. Or at least this is how it looks from Lily's perspective: what really irks Lily is not only that Gaston betrays her by *not stealing* Mariette's money, but that he also and more fundamentally betrays himself, or rather what he stands

---

17 Compare this with the standard tragic situation where the hero is forced to choose between either selling out or maintaining his integrity. If he refuses to sell out, he is materially ruined, his life is destroyed. If he does sell out, he enjoys worldly success but at the cost of inner spiritual collapse. The brilliance of the break-up scene is that while Lily refuses to sell out ("I don't want your money!"), she nonetheless manages to find a comic solution so that she can enjoy the same material benefits as if she had prostituted herself.

for, the (symbolic) Thief-Ideal. "Darling," she implores, "remember you're Gaston Monescu. You're a crook. I want you as a crook. I love you as a crook. I worship you as a crook. Steal, swindle, rob—but don't become one of those useless, good-for-nothing gigolos!"

One of the key questions debated by critics of the film concerns the relation between the two couples. Which is the true couple, Gaston and Lily or Gaston and Mariette? (In fact, there are really three couples in the film: one should also include the two bumbling suitors, Monsieur Filiba and the Major, whose imaginary rivalry provides a kind of comic relief from the main comic plot; eventually they reconcile over their shared failure to win the desired woman, proving that one of the best ways for men to become friends is through the solidarity of amorous rejection). Gaston and Lily seem to be truly made for each other, but perhaps too much so; they are more partners than lovers, Lily missing that certain *je ne sais quoi* which Mariette has in abundance. Mariette, on the other hand, is far less intrepid than Lily, but oozes with mystery and passion: the slow burning fuse. In Lubitsch's topsy-turvy universe, it's uncertain exactly what is "trouble" and what is "paradise." Perhaps the greatest irony of the film is the way that the slick criminals are positioned as a dull bourgeois couple while the high society lady stands for the Fall: the dangerous transgression of the crooked duo's "normal transgressive" routine. This has been argued by James Harvey:

> But Gaston in *Trouble in Paradise*, in the back of his taxi with Lily, has run out on Kay Francis. It's clear that he is returning to a challenging and rather dangerous career: he and Lily are both committed thieves, and they even show off their skills for us in this last scene by picking each other's pockets before the final clinch and fadeout. Still, in every respect but their thievery, Gaston and Lily are (one of the film's basic jokes) a quintessential bourgeois couple, conscientious professional types with expensive tastes—yuppies before their time. Gaston and Mariette, on the other hand, are the really romantic pair, the adventurous and risk-taking lovers. In returning to Lily and lawlessness, Gaston is doing the sensible thing—returning to his "station," as it were, opting for the mundane life he knows. And he does so with full regret, apparent in his lingering final exchange with Mariette, full of rue and stylish ardor on both sides. Here, as elsewhere, Lubitsch and Raphaelson have chosen just those possibilities that ironize or undercut the elements of romance and adventure.[18]

---

18   Harvey, *Romantic Comedy in Hollywood from Lubitsch to Sturges*, 56.

William Paul, on the other hand, defends the idea that Lily and Mariette represent "exclusive but, for Lubitsch, equally valid notions of love."[19] They are two types, neither one better or worse, defined by structural oppositions rather than dialectical reversals. These oppositions have to do fundamentally with how the characters inhabit space and time. Lily is filled with a hyperkinetic energy; Mariette, on the other hand, possesses a glacial poise. While Mariette "luxuriates in a kind of helpless passivity" which has a "masochistic coloration"—in her first meeting with Gaston the high point of seduction is his playful threat to spank her—Lily "is constantly on the move": when speaking to Madame Colet she even has to sit on her hands to restrict her too mobile impulses.[20] The ethereal longing of Gaston and Mariette, beautifully portrayed by the frozen tableaux of the lovers in mirror reflections and silhouettes, presents the polar opposite to the physical closeness and intimacy of Lily and Gaston's mutual pickpocketing games. In sum, Gaston's love for Mariette embodies the passionate intensity and longing of desire, while the tangible pleasures he and Lily share are more akin to the freewheeling play of the drives: a "bouncy allegro" versus a "sensuous adagio."[21] Desire feeds on shadows, with dreams of dissipation and oblivion never far off, and thus it is fitting that the affair with Mariette takes place in the closed and abstracted universe of her mansion, a kind of gated paradise. By returning to Lily, Gaston makes a risky choice for the outside world against the lure of timeless fantasms. We thus arrive at exactly the opposite conclusion from Harvey: "The stasis of Mariette's safe harbor must yield to the uncertain journey of a taxi cab in the dead of night."[22]

Both these interpretations are illuminating, but neither is quite right. Harvey captures the exquisite irony by which Lubitsch flips transgression and the norm, and Paul the structural differences that separate Mariette and Lily down to the ways they formally embody space and time. But ultimately the question of love that is posed by the film, and which deserves to be seen as a veritable philosophical question, is not that of the couple but that of the *object*. Remember Pickford's complaint, Lubitsch is a director of doors. In a sense she is right: the debate over which is the true couple, Gaston-Lily or Gaston-Mariette, still remains too focused on persons and not enough on doors, or in this instance, a handbag.

19   Paul, *Ernst Lubitsch's American Comedy*, 65.
20   Ibid., 57.
21   Ibid., 65.
22   Ibid., 68.

And if there is something truly transgressive in Lubitsch's presentation of love, it has to do precisely with this emphasis on the object. As I have already remarked, things in the film tend to be missing from their place, and none more so than Madame Colet's jeweled handbag, which is in fact doubly if not triply displaced. Not only has Gaston lifted it from Mariette, but in explaining where he found it he claims that Mariette left it at the opera in that little niche with the statue of Venus, a place where, she points out, she never was—this leads to the wonderful reply, "You were never at the niche? Then this must not be your handbag..." similar to Hitchcock's joke about the MacGuffin, "There are no lions in the Scottish highlands? Well then this is not a MacGuffin..." Furthermore, as the Bolshevik barks, owning such an extravagant handbag "in times like these" is already tantamount to larceny; her purchase is tainted with the decay of a decadent order. (One thinks of Ninotchka's verdict about the fancy hat she sees in a Parisian shop window, "It won't be long now, comrades...") This dizzyingly displaced accessory—stolen from Mariette's illegitimate possession and falsely discovered where it never was—will then reappear at the very end of the film where it plays the clinching role. Lily and Gaston are finally reunited, but the key question is how is this reconciliation accomplished? Put simply, through the repetition of the original scene of seduction, the game of mutual pickpocketing that is at once friendly rivalry (contest of talents), shared complicity (in the Thief-Ideal), and sexual foreplay (enjoyment of the drives). But with one key difference: with perfect nonchalance, Lily produces from behind her back that most troublesome object, the jeweled handbag, which she apparently pilfered from Madame Colet's house before leaving—this is the marvelous detail, the "sweet nothing" that contains the whole dramatic sense, and almost magically reestablishes their amorous rapport. Repetition is itself doubled, what is repeated is not only the original scene of seduction, but also, one might say, the thing that was missing from it. The Lubitschean lesson: You always have to steal a handbag twice.[23]

The style is the object, the style is the handbag. It has no proper place, but it cannot be replaced (when Filiba attempts to buy Mariette a new one, it's an abject failure); it's rightfully possessed by no one, but itself possesses whoever happens to be holding it. This is not just any handbag, but the handbag of Venus, goddess of love—it's her ornament, her treasure, her *agalma*. And let us not forget the

---

23 If one wanted to formalize this in Lacanian terms, one can detect in this brief concluding scene all the elements required for the formation of fantasy: the registers of the imaginary (playful rivalry), the symbolic (the Thief-Ideal), and the real (enjoyment), as well as the object that knots them together (the handbag).

obvious sexual symbolism, which Lubitsch certainly doesn't: to seal love's bargain, Gaston stuffs Lily's purse full of his hard cash. As there is a Lubitsch touch, so there is also a Lubitsch solution, to follow the phrase of Truffaut.[24] In this case the solution is nothing other than the destiny of the object, whose reappearance marks the rebirth of love and the reconstitution of fantasy after its brutal shattering. Is this happy or unhappy? Does it matter? In the end, *Trouble in Paradise* is the story of Love's lost handbag, a distinctly modern retelling of the ancient myth of the birth of Eros from the illicit union of Craftiness and Poverty. And perhaps there has never been a more elegant illustration of the old saying, to love means giving what you don't have.[25]

24 Truffaut, *The Films In My Life*, 52.
25 I wish to thank Tatjana Jukić and Alenka Zupančič for stimulating discussions about the film and the significance of the ending.

RUSSELL GRIGG

The Joyful Art of Ernst Lubitsch:
Trouble in Paradise

That's paradise while arms entwine and lips are kissing
But if there's something missing, that signifies
Trouble in paradise

Lubitsch's 1932 film *Trouble in Paradise* was of limited commercial success. While the film was not exactly a flop initially, it grossed less than its production costs and was less successful than other films by Lubitsch. Shortly after its release the film fell foul of the Motion Picture Production Code, also known as the Hays Code, introduced in 1934. It was not approved for re-issue in 1935 and, incredibly, became generally unavailable after that until it was seen again in 1968. The film was never released on videocassette and only became available on DVD in 2003. It is nevertheless widely, though not universally, regarded as one of the finest films of early Hollywood cinema, and is also seen, though probably incorrectly, as an inspiration for the screwball comedies of the 1930s, and, with more justification, as a major influence on the cinema of Billy Wilder and others.

It should be added, however, that the praise for the film has been not only high but also highly qualified. The frequently quoted comment by contemporary critic Dwight Macdonald, drawing attention to its "endless" virtues and deeming it "as close to perfection as anything I have ever seen in the movies," is a case in point, for it appears less impressive in the context of the condescending qualification that it is so "within the admittedly drastic limitations of its genre."[1]

---

1   http://www.tcm.com/tcmdb/title/93978/Trouble-in-Paradise/articles.html (accessed June 20, 2013). Consider also Pauline Kael's qualified praise when she writes, "In its light-as-a-feather way, it's perfection." *5001 Nights at the Movies* (New York: Holt, Rinehart and Winston, 1982).

There is some justification for thinking of some of Lubitsch's work as screwball. One thinks of *Bluebeard's Eighth Wife* (1938), with Claudette Colbert and Gary Cooper and scripted by Billy Wilder. It contains the key elements of screwball. There is a woman who triumphs over the man through her unpredictable and extravagant actions. There is a male protagonist who is ridiculed throughout the film for his obsessional but futile efforts to bring order to a world that is escaping his control. His efforts are constantly undermined by the spirited and defiant gestures of the woman, who is a figure of lawlessness, a lawlessness that leads to his humiliation. Because this lawlessness and humiliation are essential features of screwball, the resolution and reconciliation that often occur at the end of a screwball comedy invariably have a note of dissonance and falseness about them; they are not consistent with the logic of the drama that has previously unfolded but seem to be a response to other, extraneous requirements.

It seems clear that although there are precursors, "screwball" really came into its own as a genre in response to the Hays Code of 1934, under whose puritanical gaze it was no longer possible to deal with anything near the full panoply of human sexual experiences. The foolish obsessiveness of the Hays Code has been well documented. We're not just talking or even particularly talking about the censorship of deviant sexual practices, but sexual practices such as homosexuality, prostitution, adultery, even sex within marriage.

The effect of the Hays Code on Lubitsch's films can be clearly seen if you compare his 1938 film, *Bluebeard's Eighth Wife* with the simple frankness about sex in *Trouble in Paradise*. The first big scene in *Trouble in Paradise* is a seduction scene between Lily the Countess (Miriam Hopkins) and Gaston Monescu (Herbert Marshall) in which she arrives in secret, afraid, or so it seems, that she might have been seen on her way to an obviously clandestine rendezvous with a man who, we are led to believe, may become her lover by the end of the evening. Gaston's intentions are unambiguous. As he says to the waiter, the dinner "must be the most marvelous supper—we may not eat it but it must be marvelous." And any pretence that she is not a willing partner is just that—pretence. There is never any explicit sex scene in this or in any other of Lubitsch's films—here there is only the mere suggestion of an embrace, which ends when a hand reaches out from the room to hang a "Do not disturb" sign on the door. Note that the pretence is twofold: there is a pretence at pretence, a naked pretence as it were. If it were just pretence we—and they, the characters—might be taken in by it, but no one is fooled. While Lily is pretending to be someone she is not, she is perfectly happy for Gaston to discover that this is all pretence, and vice versa. The scene, delightfully scanded by mundane moments ("Pass the salt"), is both fun and sexy—and as such it counts as a perfect illustration of the erotic role that the semblant, as articulated by Lacan, plays in sexual relations, where appearance of course triumphs over reality, but where the appearance is non-deceptive, where there is a joyful and erotic element of make-believe. It excites precisely because the subject both accepts it at face value but also recognizes it as appearance. This is brilliantly captured by Lacan with his notion of the semblant, which, in the words of the philosopher Jankélévitch, is a "transparent appearance," but which also, as a transparent pretence, creates something erotic that cannot be produced "authentically," only deceptively. Lily and Gaston's mutual seduction is thus a beautiful illustration of this semblant, engaged in a make-believe that is more erotic than reality itself.[2]

The explicit treatment of the intentions of both man and woman and the assumption that if things go well, as in fact they do, then they will end up in bed together was no longer possible with the introduction of the Hays Code, hence the effective banning of the film in 1935. This did not prevent Lubitsch from portraying seductions in his films after the introduction of the Code; he just had to resort to other means to do it. In *Bluebeard's Eighth Wife*, Lubitsch employs the artifice whereby the couple get married *and then* the husband is obliged to seduce his own wife to get her to sleep with him. The reason for this unlikely scenario is the even more unlikely scenario whereby, on the eve of their wedding, his future bride discovers that she is about to become not the first or second but the eighth Mrs. Bluebeard and that the nuptials will be based on a sound and business-like pre-nuptial arrangement whereby, should they divorce (and the future Mrs. Bluebeard learns that the previous marriages have lasted 12 months on average), the fabulously rich Mr. Bluebeard will leave generous provision for his new ex-wife. Grasping the logic of the situation, Mrs. Bluebeard refuses to be bedded by her new husband, in the knowledge that while her fate may not be as bloody as that awaiting Scheherazade, it is as ineluctable, and so she refuses to have sex with him until she knows he has fallen in love with her. The clever device is, then, that the intention of getting someone into bed underlies the motives of characters who

---

2   It is this that the writer Villiers de L'Isle Adam has in mind when he asks, rhetorically, "Les semblants de l'amour ne sont-ils pas devenus, pour presque tous, préférables à l'amour même?" ("Have not the semblants of love become preferable, for almost everyone, to love itself?"). A. Villiers de L'Isle Adam, *Contes cruels* (Paris: Calmann Lévy, 1883), 341. For more on Lacan's concept of the semblant, see my "Semblants and the Phallus," *Hurly-Burly*, no. 5 (2011), 103–11.

are already married. And no one could possibly object to a man seducing his own wife or vice versa, now, could they?

The smooth transition in Lubitsch's films from the freer expression of sexual comedies in the pre-Hays period through to the time of its strict implementation after 1934 is assisted by the already frequent use of visual metaphors in his films. In the early films, the sex could be portrayed through metonymy, or displacement, such as the part for the whole: hence, the "Do not disturb" sign, where something attached to the act takes the place of the act itself.

Under the censorship restrictions of the Code, however, the expression is more metaphorical, hence more disguised, and expresses its meaning more indirectly. Lubitsch makes a virtue of this necessity, exploiting the censorship in a way that gives that release of pleasure that Freud noted we obtain when the superego is circumvented. With Lubitsch the innuendo is so light, clever, and, above all, deliberate that we can enjoy the joke with him at the expense of an idiotic Code. The constraints of the Code did not restrict Lubitsch, one feels, so much as open up new possibilities for his wit. It was not that Lubitsch's ridicule by innuendo "subverted" the Code; rather, he made use of the Code for his humor. And this is where much of the famous Lubitsch touch finds expression. Let me quote Billy Wilder and Charles Brackett:

> Directors confronted with the problem of putting a wedding night on the screen, tune it to violins. They write innuendoes and rogueries. They drown it all in blue moonlight and dissolve into dawn creeping through gossamer draperies. Not the professor, Lubitsch! He didn't give a hoot for the wedding night. He skipped it entirely. He photographed the lovers having breakfast. And he put more delightful connotations of sensuality in the bride cracking the shell of a soft-boiled egg than could be evoked by the moistest of lips meeting the most censorable kisses.[3]

The other thing is that *Trouble in Paradise* always remains too close to parody for it to qualify as a romantic comedy. Herbert Marshall distances himself from his character, as does Kay Francis, while Lubitsch almost makes fun of a genre that has scarcely been born. It seems that neither screwball nor romantic comedy can be said to define Lubitsch's work. Many critics have seen *Trouble in Paradise* as the

---

3   Quoted in Thomas Patrick Doherty, *Hollywood's Censor: Joseph I. Breen and the Production Code Administration* (New York: Columbia University Press, 2009), 108–9.

apotheosis of the Lubitsch style, which accords with Lubitsch's own view that it is his most Lubitschean film from the point of view of its style.[4] And so, given that this is the film that best represents the famous Lubitsch style, it follows that there is a uniquely Lubitschean style that is neither screwball nor romantic comedy.

What I am calling the Lubitsch style should not be confused with the Lubitsch touch. The problem with the latter term is that, as Richard Wallace observes, "Pinning down a precise definition of the 'Lubitsch Touch' is extremely problematic as no two critics agree on what the term actually represents."[5] The Lubitsch touch was never given a definition but, according to a comment frequently attributed to Scott Marks, it was simply introduced as a marketing device by the studio public relations men eager to turn the great director Ernst Lubitsch into a brand name.[6] As a result, different elements of Lubitsch films have been singled out to fit the term. Some refer to it as Lubitsch's wit. Billy Wilder is said to have picked out the Lubitsch "superjoke," where "you had a joke, and you felt satisfied, and then there was one more big joke on top of it. The joke you didn't expect."[7] Roger Fristoe referred to "a subtle and soufflé-like blend of sexy humor and sly visual wit."[8] Others also zero in on Lubitsch's undeniably subtle and clever treatment of sexual themes. Saul Austerlitz describes "a style that hinted at sex, that was playfully adult in its themes, without ever crossing the invisible boundary line that separated smut from genius."[9] Still others refer to the metaphorical condensation that Lubitsch was so effective at bringing about in visual form. Ephraim Katz has this condensation in mind when he refers to "a parsimonious compression of ideas and situations into single shots or brief scenes."[10] Leland Poague refers to Lubitsch's "ingenious ability to suggest more than [he] showed." Greg S. Faller evokes Lubitsch's capacity for "focusing on objects or small details that make a witty comment on or surprising revelation about the main action."[11]

---

4   "As for *pure style* I think I have done nothing better [than] or as good as *Trouble in Paradise*." Quoted in Herman G. Weinberg, *The Lubitsch Touch: A Critical Study*, Revised edition (New York: Dover, 1978), 268, emphasis added.

5   Richard Wallace, "Understanding the 'Lubitsch Touch': Does it Increase Our Appreciation of *Trouble in Paradise*?", *Off Screen* 12 (2008), http://www.offscreen.com/index.php/pages/essays/trouble_paradise

6   See http://www.lubitsch.com/touch.html

7   Quoted in Scott Eyman, *Ernst Lubitsch: Laughter in Paradise* (Baltimore: Johns Hopkins University Press, 2000), 169.

8   See http://www.lubitsch.com/touch.html

9   Ibid.

10 Ibid.

11 Ibid.

For Herman G. Weinberg, on the other hand, it "meant going from the general to the particular, suddenly condensing into one swift, deft moment the crystallization of a scene or even the entire theme."[12]

What is striking about these definitions of the famous touch is that they are all true of Lubitsch's movies, and collectively could be said to define it. The broadest definition, and the one that comes nearest to capturing his style, was offered by Peter Bogdanovich: "One can feel this certain spirit … not only in the tactful and impeccably appropriate placement of the camera, the subtle economy of his plotting, the oblique dialogue which had a way of saying everything through indirection, but also—and particularly—in the performance of every single player, no matter how small the role."[13]

This last point—referring to the acting style of Lubitsch's actors, the dialogue (often written in collaboration with Samson Raphaelson), and the care taken with the mise-en-scène—is very interesting. As we know, Lubitsch started his career in theater, joining Max Reinhardt's Deutsches Theater as an actor at the age of 19 in 1911, but by 1920 he was making films that were reaching an international audience, particularly in the USA, which he emigrated to in 1922 and started making films in Hollywood. It is recorded that in making a movie Lubitsch was obsessively attentive to the acting of his actors as the film was being made. Incredibly, he would act every part in every scene for every actor. The significance of this is apparent in the unusual relationship, unusual for cinema, between the actor and the on-screen character in Lubitsch's films; namely, a discordance between the actor and the character that is so unusual and, particularly for the time, unexpected that it can look like a stilted and rather formal style of acting. In *Trouble in Paradise*, for instance, Herbert Marshall is not just playing the role of Gaston Monescu, he is not totally "in" the character; rather, he plays, at one and the same time, the actor *and* the character. In the famous seduction scene with Miriam Hopkins (at 6:13 to 10:18 and 12:34 to 17:06) Marshall plays the role with a cool superciliousness that is in part an expression of the character of Monescu but also conveys a sense of distance from the action, a slightly mocking superiority, as if it were all a charade and a slightly ridiculous one at that. Monescu is reminding us of the role of semblance and make-believe in seduction, where both participants know it is inevitable but pretend otherwise, and where, as already observed, the

---

12   Herman G. Weinberg, *The Lubitsch Touch—A Critical Study* (New York: Dover, 1977), 25.
13   Video introduction with Peter Bogdanovich, Criterion DVD release of *Trouble in Paradise*, 2003.

semblance is one of the essential ingredients in the art of love. Dan Sallitt refers to the influence of operetta and vaudeville on Lubitsch's filmmaking technique. He writes: "Lubitsch's actors, like their theatrical counterparts, tend to establish a direct relationship with the audience, an understanding based on a shared knowing perspective on the fiction."[14] In his early work of the 1930s using the new sound technology, Lubitsch contributed to the development of the musical genre, seeking inspiration in both operetta and vaudeville. Sallitt observes that in Lubitsch's musicals, several of which figured Maurice Chevalier, he and other characters "feel free to address the audience directly, and walk through the plot with the smiling detachment of vaudeville entertainers; they are as much narrators of as participants in the drama." Lubitsch also finds more subtle means to capture the same narrative role for his actors. At the beginning of *Trouble in Paradise*, in a self-referential, meta-commentary, Gaston remarks that "beginnings are always difficult," which then turns into a joke as Gaston asks the waiter, "How would you start?" and the waiter replies, "With a cocktail." At this moment Gaston takes on the role of the Hollywood director who adds, picturesquely, "I want to see that moon in the champagne glass."

This smiling detachment is particularly pronounced in Herbert Marshall's portrayal of Gaston Monescu, where the aloofness of Monescu the character is compounded by an added dimension of aloofness conveyed by Herbert Marshall the actor. Similarly, when Monescu returns Madame Colet's (Kay Francis) lost handbag for the advertised reward, which was Lily's idea, Madame Colet immediately engages Gaston as her personal secretary, a role he then plays with the same sort of excess that Sartre brilliantly describes concerning the waiter in a café:

Let us consider this waiter in the café. His movement is quick and forward, a little too precise, a little too rapid. He comes towards the patrons with a step a little too quick. He bends forward a little too eagerly; his voice, his eyes express an interest a little too solicitous for the order of the customer. Finally there he returns, trying to initiate in his walk the inflexible stiffness of some kind of automaton while carrying his tray with a recklessness of a tight-rope walker by putting it in a perpetually unstable, perpetually broken equilibrium which he perpetually re-establishes by a light movement of the arm and hand.[15]

---

14 Dan Sallitt, "Ernst Lubitsch: The Actor vs. the Character," in Greg Rickmann (ed.), *The Film Comedy Reader* (New York: Limelight Editions, 2001), 154; also at http://www.panix.com/~sallitt/lubitsch.html (accessed June 20, 2013).

15 Jean-Paul Sartre, *Being and Nothingness*, trans. Hazel Barnes (London: Methuen, 1969), 59.

In the film Monescu is playing at being personal secretary to a wealthy woman and the exaggeration of solicitous movement and deferential attention indicate precisely that he is playing. But what is striking is that Marshall—and remember that Lubitsch directed his actors down to the last gesture—achieves this by introducing an ever-so discreet mocking, cynical gap between the actor and the character. Rather than simply acting as a refined and classy thief who is, more or less successfully, playing at being a rather refined and classy personal secretary to Madame Colet, Herbert Marshall is addressing the audience with an implicit nod and a wink, as if to say: "See what a refined secretary I can play at being!" Compare this with Cary Grant's role as the "cat burglar" in Hitchcock's *To Catch a Thief* (1955), where there is a profound ambiguity that lies entirely within the character as played by Grant. Of course, the two situations are different in that we know that Marshall is in fact a thief, while the audience is kept wondering in the case of Cary Grant. Nevertheless, in *Trouble in Paradise* the audience is constantly reminded of the pretence by the manner in which Marshall acts with one eye to the audience. In musicals, this presence to the audience, in which the actor sometimes addresses the audience directly, is not just a vestigial hangover from vaudeville and burlesque but relieves the audience of the sometimes impossible task of making believe that the actors and the action are real. In Lubitsch's hands make-believe serves as more than, or rather other than, a reminder that this is not real, becoming a crucial part of the narrative.

One direct consequence of this schism between actor and character is that it negates the naturalism of cinema and inhibits the development of character. While Cary Grant as the "cat burglar" looks mysterious because there are depths to his character we are unable to fathom, there is no psychological depth to Gaston Monescu. He is a vehicle for the drama of the film, a subliminal narrator, just as there is a rupture of the illusion of reality and we know that we are watching actors acting at being lovers, thieves, and gentlemen.

Critics who chastise Lubitsch for being light and superficial have missed this point about the acting of his actors. In musicals, as just noted, the actors will sometimes address the audience directly, in a style that directly reflects the conventions of the music-hall or vaudeville, while in *Trouble in Paradise*, for instance, the technique keeps the actor at a cynical distance, superior in a sense to the passions of love and desire, not entirely moved by them but almost mocking them as foibles of the pathetic human heart that is either unable to appreciate the absurdity of it all or apt to appreciate the absurdity and play along. In either case, they are not be viewed realistically, as if the events and people depicted on the screen are real events and real people with real psychological desires and beliefs making real decisions and performing real actions. This is why there is minimal character development in *Trouble in Paradise* and a tendency to stereotype characters, so that the criticism of this and other Lubitsch films misses the subtlety of his craft. The viewer who approaches a Lubitsch film realistically is liable to make the mistakes of looking for a psychological depth that the characters don't have and of missing the finesse in Lubitsch's construction. The fact that the construction of *Trouble in Paradise* involves a more complex technique than do other films of the time explains both its muted success on release and the recent recognition of the film as a cinema masterwork.

Actor, Character, Plot

It is no objection to the minimal character development to point out that the relationship between Lily and Gaston develops over the course of the film. The movie portrays four major moments in their relationship: the initial joyous and beguiling seduction scene in which, having come together in playful pretence, they end the night in one another's arms, now well beyond any playful embrace ("I love you. I loved you the moment I saw you"); the moment when, living as a comfortable couple, Lily, reclining on a chair, remembers the time "over a year ago" when Gaston stole a Chinese vase and turned it into a lamp for her nightstand, and he replies (using the stolen object to signify his love): "I remember the vase—and I remember the night"; the crisis introduced by the triangle with Madame Colet, again revolving around a stolen object in the form of Madame Colet's handbag; and the final scene where Lily and Gaston are in the back of a taxi, in flight, which recapitulates the playful seduction at the start with each producing objects stolen from the other.

It would be possible to view these four scenes as moments in the life of a couple: the initial seduction, the couple's routine life together, the threat posed by an intruder to their stability, and the final moment of resolution in which the couple triumphs. It would, moreover, be a reading perfectly suited to the romantic comedy genre: a man and a woman meet and fall in love, their relationship is challenged and risks falling apart, but ultimately they meet the challenge and reunite happily. Such a reading is possible, but there are problems with it, created mainly by the Lubitsch touch. There is, for instance, the problem that the scene in which Gaston and Madame Colet say their farewells is almost parodic of the "what might have been" moment when two people nobly forsake the happiness they could have found with one another. The stilted delivery of banal lines (at 1:19:56) is notably devoid of emotion—it is striking that two characters so attracted to one another as these can part not only without the least display of emotion (compare the draining last scene of *Brief Encounter*, 1945) but with a Mozart-like parody of what had not yet become a genre (one thinks of the "Di scrivermi ogni giorno" ["I will write you every day"] quintet in *Così fan tutte* in which the deliberately banal libretto belies the poignancy of lovers parting).[16] There is also the problem that if Gaston has been at the point of losing his heart to Madame Colet, as Lily surmises, then the joyous finale with the two lovers gaily invading each other's clothing is highly dissonant with the preceding scene. In short, the idea that *Trouble in Paradise* expresses a thematic development, or deploys a strict narrative, does not stand up to scrutiny. Dan Sallitt makes the observation that in Lubitsch's films "his actors characteristically come to a dead stop after every line, and that a beat of silence separates each bit of dialogue from the next."[17] This is clearly overstating the case but there is some truth in saying that "a beat of silence" separates successive scenes in *Trouble in Paradise*, as if there is no character development linking the narrative elements of successive scenes. Thus, Dwight MacDonald, troubled by Lubitsch's lack of interest in narrative, famously claimed it was "close to perfection" even as he referred to the "drastic limitations" of its genre and the "banal" narrative.

It is because of this relationship of actor to character that any attempt to read the film in terms of classic Hollywood categories like "romantic comedy" or "screwball"—which emphasize content and character—will fail to get the point of the film and will never do it justice. A more formal description is required where Lubitsch's techniques are concerned. I will go on to discuss some of these formal techniques, after introducing a key concept taken from Freud.

What Freud analyzed as wit, *Witz*, as distinct from the comic, has the closest of relations to the unconscious. This makes for something of a suggestive idea, and the distinction between wit and the comic will follow this insight.[18] Freud's analy-

---

16 It is worth noting that the parody of the genre here, as with Mozart, is introduced at the very same moment as the genre is invented; I do not know if this is universally so, but there are cases, like here, where parody is not a later response to the genre but is coeval with it.

17 Sallitt, "Ernst Lubitsch: The Actor vs. the Character," 154.

18 Freud considers that the comic behaves differently from jokes. As he says in his classic work on *Witz*, the comic may involve only two persons: "a first who finds what is comic and a second in whom it is found. The third person, to whom the comic thing is told, intensifies the comic process but adds nothing new to it. In jokes this third person is indispensable for the completion of the pleasure-producing process; but on

The romantic couple: Mariette (Kay Francis) and Gaston (Herbert Marshall). *Trouble in Paradise*

sis of wit examines the formal aspect of witticisms, something that is particularly emphasized by Lacan in *Seminar V* where he calls it the signifying articulation. As Freud explains, the actual word form is essential to the working of *Witz*. The content, the idea behind a joke, is not necessarily all that funny. The content may be insulting or bawdy or insurrectionary or racist or otherwise not politically correct, but a *Witz* generally won't make you laugh unless at the formal level there is something clever and well constructed, as when Madame Colet (at 19:35) puts down one of her suitors, the feckless François Filiba, with the comment, "You see, François, marriage is a beautiful mistake which two people make together. But with you, François, I think it would be a mistake."

This is not invariably the case in cinema. Somehow the visual element of film and the mise-en-scène of the events portrayed make a difference. In slapstick you might be laughing because someone has got hurt or done something really stupid, or because something ridiculous has happened, and so on. Moreover, cleverness is not a characteristic that comes to mind where slapstick is concerned; what cleverness there is lies in the production skills that make it possible for this death-defying stunt or that realistic but physically impossible situation to be portrayed on the screen. In our fantasies and desires we are capable of extremely vicious attitudes towards others, of intending gratuitous harm to people whether we bear a grudge or not. On screen we laugh at people, anonymous people, getting hurt. And this needn't be acted or make-believe hurt; the success of *Funniest Home Videos* is built around people doing harm to themselves, as puerile as the humor might be. It must be said, though, that the realistic nature of the scene is tempered by technical means so that the serious implications of a "blooper" are undermined by the avoidance of too much information, such as visuals of nasty cuts and abrasions, etc. Cinema is said to be the most realistic of art forms, but the formal markers of cinema invariably introduce an element of non-reality into the scene.

Ultimately, as Freud saw, *Witz* relies upon verbal means of expression to bypass the censor that makes us good, ideological subjects.

---

the other hand the second person may be absent, except where a tendentious, aggressive joke is concerned. A joke is made, the comic is found—and first and foremost in people, and only by a subsequent transference in things, situations, and so on, as well. As regards jokes, we know that the sources of the pleasure that is to be fostered lie in the subject himself and not in outside people ... Jokes can sometimes re-open sources of the comic which have become inaccessible, and that the comic often serves as a façade for a joke and replaces the fore-pleasure which has otherwise to be produced by the familiar technique. None of this precisely suggests that the relations between jokes and the comic are very simple." Freud, *Jokes and Their Relation to the Unconscious*, SE 8, 181.

Couplings

While romantic comedies revolve around seductions in which a couple fall into bed or love or both, *Trouble in Paradise* establishes a number of couples, all fundamentally different. All are in libidinal relationships even if not all qualify as "romantic" in the proper sense of the term. Let us look at the relations between three couples: François Filiba and the Major; Lily the Countess and Gaston Monescu; and Gaston and Madame Colet.

There is a comedic element to all three, though it is less prominent in the Gaston–Madame Colet relationship, which comes closest to being wistfully tragic. In comedies generally, some actors play characters who are funny because of their response to what happens to them in funny situations, while some actors are comic actors, whatever happens to them. Cary Grant in *Arsenic and Old Lace* (1944) is funny because of his response to the situation he finds himself in: his sweet and gentle but quietly insane aunts turn out to be murdering lonely old bachelors. Then there are properly so-called comic or comedic actors—think of Ben Stiller, Adam Sandler, or Rowan Atkinson—who react in a humorous way to ordinary circumstances. Theater has always had comic characters and many of the minor characters in Shakespeare are comic in this latter sense. Cinema follows the same tradition, with the difference that it is often enough the case that the actors themselves are comic actors, not just the characters they play. They are known for playing comic roles, they choose comic roles, and their films are marketed with them in that role—a phenomenon so well analyzed by Stanley Cavell.[19]

The Major and François Filiba

Trouble in Paradise, then, revolves around three couples. The first is the pairing of the two minor characters who play a large, comic role throughout the film: the Major (Charles Ruggles) and François Filiba (Edward Everett Horton). The film pairs them as indistinguishable rivals and the comedy plays on the two dimensions of their indistinguishability and their rivalry. They are as indistinguishable from one another as Tweedledum from Tweedledee, or Rosencrantz from Guildenstern—these are their ancestors, bound together in the imaginary, and, like any imaginary couple, their destinies mirror and parallel one another's. Their indistinguishability plays out in a rivalrous courtship of the beautiful Madame

---

19   See the chapter, "Audience, Actor, and Star," in Cavell's *The World Viewed: Reflections on the Ontology of Film*, Enlarged edition (Cambridge MA: Harvard University Press, 1979).

The comic couple: François Filiba (Edward Everett Horton) and the Major (Charles Ruggles).
Trouble in Paradise

Colet, where the joke running through the film is that while each sees the other as a threat to his own success with Madame, neither realizes that he has no chance of success at all. Madame Colet loses her valuable handbag; the two suitors run into one another at the accessories shop as they each search for a replacement, and much humor is made of the fact that each tries to hide from the other their reason for being there. Moreover, both have hastened to fill the gap of the missing bag with another, Filiba even choosing the one that (as we have seen earlier in the film) Madame Colet thought wasn't worth the money—as if in further indication that he has no idea what her desire is. They are of course bound together by their rivalry; it is this that homogenizes them, turning them into images of one another. This bonding results in a fraternal, libidinal tie—what Freud called "aim-inhibited libido"—demonstrated near the end of the film when they are found sitting together side by side, disconsolate and denigrating as unworthy of Madame Colet the talents of the favored Gaston.

The humor of many doubles stems from the fact that the pair, unaware of their identity, are perpetually engaged in a struggle to differentiate themselves from one another. The identical Tweedledum and Tweedledee "go to war" in a humorous illustration of the rivalrous, or even murderous, dimension of the imaginary relationship, while Hergé's celebrated Dupond and Dupont, on the other hand, identical but for their different moustaches, embody the narcissism that valorizes minor differences just because these differences differentiate otherwise indistinguishable elements.

The Major and François Filiba, on the other hand, are not indistinguishable, even if they are two of a kind, issued from a social class in which an essential role is played by mutual recognition. They are united as a couple by their desire to be Madame Colet's beloved. Both are wealthy bachelors accustomed to paying for sex, while being suitors to Colet whose benign indifference towards both is so blatantly apparent to the audience as to make them look fools for not realizing it themselves. For instance, when asked by Madame Colet why he was offensive to Filiba, the Major replies (at 21:28), "Because I hate him. Because I love you." Madame Colet, as if speaking to an ill-behaved child, scolds him and says, "I want you to go out and apologize. Immediately." Or, again, when she says to Filiba, with that *Witz* referred to earlier: "Marriage is a beautiful mistake which two people make together. But with you, François, I think it would be a mistake." It is this common object of desire where each wants what the other wants, and above all their blindness over its inaccessibility and the futility of their quest, that unites this comic couple as brothers, as siblings. They each desire to be the Other's desire, to be the phallus for the beautiful Madame Colet. But try as they might to occupy this place themselves, her desire lies elsewhere, leaving them to swallow their bitterness and manifest their resentment, the remnant of their loss, against the person of Gaston Monescu. Gaston on the other hand is the sole person not to offer himself to Madame Colet and his seduction of her turns on a play between his role as her personal secretary—a role in itself ambiguous if not suspect from the outset—and an assumed intimacy that, because its audacity verges on the impertinent, thrills and stirs something inside Madame Colet that no other man does. Gaston knows very well the game he is playing, ambiguously suspended between the role of the perfect personal secretary, Sartrean in his correctness, aloofness, and efficiency, and a seductive presence who, though Madame Colet never seems to notice, stands too close, far too close for a secretary…

In the Major–Filiba couple we see that they are homogenized by the relationship to the phallus as lack in the Other. This makes them into copies of one another, identified along imaginary lines while they assume the same identification with the phallus as object. The result is a touch of perversion easily traceable in the relationship that each has to the objects and accessories of the woman. Whether it be the woman's handbag, stole or jewelry, the metonymical object symbolizes, at least for these two, the woman's lack with which they each identify.

Lily and Gaston

If the Major–Filiba couple is an imaginary, comical duo united by their identification with the object of the woman's desire, Lily the Countess and Gaston
Monescu illustrate a different and more complex relationship. They are in one
sense classic screen characters: he the gentleman thief and smooth con-man, she
the lady pickpocket. It is true that when Gaston declares that he has loved Lily
from the first time he saw her, they are the words of a man in love, to which she
responds with words of love of her own. But their relationship is based on a number of other features as well.

First, there is mutual recognition, made comical by the inversion of conven-
tional values. Both delight in recognizing their values, their skills as pickpockets,
and their ideals of thievery in one another. The hilarious and deservedly famous
seduction scene ends with each applauding the other's cleverness and embracing one another in the narcissistic pleasure of their mutual recognition. This
bonding is not that of lovers (though it does not preclude them being lovers as
indeed they are in the film) but corresponds to the libidinal ties of the group
united together around the type of ideal analyzed by Freud in *Group Psychology
and the Analysis of the Ego*. These are the aim-inhibited libidinal ties of affection
that transform sensual love into bonds that are able to establish enduring ties
between members of a group. Following Freud, we could say that by virtue of
the fact that Lily and Gaston share the ego ideal of thievery they can identify
themselves with one another in their ego.[20]

Second, their bonds are those of the form of friendship Aristotle called "im-
perfect friendship"—a relationship in which friends recognise that the other is
the source of some advantage or of some pleasure that they can benefit from in
the friendship. The association is not purely calculated or utilitarian, since there
is sincere friendship and pleasure involved, but the friendship will not necessarily last when it is no longer useful to one or both parties. Friendships in the
workplace are often of this kind. And to the extent that Monescu and Lily are
friends in this sense, it is not a romantic relationship. They are sexual partners
nevertheless, and while the romance, at least initially, has no suspense, no discomfort, no pain, neither suffering nor ecstasy, it has the romance of an assignation,
the "moon in the champagne glass," at which two kindred spirits meet, recognise
themselves in the other, and fall in love. Even though there are no dizzy spells, no

---

20   See Freud, *Group Psychology and the Analysis of the Ego* (1921), SE 18, 116.

The thief couple: Lily (Miriam Hopkins) and Gaston (Herbert Marshall). *Trouble in Paradise*

sobs, no sorrows, no sighs, and even though their relationship is convenient for both—they are partners, albeit partners in crime—their encounter climaxes in an erotic and romantic denouement.

It is not essential to their relationship that they live as man and woman, but they do, and the development of their sexual relationship is cleverly depicted by the theft of precious objects signifying the invasion of the other's person: he realizes she is stealing his wallet (which he has just stolen from Monsieur Filiba) but remains silent because "her embrace was so sweet"; he steals then returns her pin; she steals then returns his watch; he steals her garter, but this time kisses it and keeps it for himself. At this point, she can do no other than fall into his arms. In their embrace he utters the words: "I love you. I loved you the moment I saw you."

Lily becomes jealous immediately she becomes aware that Madame Colet is pursuing Monescu, and we sense her initial suspicion, unease, and discomfort over the intentions of first her rival and then of Gaston himself. "If you behave like a gentleman, I'll break your neck" (at 44:58) she warns him prior to his evening with Madame Colet. Later, tough cookie that she is, she is nevertheless saddened by the realization that she may be losing Gaston to another woman. Lily is motivated by a combination of love and self-interest; as a shrewd woman who has always lived off her wits, the figure of self-interest lies behind her love. The manner in which she is prepared to renounce Gaston and free him for Madame Colet, which I discuss below, demonstrates very well that while Lily loves Gaston, and behaves like a scorned lover, she is also a clearheaded and unsentimental swindler.

Their shared ideals are those of thievery and all that implies in terms of living off one's wits, never having to work for a living, outwitting others. This situation is made more complicated in the film by the fact that the worst crooks turn out to be the respectable and supposedly honest pillars of society. Their hypocrisy and criminality is everywhere made apparent in pointed fashion: Filiba is waiting for two prostitutes to arrive when Monescu robs him; the eminently respectable Giron, illustrious, long-standing friend of the Colet family, turns out to have been quietly embezzling Madame Colet's fortune for years. Madame Colet herself is accused of verging on criminality by the Russian Trotskyist for spending a fortune on a handbag "in times like these" (we are at the height of the Great Depression). Nevertheless, if robbery and embezzlement are everywhere, the criminality of Monescu and Lily is assessed as different in kind. Their thievery involves no hypocrisy, just the opposite; they cleave to their ego ideal, built around the virtues of thievery. In the world of Gaston and Lily an object has value if and only if it is stolen.

Because they are fraternal images of one another united under the banner of shared ideals, and despite the fact that they end up falling into one another's arms and becoming lovers, their relationship is not a romance but one of friendship. Indeed, it goes some way, though with a perverse inversion, to fulfilling the requirements for Aristotle's true friendship: I love my friend because she has a virtuous character. This is the conceit in the exchange between Lily and Gaston: each recognizes him or herself in the other as a person of "virtue"; she steals his wallet, he steals her garter! How marvelous! There is no seduction, only recognition—recognition that what they value in themselves they also find in the other. It is thus not a romance but a libidinal and narcissistic bond founded on the recognition of shared values—and the inversion of values it is built on is exploited by Lubitsch for our amusement. True to their calling, Gaston and Lily are con "artists" of the highest order.

The Object as Contraband

There is an interplay in the film between sex as plundering and the stolen object, apparent in the way the latter is constantly at play in the scenes of seduction. The seduction scene between Lily and Gaston advances by means of increasingly intimate objects more or less stolen from the other without the other's knowledge or consent: wallet, pin, watch, then garter. The metaphor of seduction as the plundering of the other's intimate object does not apply symmetrically in sexual relations, where the lover to beloved (*erastes* to *eronomos*) relationship typically goes from a man to a woman, and where the *erastes* is easily portrayed as a plunderer. The plundering of a woman's intimacy, whether she resists or consents, by a man who seduces entails a complex play of seduction and counter-seduction, but the connotation of invasion is never far away, and is consistently exploited in *Trouble in Paradise*. Lily and Gaston's sexual pickpocketing, in which Lily gives as good as she gets, is followed by a more subtle but arguably more erotic sexual invasion in the seduction scene between Madame Colet and Gaston Monescu.

The elements of the scene begin to be set up when Madame Colet buys a handbag:

SALESMAN: This one, Madame Colet, is only 3,000 francs.
MADAME COLET: Oh, no, that's entirely too much. How 'bout that one?
SALESMAN: Oh, this one Madame? Well that's 125,000 francs.
MADAME COLET: But it's beautiful. I'll take it.
SALESMAN: Thank you, Madame Colet.

Madame Colet later loses the handbag at the Opera, though not before it has been observed and its value noted by Gaston Monescu. In fact, what Gaston first sees is the handbag. The camera goes first to the handbag as the object, then to Madame Colet, back to the bag, back to Madame Colet and then, finally, back to the handbag. It is not she who gets the last look from Gaston, but the object. When the handbag goes missing we can presume that Monescu is the thief; we are not told how he does it but we can imagine the "how" presents no problem for a man who can "walk into the Bank of Constantinople and walk out with the Bank of Constantinople." It is, however, the return of the handbag that is of interest. The two impotent suitors, Filiba and the Major, ineffectively try to buy replacement handbags with their wealth and their knowledge of what shops a chap shops at leads them to the very shop where Madame Colet originally bought the handbag. Monescu is much more to the point, to the point of Madame Colet's desire, in that, having found the handbag, he returns it to her … in exchange for the reward she has offered for its return.

In the scene in which Gaston returns the handbag, he gradually but relentlessly penetrates Madame Colet's intimate spaces. As if he were exploring some sort of *Carte du Tendre*, Gaston begins by peering around the quasi-public downstairs room in which Madame Colet receives her visitors. He then proceeds (at 30:30) to an inventory, under the mildest of protests from Madame Colet, of the contents of her handbag, even to the point of brazenly declaring he has read a love letter from her suitor the Major. Lubitsch gives this moment beautifully sexualized imagery. As Gaston is entirely focused on rummaging around in her intimate belongings (one purse, one vanity case, two hairpins, one cigarette lighter, one box of real matches, a letter from the Major…), Madame Colet (Kay Francis clearly acting under Lubitsch's instructions) takes no interest in the bag, shows not the slightest alarm over what Gaston may find there, but is completely entranced by the rummaging Gaston. As he rummages, head bent over the bag, she looks at him transfixed. It is a beautifully metaphorical representation of love, seduction, and sexual intimacy.

The penetration of Madame Colet's intimate spaces continues. Gaston runs up the stairs to her private space, uninvited. He follows her, again uninvited, into her personal secretary's office and even closes the door behind him. He enters her secretary's private room, again uninvited, and is found by Madame Colet staring at the double bed previously used by her secretary, who, she declares, was sacked because she was "too happy" in the bed. And, finally, he discovers where Madame

Colet's safe, the most secret treasure of all, is located and detects the combination of the lock. In the penetration of Madame Colet's world, sexual penetration, invasion of private space, and theft of her belongings are intermingled in the rich visual text of Lubitsch's film. The sexual content of the encounter with the increasingly invasive Gaston Monescu, and the final submission (at 36:48) of Madame Colet who, ultimately, "can do no other," are rendered by making the sexual innuendo explicit:

> **GASTON**: If I were your father—which, fortunately, I am not—and you made any attempt to handle your own business affairs, I would give you a good spanking, in a business way, of course.
> **MADAME COLET**: What would you do if you were my secretary?
> **GASTON**: The same thing.
> **MADAME COLET**: You're hired.

This interweaving of sex and money in relation to theft continues throughout the film. Thievery is a turn-on for Lily and Gaston. Theft is more than a source of income, it excites them; it is the currency of their erotic attachment. The final scene between Lily and Gaston in the back of a taxi as they flee the residence of Madame Colet and their own detention by the police is a comic recapitulation, in silence, of the first scene, the seduction scene, between them. He reaches into his jacket for the coveted necklace, the one object of Madame Colet's that Lily had specifically requested they steal, but it is gone. With a shy glance at Gaston, Lily produces it, along with Madame Colet's stolen handbag. Taking out her own purse, Lily is surprised to find it empty of the 100,000 francs she herself has stolen from Madame Colet … which Gaston then produces from out of his own jacket, thrusting it forcefully into her purse. At this point, in a reprise of the first seduction scene, they embrace. "Gaston!" she cries. The credits roll.

Gaston Monescu and Madame Colet

Gaston the penetrator is also the perfect servant to Madame Colet. At least in appearance, he is efficient, dependable, deferential (mock-deferential might describe him better), he gives wise counsel, and moreover, though a gentleman, he is a destitute one and not too proud to enter into the service of a wealthy woman. With Madame Colet his behavior is impeccable. He makes no overt display of sexual interest in her, acts properly and respectfully towards her at every turn.

Madame Colet becomes increasingly fascinated by him and makes it increasingly apparent that she is available. There is a marvelous passage involving a sequence of clocks (at 44:50 to 47:15, displaying what can only be called the Lubitsch touch) when, having said goodnight to one another, we hear first the key turn in the lock of Gaston's door and *only then* the locking of Madame Colet's door in the adjacent room—indicating that she has been waiting at her door for Gaston and only locks it when she knows that he is not coming to her bed. This is a most subtle and erotic moment, replete with the frustration and tension that she feels about this man who hesitates to come to her. It is following this that his presence in her life starts to take on the whiff of scandal, as her friends start to speak sarcastically of the "secretary."

For most of the film Gaston is the scheming con-man determined to prey on a beautiful, rich woman whose confidence he has won, and who has fallen in love with him. It is not necessary that she fall in love with him; he only needs her trust. But she does fall in love with him, and indeed does so at first sight. He of course subsequently falls in love with her, but even then he plans to spend only one night with her and then abscond with her money and jewels and rejoin Lily to flee Paris together (as they must, once he realizes that sooner or later Filiba will recognise him as the man who robbed him in Venice).

As the perfect servant, he is also part of the hired staff. Madame Colet, who has more wealth than she needs and is indifferent to the value of money, falls in love with a man she pays for. She raises Lily's salary in order to spend more time alone with Gaston, and this immediately arouses Lily's suspicions. Lily's response to this, in perhaps the single dramatic moment of the film, is complex. It occurs in an intricate scene towards the end of the film when it has become apparent that Gaston has fallen for Madame Colet, that he is about to be unfaithful to Lily (about to "act like a gentleman," as Lily pointedly remarks earlier), and that Madame Colet intends to spend the night in his room (remarking, as if in counterpoint, that she has no desire "to be a lady"). Thinking Gaston is about to betray her, Lily (at 1:11:35) steals Madame Colet's 100,000 francs from the safe, declaring "This is what I want. This is real. Money. Cash." In a complicated exchange, Lily will effectively release Gaston to Madame Colet for this not inconsiderable amount, which nevertheless remains less, as Lily later points out, than the 125,000 francs Madame Colet paid for a single handbag. Clear-sighted Lily says, "Madame, the only thing that seems to stand between you and romance … is a hundred thousand francs." Madame Colet, oblivious to the value of money as the film emphasizes time and again, cannot understand how Gaston could intend to rob her rather than love her. Lily, on the other hand, remains faithful to the ideals of thievery that Gaston has started to eschew. When Gaston realizes that a member of the establishment, in the person of Monsieur Giron, can embezzle funds with impunity, while a "self-made crook" like himself will be handed over to the police without a moment's hesitation, he realizes that he is forever excluded from the circle of privilege. Gaston has started to fall in love with Madame Colet and, in the words of Lily, to behave "like a gentleman" and embrace the glamour of Madame Colet at the expense of the wifely Lily. Interestingly, Lubitsch doesn't at all suggest that this is a calculated move on Gaston's part. He has no thought of becoming Madame Colet's lover, perhaps even eventually her husband, for her wealth. He is in his way a man of integrity, in that he lives and abides by the ideals of a thief but is no gold-digger. He will rob Madame Colet, even as she loves him, but will not make love to her or marry her under false pretences. Indeed, one of the major things this scene shows is that as Gaston becomes increasingly romantically involved with Madame Colet, he is less inclined to rob her. He is caught between two codes in conflict: the code of love which requires a certain fidelity to the love object, and the code of the self-made crook which requires fidelity to the stolen object—and here, *stealing* her object is an act of betrayal for a lover, while being given an object is part of the code of love.

However, when Lily confesses that she and not Gaston stole the money, and declares that the only thing standing between Madame Colet and romance is 100,000 francs, her intervention has the effect of rupturing the separation between the two codes, always a fictional one anyway. It is effectively equivalent to an analytic intervention because it changes the discourse of the protagonists, Gaston and Madame Colet. Here, the sentimental thought that romantic love might rupture or transcend the economy of goods is never indulged in. Love comes at a price, and because the price varies from one person to the next, each must decide whether or not he or she is ready to pay it. For Gaston the price is his freedom, for Madame Colet her reputation. Lily, for her part, consistently measures everything against its monetary value, and the fact that she does so allows something very interesting to happen. When Madame Colet dismisses her with the remark, "You have your money, [now go]," Lily responds, "I don't want your money. You wanted to buy him for 50 francs. Well, you can have him for nothing!" and throws the 100,000 francs on the bed in a scornful gesture indicating that Gaston has no value for her now that he has rejected the ideals of the thief for the sake of mere romance. "You were willing to sacrifice a hundred thousand francs for her!" she scoffs to him, accusingly. She then turns on Madame Colet, pointing out that if she was prepared to pay 125,000 francs for a handbag, she can easily pay 100,000 for Gaston Monescu. She then gathers up the money she had earlier thrown down on the bed and storms out.

This is the most unusual exchange in the entire film. What does it mean? It is effectively an interpretation by Lily of Madame Colet's love for Gaston. Her initial gesture apparently accepts Madame Colet's claim to Gaston on Madame Colet's financial terms, thus deriding her pretence to the discourse of love: you try to buy him for 50 francs, well you can have him for nothing! This has the appearance of an analytic interpretation, for it has the effect of exposing Madame Colet's obliviousness to the fact that she is making use of her wealth and position to get her way while pretending that she and Gaston are engaged in lovemaking as equals. Madame Colet remains impervious, willfully so, to the true social relationship between them. As I have already mentioned, her friends snigger about his being "her secretary"; she declares she would have no hesitation "ruining his reputation"; and so on. But when Lily makes a truly analytic interpretation by taking the money in exchange for Gaston and walking out, this tests Madame Colet's love for and commitment to Gaston. The money she pays is of no consequence; she has after all paid more for a handbag, so what a trifle to pay for a lover? But while she is now free to have her lover, she finds that he actually comes at too high a price, since the day after their night of romance he will be bundled off to the commissariat of police and charged with a long list of crimes. True to his ideals, he spares her the scandal, cutting the bonds of love, not just by leaving, but also by declaring his final allegiance to Lily when, as he leaves, he shows Madame Colet the necklace he has just stolen from her—the very necklace Lily had wanted him to steal for her benefit. True thief that he is, Gaston steals the necklace from the woman he might have loved to give as a gesture of love to his beloved—an intriguing gesture that Madame Colet allows and indeed seems to endorse. In a final intermixing of the themes of theft and sex, instead of sleeping with her, Lubitsch has him rob her, an act that terminates their nascent romance and returns him to his partner.

Lubitsch here avoids any suggestion of sentimentality, of the kind normally associated with the scene of two lovers forsaking one another in the name of something more noble, more pressing, or more "bourgeois," as has so often been the case in the movies (again, *Brief Encounter* springs to mind). Lubitsch achieves this, first, by having his parting lovers use such clichéd language that the scene appears almost as a parody; second, by maintaining the very controlled gap between actor and character I have already discussed, which keeps the characters at a distance from any authentic emotional involvement with one another. The "It could have been marvelous—Divine—Wonderful" scene (at 1:19:55) between Kay Francis and Herbert Marshall displays both of these strategies clearly. In this sequence of mock-romantic statements by the two actors about what could have been, verging on parody, Lubitsch manages to keep the moment's poignancy while deliberately avoiding the sentimentality of romance by an ironic distancing of the actors from the characters they are playing and the emotions and desires they are subject to. It is as if they are just saying their lines, lines the characters themselves know they are supposed to say. And they mirror Lily saying her lines in her first scene when she says "I shouldn't have come," and then lets herself go, and then, having said her lines, stays—to which Gaston replies "Oh don't stop complaining [that is, pretending]; it's beautiful." But when Madame Colet and Gaston say their lines, "It could have been wonderful," etc., they do leave each other—just the opposite of the opening scene.

It is not difficult to agree with Lubitsch's observation that *Trouble in Paradise* was his best film in terms of *pure style*. It is the most stylized and stylish of his sound films and displays in a highly enhanced form the characteristics of Lubitsch's filmmaking style. A notoriously strong director of his actors, we can see his mark upon the stylized relationship portrayed between actor and character. It may be true, as has been remarked, that this feature of his films originated with vaudeville, but he uses it to such refined effect that it becomes a novel cinematic device in his hands, as *Trouble in Paradise* testifies. The result is a beautifully weighted sense of subtle irony about seductions, sexual encounters, and the things we humans do in the face of the absence of any straightforward sexual rapport between the sexes. The naturalness and candidness of Lubitsch's treatment of sex is of course deservedly celebrated, but one should also note his frank treatment of the passions of the human soul. Lubitsch never exploits our emotions, he spurns nostalgia, and scorns self-indulgence. It's not that love is just a game, but rather that love can and ought to be playfully erotic, and becomes a mere shadow if it loses touch with seduction and uncertainty.

Indeed, the *Witz* that runs all the way through *Trouble in Paradise* in the form of an interweaving of the themes of sex and theft provides much of the formal pleasure of the film, along with the visual metaphors (one thinks of the clocks sequence) in which Lubitsch delights and at which he excels. The interweaving of sex and theft creates much humor but also gives a subtly erotic and unstated, almost subliminal dimension to the film. The inversion of values for the two thieves Lily and Gaston is erotic and playful, as they acknowledge their mutual expertise at "touching up" one another. Equally, the relationship between Gaston and Madame Colet revolves around theft and sex. He penetrates her private quarters. She in turn is happy to pay good money to buy Gaston. The fact that she intends to buy him on the cheap, as Lily caustically remarks,[21] is of more significance for Lily and Gaston than for Madame Colet, who with her vast wealth is, for the time, culpably ignorant of the value of money. The question of what one is prepared to pay for love (the price of sex is a much more straightforward issue, as Filiba and the Major both know) is raised when Madame Colet becomes aware that Gaston, with the aid of Lily, means to rob her and had never intended to become her lover. He leaves, not because of her but for fear of being apprehended by the police. What might have been a sad but obviously clichéd lovers' farewell is acted—and here it's all in the acting—in a way that borders on parody. And there is a lack of sentimentality in the fact that in the end it is Lily who remains true to her values. For while Gaston has to be reminded that he is a con-man and a thief, when Lily realizes she is on the point of losing Gaston anyway, she is prepared to sell him to Madame Colet for 100,000 francs and head for the door.

And finally, the funny, joyful and, as a recapitulation of Lily and Gaston's initial assignation, clever final scene in the taxi is a scene of reconciliation in which the couple are reunited, at least for the while if not for good: no ring, no flowers, their renewed alliance romantically cemented with Gaston thrusting his (Madame Colet's?) wad of money into Lily's open purse—one last brilliant piece of sexual wit from the master Lubitsch.

---

21   Gaston: "Well, what does she want?" Lily: "You! And she's willing to pay as high as 50 francs" (at 43:40).

Robert Pfaller

What is so Funny About Multiple Love? The Polygamous Lubitsch Touch

One absolutely stunning thing about Ernst Lubitsch's comedies is their optimistic, frivolous view on polygamy. Not only do they show, like other comedies, a preference for erotic troubles, sidesteps and triangulations, Lubitsch's films even present erotic plurality as a possible happy ending: an outcome with, for example, a woman and two men (*Design for Living*, 1933), or even three (*To Be or Not to Be*, 1942). What has been called the Lubitsch touch stems, in no small part, from this "polygamous" position in his understanding of comedy. With Lubitsch, one is often reminded of Adam Phillips's twist on an old English proverb: "Two is company, but three is a couple."[1]

Obviously polygamy is not in itself necessarily funny or comic. Yet, on the other hand, comedy seems unable to exist without something that refers to polygamy. So one has to ask which type of polygamy is at stake here and what it is precisely that makes it so useful for comedy's purposes. One may furthermore feel tempted to approach these aesthetic concerns in terms of their ethical and political consequences: Can a political ethics be derived from a successful aesthetics? In other words: Can real life follow the laws of comedy? Is real life pleasant (for the people involved) when comedy is funny (for the observers)? Is there such a thing as a real life with a Lubitsch touch?

---

[1] For this quotation see the back cover of Adam Phillips's brilliant book *Monogamy* (London: Faber and Faber, 1996). I am grateful to Camilla Nielsen, Vienna, for this precious hint.

Polygamy

The pertinence of the issue of polygamy in Lubitsch's films can already be seen from an overview of some of their titles (in either their English or German versions), for example: *Die Ehe im Kreise* (*The Marriage Circle*, 1924), *Küss mich noch einmal* (*Kiss Me Again*, 1924), *Liebesparade* (*The Love Parade*, 1929), *Serenade zu dritt* (*Design for Living*), or *Ehekomödie* (*That Uncertain Feeling*, 1941). The same predilection for multiple love can also be discerned in the titles of several screwball comedies, for example: *Double Wedding* (1937, Richard Thorpe), *My Favorite Wife* (1940, Garson Kanin), or *I Love You Again* (1940, W. S. van Dyke II).

Of course, polygamy does not appear only at the level of titles, but also at the very heart of the comedy plots of the time. This can most clearly be seen in, for instance, the screwball comedy *Libeled Lady* (1936, Jack Conway), in which William Powell has to fake a marriage to Jean Harlow just in order to seduce the millionaire's daughter Myrna Loy into an affair with a married man (a certain extra-diegetic comicality, by the way, here stems here from the fact that in real life Jean Harlow actually was Powell's partner). Even in post-war comedies we can observe a certain recurrence of multiple love, for example in *Kiss Me, Stupid* (1964, Billy Wilder) or *Good Neighbor Sam* (1964, David Swift). In all these comedies multiple love is acknowledged as a necessity and becomes established (sometimes—as in *Kiss Me, Stupid*—by the very attempt to avoid it), if only temporarily. In most cases it gets dissolved in the end.

Herein lies the uniqueness what might be called the polygamous radicality of Lubitsch, who, far from treating polygamy as a transitory state of affairs, repeatedly presents it as the successful outcome of the story and the mark of its happy ending. Only once in recent mainstream cinema history, to my knowledge, this has been handled with similar nonchalance: in the 2001 US comedy *Bandits* (Barry Levinson), at the end of which not only do the two young bank-robbing accomplices get married, but also the three heroes—Bruce Willis, Billy Bob Thornton, and Cate Blanchett—stand up at the priest's request that the engaged couple rise from their seats.

Comedy and Multiplicity

Already it might be guessed that this certain bias in comedy towards polygamous love is due to comedy's inherent tendency to multiply characters and objects.[2]

---

2   For the double as a recurrent concern of comedy see Mladen Dolar, "Comedy and Its Double," in Robert Pfaller (ed.), *Stop That Comedy! On the Subtle Hegemony of the Tragic in Our Culture* (Vienna: Sonderzahl, 2005), 181–209.

So, for example, in Lubitsch's *To Be or Not to Be* we find two concentration camp Ehrhardts, two Professor Siletskys, two Hitlers, two false moustaches. No wonder, then, that we may also find at least two husbands. Their comical effect may be described by paraphrasing a sentence from Blaise Pascal: Two husbands, neither of whom is particularly funny by himself, can make us laugh by their mere duplication. The comicality of such a proliferation of husbands stems not only from the Freudian "narcissism of small differences"[3] (i.e., the fact that the one man appears as a slight criticism of the other), but also from the appearance of an impossibility—that of one person existing in two places at the same time, which, while we know very well it can't happen, nevertheless someone may believe that it has. (The line "To be or not to be" could here be read as a kind of magic spell that always conjures up multiple husbands.) It has to be added here, that, unlike in some French comedies of the "secret-lover-hiding-in-the-closet" type, in Lubitsch's films every man in intimate contact with a woman is to be regarded not only as a lover but as a husband. This is due to the prevailing "appearance counts" principle:[4] in comedy, whoever looks like a husband is a husband.

However, as Georg Seeßlen has perspicuously remarked, one never really knows what happens in the affairs of Lubitsch's characters[5]—between, for example, Maria Tura and her loving pilot. In a line that was cut after Carole Lombard died in an airplane crash shortly before the release of the film, she says, having been invited by her airman for a flight, "What can happen on a plane?" This line highlights a trick specific to Lubitsch's heroines, and a nice parallel between the pilot and the Hamlet actor Joseph Tura: apparently Maria is able to push her men to a point of male imposture at which she becomes completely safe from them. Precisely when they think they are performing at their very best and most impressive (whether as an actor or as a pilot), they can neither get close to her nor control her. Similarly, the heroine in *Design for Living* initially escapes from love by driving her two lovers forward towards artistic success. One consequence of this strategy, when lovers blossom and proliferate, is that love—or sex—may sometimes seem to disappear (almost like in courtly love). Yet we have to ask whether the aim of Lubitsch's comedies does not consist precisely in letting it

3   Cf. Sigmund Freud, *Civilization and Its Discontents* (1930), SE 21, 114.
4   Cf. Robert Pfaller, "Materialism's Comedy," in *Bedeutung Magazine. Philosophy—Current Affairs—Art—Literature—Review—Analysis*, Vol. 1 (London: Bedeutung Publishing Ltd., 2008), 20–28.
5   Cf. Georg Seeßlen, "Vom Verlust des Paradieses der Schwäche und der Sinnenfreude," in *Sein oder Nichtsein*, Deutsches Theater Berlin (Programmheft), 37: "Fast immer ist das Zentrum eine Dreiecksgeschichte, und fast immer läßt es das Drehbuch im Vagen, wie weit dabei die Untreue eines Partners gegangen ist."

reappear again. If, as Stanley Cavell has suggested, certain Hollywood comedies can be regarded as comedies of re-marriage, then certain of Lubitsch's comedies can be regarded as comedies of "re-polygamy."

Multiplicity of Love, and Funnyness

Of course, it has to be admitted that multiple love is not always funny, as can be seen in classic melodramas such as *Jules et Jim* (1962, François Truffaut). More recent cinema too is full of sad examples—just think of the odd description of partner-exchange games in *The Ice Storm* (1997, Ang Lee), or of the ultimately tragic presentation of the polygamy issue in *Marie-Jo et ses deux amours* (2001, Robert Guédiguian). In particular, a certain genre that I would like to call "post-sexual cinema," beginning around the year 2000, has specialized in elaborating on the sadder aspects of non-monogamous love, invariably portrayed as ending in inevitable failure and frustration. Typical of this approach are, for instance, *Intimacy* (*Intimité*, 2001, Patrice Chéreau), *Romance XXX* (1999, Catherine Breillat), *Une liaison pornographique* (1999, Frédéric Fonteyne), *Le Pornographe* (2001, Bertrand Bonello), as well as novels by Michel Houellebecq and Cathérine Millet.

Cinema can here be taken as registering a shift in the mood of Western society more generally, a shift also apparent in some recent real-world cases—think of Dominique Strauss-Kahn, Julian Assange, or the German weather forecaster Jörg Kachelmann. Of course it is impossible from the outside to make any judgments about what actually happened between these men and their women, but one can nevertheless analyze the general interest and public passion these cases provoked. It seems to clearly express one desire: the desire that affairs should always be suspected of being cases of rape; that multiple love of this kind should generally be regarded as a crime; that there be no such thing as innocent multiple love.

Apart from this sinister contemporary perception which condemns it, multiple love is also definitely not funny under another condition: when it is openly affirmed and confessed. Such is the case with the so-called "slut ethics" of certain sexual minority groups who indulge in ideas of "openness," "honesty" and "negotiated consensuality."[6] One "practical guide" to this ethics recommends that partners share all their experiences of other partners with each other, that they attempt to meet each other's partners, and even do one's best to fall in love with

---

6   Cf. Dossie Easton and Janet W. Hardy, *The Ethical Slut: A Practical Guide to Polyamory, Open Relationships and Other Adventures*, Second edition (Berkeley: Celestian Arts, 2009), 21, 26, 32.

them too, etc.[7] Assuming such a life is possible at all, it is certainly not wrong, but it is definitely not comical either. Similar principles prevail in the German "Polyamori" movement, which has generated a new genre of partisan literature—confessional texts about love with multiple partners, be they hetero- or homosexual, which often read like "A loves B, and B loves C, and both love D, and they all tell E," i.e., as boring as a telephone-book.[8]

It would seem that, in order to produce comical effects (at least intended ones), polygamy has to be treated as a *secret*. For only when treated as such is polygamy respected as something belonging to the order of the impossible. It thus makes a great difference whether the people involved agree that they need not know everything about their love partners or, on the contrary, whether they feel obliged to know all there is to know. The need to know and to openly confess destroys the care for appearances—which is comedy's central concern. Comedy can also be seen as a civilized attempt to moderate the lover's desire for knowing the truth (*The Awful Truth*, as the title of Leo McCarey's brilliant screwball comedy from 1937 puts it). It emphasizes the human right to decide what one does not want to know—a right which is considerably threatened under postmodern conditions, wherein more and more people appear convinced that they have to tell their alleged best friends at any price "what they must know."[9]

The Order of the Impossible
Since polygamy is not funny in itself, in order to become funny it has to follow the laws of comedy. One fundamental law of comedy is that comedy deals with the *impossible*. This can be seen at a number of (typically Lubitschean) points: the appearance of doubles, or doppelganger, the repetition of scenes; equally the "magic" or "symbolic efficiency" typical of comedy, e.g., the fact that a man's saying to himself "I am a girl" will have an effect on himself as well as on other men (cf. *Some Like It Hot*, 1959), or, as in Woody Allen's *Scoop* (2006), the fact that even the poorest variété magician at some point manages to invoke a real ghost (in this case, that of a dead journalist who even after his death still has to go after the big story). In Lubitsch's *To Be or Not to Be* this symbolic efficiency is a constant

7   Ibid., 202.
8   For this example see Cornelia Jönsson and Simone Maresch, *Gründe, offen zu lieben. Ein Loblied auf offene Beziehungen, Polyamorie und die Freundschaft* (Berlin: Schwarzkopf & Schwarzkopf, 2010), Chapter 1.
9   I have elaborated on this problem in my recent book *Zweite Welten. Und andere Lebenselixiere* (Frankfurt am Main: Fischer, 2012), Chapter 5: Das Ungesagte und das Nichtgewusste, 81–95.

issue—beginning with the fact that a theater piece about the Gestapo performed on a Warsaw stage is seen as a real provocation to Hitler, and is duly censored, which ironically means that now "Hamlet" triumphs over "Gestapo" on the billboard, until the final development that the actors, simply by their acting, are able to bring about real acts of political resistance.

The symbolic efficiency—the fact that mere words or even the poorest stagings can become true and bring about the real thing—is a consequence of one major principle of comedy, namely *success*. Success means here precisely that the impossible happens: In comedy, the most incredible endeavors succeed, and the most unlikely heroes and heroines manage to make it. This principle of success as a source of comicality is clearly visible in *To Be or Not to Be*, for example in the fact that the director is not satisfied with the authenticity of the Hitler costume, and even a little Polish girl is not fooled by it, whereas the real Nazis always take the disguised actors for real. Another typical example occurs when Joseph Tura, with the help of a second false moustache, manages to maneuver himself out of a trap in Gestapo headquarters with the dead Professor Siletsky, and equally when his actor comrades subsequently succeed in "rescuing" him by revealing him as an impostor. Here it also becomes clear that success in comedy is of necessity always *too much*—a *surplus-success*, we may say. Since success is the happening of the impossible, the surplus is its indicator. Thus we can say that tragedy and comedy may be understood as two different ways of dealing with the impossible: tragedy refers to the impossible through its absence, whereas comedy represents it through surplus.

Now since love is regarded by comedy as something of the order of the impossible, and since comedy allows the impossible to happen, always in the manner of a surplus of success, comedy has an inherent connection to polygamous love, as an instance of the (surplus-) successfully happening impossible. Herein lies the difference between comedy's polygamy and that of contemporary "polyamori" movements: the latter treat polygamy simply as belonging to the order of the possible. Taken as such, polygamy completely lacks any comic potential. In comedy, on the contrary, the surplus of love and lovers is not to be taken as a simplistic assumption of their possibility. Rather, *the surplus is, as it were, the mathematical operator of comedy's metaphysics*: precisely by presenting too much of something, comedy attempts to show us that it is something of the order of the impossible. It is impossible, but still it happens—too often even—and therefore it becomes comical.

The Impossible as a Requirement for Comicality—and the Conditions for the Comicality of the Impossible

In order to be funny, then, polygamous love has to be treated as belonging to the order of the impossible. Comicality arises precisely when the impossible happens. But we have to make one more specification here, since not every impossible thing that happens is funny. Just as with polygamy, so too with the impossible: we have to identify which specific part of it is able to produce comic effects.

Usually when the impossible happens it leads to an experience of the *uncanny*.[10] In order to become comical, the uncanny has therefore to undergo a further transformation—a displacement. I would like to demonstrate this with a small example. Close to Vienna there once lived twin brothers, who were both policemen. They are said to have had some fun in the following way: One of them would stop all speeding cars and reprimand the drivers for their risky driving. A few kilometers down the road, the other brother would be waiting. Informed by cell phone, he would stop the same cars again and ask the drivers sternly: "Didn't I just tell you not to drive so fast?" What was fun for the brothers must have been a rather uncanny experience for the drivers. I, for my part, would hesitate to tell even to my closest friends about such an experience.

From this example it can clearly be seen that one person's comedy is the other person's uncanny. But this is not, of course, a statement of relativism. On the contrary, it is to say that comicality arises precisely where one has managed to displace the uncanny onto someone else. As soon as this other lacks, as soon as nobody is available for displacement, the uncannyness will fall back upon the first person, as Octave Mannoni has pointed out.[11] Displacement is possible when one disposes of an explanation for the "impossible" which is not available to the other. In other words: the comical impossible is the other's impossible. In *To Be or Not to Be* the other to whom we owe this displacement is very often "concentration camp Ehrhardt," who, for example, when on the way to discovering the truth, discovers to his surprise only a false moustache—and, then, convinced now that the other moustache must be the real one, uncannily encounters a second false moustache.

---

10   Cf. Sigmund Freud, *The Uncanny* (1919), SE 17, 218–52.
11   Mannoni writes: "si sa croyance à la magie retombe pour ainsi dire sur lui-même, il est saisi d'angoisse." See *Clefs pour l'Imaginaire ou l'Autre Scène* (Mayenne: Seuil, 1985), 30.

Variants of Displacement

Comedy offers several different versions of such displacement. In the first version, as we have just seen, the other encounters the "impossible" but we do not. Here, both sides have to be "castrated." We know perfectly well that no one can exist in two places at once and that doppelganger do not exist, yet for the other (who knows the same thing equally well), that is just how reality appears. The other is not a naive believer, as in a fairy tale, where fairies and other beings are conceived of as normal, possible things. The appearance of the uncanny, on the contrary, requires an "enlightened," castrated subject.[12] In order to find the other comical, I have to dispose of some knowledge which lets his "impossible" appear possible to me. Thus I can save psychic energy and decathect, laughing off the difference of expenditure.[13]

Yet the displacement can, funnily enough, also take on a kind of opposed form. In *The Great Dictator* (1940), we see Chaplin, blindfolded by a big hat, unwittingly balancing on a narrow plank extending beyond the edge of a roof. What he takes to be a roof terrace is in fact a highly dangerous narrow strip across which he moves without the slightest worry or hesitation. In this case, the other encounters the impossible, yet does not notice, whereas we do. It is not easy to tell why we laugh here. With regard to the character, we are not able to save psychic energy; indeed, we have to spend more than he does. We are amazed and amused at the sight of things actually appearing easy to those who just do not see their difficulty. It seems that what we manage to displace onto the other here is narcissism. The other appears to live in a wishful (as Freud puts it: "wunschgerechte"[14]) world that we have had to renounce. If that seems funny to us, we have to conclude that symbolic castration brings about a saving of expenditure with regard to narcissism.

Polytheism, Polygamy, and Comedy

The difference in libidinal economy between monogamous and polygamous love seems to be that the latter denies any privilege to the One. From a psychoanalytic viewpoint, it can be said that this privilege of the One—also seen, for example, in monotheist religions—always derives from narcissism. The idea that there is only one, absolute thing to be adored must have been formed after the model of the first one and absolute thing—*the ego.*

---

12   Cf. Freud, *The Uncanny* (1919), SE 17, 218–52.
13   Cf. Freud, *Jokes and Their Relation to the Unconscious*, SE 8, 187.
14   Cf. Freud, *Fetishism* (1927), GW 14, 316; SE 21, 156.

Now, the more absolute this one thing becomes, the less it is allowed to bear specific features: monotheist gods become invisible, non-sexual, all-knowing, etc. And the same, it seems, often also occurs with monogamous, unique, absolute love objects. Polygamy, on the contrary, just like pagan polytheism, concedes to every god and goddess their specific attributes, virtues, and vices, etc. This attitude allows us to see differences. It is therefore not narcissistic, but empirical, world-oriented.[15]

The ideal of monogamous love, just like that of monotheism, also brings with it the idea of its object's inaccessibility. The dramatic vicissitudes of monogamous love are therefore by necessity tragic, peaking in romantic failure. Comedy has an affinity with polygamy, then, due to the fact that comedy is about success—which is in most cases, as we have seen, a surplus of success. The heroine in Lubitsch's *Design for Living*, for example, succeeds in finding more than one love partner.

In tragedy, the impossible of love is thus represented by "not enough" of it being achieved; in comedy, by contrast, "too much" of it is achieved. Likewise, the impossible Divine appears in the tragic world in the form of lack or absence; while in the world of comedy it appears in the mode of surplus. This corresponds to what both Theo Sundermeier and Jan Assmann have argued with regard to the two basic types of religion:[16] "secondary," monotheist (in our terminology: tragic[17]) religions, which presuppose that the Divine cannot appear, are afraid of facing *too much* of the sacred and so attempt to cut it down; "primary," polytheist (comic) religions presuppose on the contrary that the Divine will appear in many forms—they are therefore afraid of venerating *not enough* of the sacred beings and build temples to "unknown gods" like the pantheon.

Gods or Atoms

In a 1910 footnote to his *Three Essays*, Sigmund Freud states:

> The most striking distinction between the erotic life of antiquity and our own no doubt lies in the fact that the ancients laid the stress upon the instinct [Trieb] itself, whereas we

---

15   On this point, psychoanalytic authors such as Grunberger and Dessuant appear too hasty in identifying ancient polytheism with narcissism. Cf. Béla Grunberger and Pierre Dessuant, *Narzißmus, Christentum, Antisemitismus* (Stuttgart: Klett-Cotta, 2000), 227ff.

16   See Theo Sundermeier, *Was ist Religion? Religionswissenschaft im theologischen Kontext* (Gütersloh, 1999); and Jan Assmann, *Die mosaische Unterscheidung oder der Preis des Monotheismus* (Hanser, 2003).

17   For this identification of monotheism with tragic religions see Pfaller, "Materialism's Comedy," and *Wofür es sich zu leben lohnt. Elemente materialistischer Philosophie* (Frankfurt am Main: Fischer, 2011), Chapter 4.

emphasize its subject. The ancients glorified the instinct and were prepared on its account to honour even an inferior object; while we despise the instinctual activity in itself, and find excuses for it only in the merits of the object.[18]

In this distinction we can discern the difference between tragedy and comedy, regarded as two opposed strategies for dealing with the impossible of sexual love.[19] It can be dealt with either in the form of idealization (which as a rule renders sexual love ultimately impossible, as in the romantic ideal of courtly love), or it can be handled by reduction: celebrating the drive means to take the drive itself as something great and worth celebrating, and not to overcathect it with meaning and expectations of identification or intersubjective understanding (which as a rule recognizes the impossible dimension of sexual love by producing a surplus, as can be seen in skilful sexual minority cultures).

This twofold vicissitude of sexual love can be compared to the two ancient strategies for dealing with excitement as such: the Stoics sought to calm down by referring exciting events to higher meanings and Gods, while the Epicureans reduced them to meaningless random collisions of atoms. "Gods or Atoms" was thus the pithy formula coined by Marcus Aurelius to account for these two ethics of the impossible:[20] either the idealization of the object or the comically relieving disillusion of, and fascination with, the mere "acephalic" movements of the world's smallest particles.

These two strategies can lead to two different forms of solidarity: either that of romantic, monogamous love, with its sentimental enthusiasm and aspiration to melt into the one, idealized other—up to the point where finally even sex is conceived of as possible (a point which is actually rarely reached); or that of comedic love, where sex comes easily, and the partners forgive each other for perhaps not being the ideal—following a principle such as: "Let's not make a fuss about that little bit of divine folly to which we are necessarily subjected,"[21] or, as the final line of *Some Like It Hot* puts it: "Nobody's perfect."

---

18 Freud, *Three Essays on the Theory of Sexuality*, SE 7, 149, fn. 1. In what follows I will refer to Freud's notion of "Trieb" not as "instinct" but as "drive."

19 For a Lacanian account of this issue of the impossible (or "real") of love, cf. David Monnier, David, *Le réel de l'amour. Trois modèles lacaniens* (Rennes: Presses Universitaires de Rennes, 2011).

20 Cf. Marc Aurel (Marcus Aurelius Antoninus), *Selbstbetrachtungen* (Stuttgart: Kröner, 1948), 107.

21 This is opposed to contemporary, postmodern polyamorism which requires much talking and "confession": It tries to avoid secrets, to maintain sexuality in total conformity with the ego, and aims at a total "subjectivization"—a position that Michel Foucault criticized with regard to its subjecting power

These two opposed concepts of love imply different sequences of love elements.[22] In romantic love, sex is regarded as a late event—the ultimate vicissitude of intimacy; it occurs when, so to speak, the melting together of two souls finds its "prolongation by different means." Sexuality is thus regarded as a "heart's choice," as a completely spontaneous initiative based on free will, and as the ultimate step in a continuous retreat from society. In comedic love, by contrast, sex is an early achievement—a consequence of entering into society's public space. Even if individuals may not yet feel like it, love or sexual activity follow already from the fact that other people seem to believe in it or expect it from them. Hence, in comedy, characters regularly fall in love as soon as they stage such an event for others. Eroticism is here conceived as part of the role-play of "public man"[23]—and as something obligatory, independent of any individual, spontaneous, "pathological" (in the Kantian sense) inclinations. (This respect for the public dimension may explain the importance of sexual role-play among those who, in their love, follow the comedy model.[24])

Romantic Love or Solidarity of the Driven?

Lubitsch's modernism draws a lot of its glamour and comicality from its break with, and mockery of, nineteenth-century bourgeois customs as well as romantic notions of love. Against such notions, Lubitsch offers an alternative utopia of solidarity between the mutually attracted sexes, a utopia that expresses the modernist attitude of heterosexual comradeship or complicity (a type of relationship

---

    dimension. This shows how a metaphysical ignorance of the dimension of impossibility connected with sexual love leads to the political support of subjection.

22 This idea of a sequence of love elements is crucial to Paul Watzlawick's clever analysis of the widespread misunderstanding between American men and British women during World War II, as a result of which both sides accused each other of behaving shamelessly. Watzlawick argues that the sequence of love practices was different in both cultures. In the US, a little kiss was regarded as quite innocent and came early (say, step 5), whereas in Britain it came very late (say, step 25) and required either an ending of the relationship or a substantial reaction. See Paul Watzlawick, *Wie wirklich ist die Wirklichkeit? Wahn, Täuschung, Verstehen* (München; Zürich (13. Aufl.): Piper, 1985), 74 ff.

23 For this notion see Richard Sennett, *The Fall of Public Man* (New York; London: W. W. Norton, 1974). The thesis that tragedy (monogamy) refers to the private person whereas comedy (polygamy) refers to the public role may find support in Alenka Zupančič's brilliant observation about titles in both genres: "It would be hard to imagine, as titles of tragedies, universal or generic names—to change, for example, the title *Antigone* into *The (Untamed) Shrew*, *Othello* into *The Jealous Husband*, *Romeo and Juliet* perhaps straight into *Love's Labour's Lost*. It would indeed be hard to do this and still remain on the territory of tragedy." See Zupančič, *The Odd One In: On Comedy* (Cambridge MA: MIT Press, 2008), 37.

24 On this see Johan Huizinga, *Homo Ludens. Vom Ursprung der Kultur im Spiel* (Reinbek: Rowohlt, 1956), 48 ff.

that can be compared to the "promiscuous" comradeships practiced in—male and female—homosexual or BDSM communities).

Whereas the romantic nineteenth-century position consisted in idealizing the singular object, the modernist position, like the ancient, consists in celebrating the drive, with its multiple objects (the object being the drive's most variable element, according to Freud[25]). Multiple relationships are now produced by de-dramatizing and de-idealizing sexual love. Yet this de-idealization does not occur without a kind of second-degree-idealization: Solidarity and even a kind of "idealist" respect for one's love-comrades is now established precisely by sharing this non-idealist attitude towards sexual love. This is sometimes organized by a kind of social *contract*. Such a contract appears explicitly in *Design for Living*—in the "gentlemen's agreement" not to have sex with each other. But it also occurs in *To Be or Not to Be*, when the heroes decide that they will first have to fight the Nazis, and then settle their complicated love matters later (so they think).

When, at the end of *Design for Living*, the woman and the two men renew their "gentlemen's agreement" not to have sex, they laugh as they do so, knowing that the heroine, as she has herself stated earlier, is no gentleman. So there will be sex, but between equal "gentleman" partners. (An analogous renewal of a polygamous structure occurs, of course, at the end of *To Be or Not to Be*: here, too, the sentence that structures the movie, and the sexual relationships in it, is given a new meaning.)

The new, modern twist here is that love now happens between "parallel" partners who are in the same business (as can be seen most clearly in *Trouble in Paradise*), not between opposed partners who complement each other—love takes place, so to speak, along a "paradigmatic" axis, not a "syntagmatic" one. Or, to put it in philosophical terms, the relationship between men and women is not conceived of along the lines of a Cartesian mind-body relation, where one part can only be active when the other part is passive. It involves, rather, a Spinozist "parallelism," where the activity of one part implies that of the other.

Lovers With a Cause

In Lubitsch's films, men and women love each other because they are in the same position, because they have a common cause—which gives them a "triangulation." Their relationships are thus formed like those between equal subjects in

---

25 Freud, *Instincts and Their Vicissitudes*, SE 14, 122.

More than a couple: Tom (Fredric March), Gilda (Miriam Hopkins), and George (Gary Cooper), in *Design for Living* (above); Mariette (Kay Francis), Gaston (Herbert Marshall), and Lily (Miriam Hopkins), in a publicity still for *Trouble in Paradise* (below).

a Freudian "mass." The partners form not a dual Freudian "Masse zu zweit" ("a group formation with two members"[26]), with one of the members as the big Subject at the center, and the other its small subject at the periphery; rather, both (or all) of them occupy equal, peripheral positions, grouped around a center which is that of their common cause.

This triangulating cause is at the same time the element that displaces or suspends the impossibility of the surplus: the impossible can be lived so long as ordinary life is displaced by some urgent necessity or higher goal. (This can be compared to the way in which promiscuous sexual minority groups manage to inhabit their group utopia in relative harmony so long as they feel suppressed by the alleged "heteronormative" majority.)

The happy ending, of course, in achieving the higher goal, eliminates this triangulating, displacing instance. Thus every polygamous happy ending in Lubitsch raises the question of how the impossibility of multiple love will from now on be constructed and sustained. But this is also the case with classical, monogamous happy endings—think for example of John Wayne and Claire Trevor's escape into the night at the end of John Ford's *Stagecoach* (1939): we have no idea what their future life might look like or how it will continue to function.

Brotherhoods With Benefits: The Sacrilege of Monogamy

This social relationship between love partners might be compared to that between the equal brothers after their killing of the primordial father in Freud's construction of the origin of social bonds.[27] In *Design for Living*, human beings become brothers, just as in the Enlightenment's and the French Revolution's utopia: "Alle Menschen werden Brüder," as Friedrich Schiller's 1786 poem announces it. Yet there are no sexual taboos between them: they are "brothers with benefits," as Easton and Hardy might put it.[28] The "gentlemen's agreement" allows for sex between male and female "brothers," since it excludes something else: what is now taboo is precisely monogamous marriage.[29] The three heroes of *Design for*

---

26 Freud, *Group Psychology and the Analysis of the Ego* (1921), GW 13, 142; 160; SE 18, 127; 142.
27 Cf. Freud, *Totem and Taboo*, SE 13, 1–161.
28 Cf. Easton and Hardy, *The Ethical Slut*, 48.
29 As we know, monogamous marriage was for long time regarded as a crime. It broke the laws of tribal "club marriage," and the monogamous "usurpator" had to pay tribute for this crime to the brothers. Cf. Johann Jakob Bachofen, *Das Mutterrecht. Eine Untersuchung über die Gynaikokratie der alten Welt nach ihrer religiösen und rechtlichen Natur* (Frankfurt am Main: Suhrkamp, 1982 [1861]), and Friedrich Engels, *Der Ursprung der Familie, des Privateigentums und des Staates* (Berlin: Dietz, 1973 [1884]), 12, 60.

Living can enjoy their promiscuous bond on the condition that they have not only killed or overcome the real, boring husband but have also abandoned his structural position. From now on, no man is allowed to usurp the position of the singular, monopolist husband. This excluded Third can also now function for the loving multiplicity as its necessary triangulating and displacing instance.

The Romantic and the Comedy Couple

The parallelism between men and women as Lubitsch conceives it has important consequences for the plots of his films, as well as for the structure of his couples (if there is one). Many comedies from the 1930s and early '40s (such as *The Awful Truth*, *His Girl Friday* (1940), *Libeled Lady*, etc.) can be read as a struggle between a funny "comedy couple" and a serious "romantic couple." Often the starting point involves the establishing of an alliance between people who either fake a relationship or marriage in order to reach some utilitarian goal (such as saving a newspaper from a lawsuit, as in the "fake" marriage between William Powell and Jean Harlow in *Libeled Lady*), or who, on the contrary, dissimulate an existing relationship in order to reach such a goal (as in *Trouble in Paradise*, when Miriam Hopkins and Herbert Marshall become personal assistants to Kay Francis). This is the comedy couple: the bond between the two partners consists precisely in their solidarity in *establishing and maintaining the illusion*—be it one of solidarity or of separation.

This leads in turn to another, quite different couple, when one (usually the male) partner of the comedy couple encounters someone else connected with the utilitarian goal, such that the goal itself becomes threatened with suspension by the existential question concerning true love. This linking between the comedy hero and the new love partner can be called the romantic couple. Between them there seems to develop an uncanny "true love," which appears doomed to failure due to the fact that only one partner knows about the fakery on which it is based. The bond between them exists at the level of the *content* of this fake or illusion. So, whereas the comedy couple loves at the level of the construction of an illusion, the romantic couple loves at the level of its content. Or, to put it in Lacanian terms: the solidarity of the comedy couple occurs at the level of the *enunciation* of the comedy fake, while the solidarity of the romantic couple occurs at the level of the *enunciated*.

Lubitsch's comedy couples, of course, typically take the form of business alliances between men and women. And their business almost always consists precisely in creating some semblance in order to deceive other people. Establishing a semblance for others is a typical starting point for a comedy, but the staging of love almost always brings about real love, in accordance with comedy's laws of symbolic efficiency. Yet in very few other comedies is the struggle decided with such regularity in favor of the comedy couple as it is in Lubitsch. In *Libeled Lady*, for example, it is the two romantic couples who triumph in the end. In Lubitsch, by contrast, comedy love triumphs over romantic love in *Trouble in Paradise*, in *Design for Living*, and even in *Cluny Brown* (1946). Just as polygamy is for Lubitsch not only a transitory state but also a happy end, so his comedy couple is not only a transitory necessity required to trigger the comic plot, but apparently also the best outcome a comedy has to offer.

Lubitsch's Lessons: Loser's and Winner's Bliss

To speculate on what conclusions might be drawn from these structural features of Lubitsch's comedies for real life, and what specific relevance they might have for our time, we can start from the following rough picture: Forty-five years after the sexual revolution of 1968, we observe not only a reinforcement of the "monogamous matrix" (even among homosexuals) but also a predominance of sexual-harassment claims, low sexual desire (LSD syndrome), and so-called "post-sexuality." We should not fall into the trap here of supposing that such a hostility towards sexuality is a reaction against an excessive liberation; that the younger generation is now pushing back the pendulum, after their euphoric hippie parents had taken things too far. Rather, the liberation *of* sexuality has already in itself been a liberation *from* sexuality. Post-sexuality is the truth of sexual revolution.

This is currently accompanied by a political development in which the state is systematically cut back to its repressive functions against individuals. And strangely enough it is mostly today's "anti-authoritarians" who call upon the police to protect them (or weak others) not only from sexual harassment, but from all manifestations of erotic life, be it adult language, joking, flirting, or even smoking. A kind of fundamentalist sex-negativity has become widespread within formerly emancipatory movements, and is almost always an indicator of their turning reactionary. Thus they contribute today to the neoliberal cleansing of public space and the establishing of a repressive, "minimal" society in which everybody has almost no civil rights except that of the right to complain about somebody else.

As Richard Sennett remarked back in 1974, Western societies have been moving "from something like an other-directed condition to an inner-directed condition."[30] Whereas for the parents of the '68 generation marriage was a formal institution, the '68 rebels themselves opted for "the heart's choice"—a path that often led to loving couples without marriage.[31] (This "generation gap" can be clearly observed in, for example, Mike Nichols movie *The Graduate*, from 1967.) A massive "romantization" and "interiorization" of love was thereby effected: whereas for the older folks monogamy was an appearance that had to be maintained in order to avoid public scandal, for the younger generation monogamy became an inner wish, dictated by the heart. The rebellious insistence on asserting what one really wants, and defending it against all objections and obstacles, turned into the ambiguous conviction that, henceforth, one should do only what one really wants and what one truly believes in. As it turned out, what people really wanted and could truly believe in was in fact very little. Once again, the radicalism of romantic love amounted to rendering love almost impossible. Deep in their heart, the romantics discovered little more than post-sexuality. Sexual liberation consisted in actually forbidding oneself what one had previously been forbidden by others. Where the older generation had at least partly yielded to the surveillance of society, if not without having their little secrets (uncovered by, among others, the Kinsey report), the younger generation began to yield only to the inner surveillance of their superego—a much more rigid master from whom nothing can be kept hidden, not only actions, but even wishes and intentions, as Freud noted.[32]

This may explain why today monogamy appears, perhaps more than ever, as "the only game in town." In particular, women who live without a partner or without children have to be ready to face questions and explain themselves. The underlying romanticism of the "sexual revolution" has thus today become a source of questionable political developments and of increasing intolerance at the level of individual life. And besides, such romanticism is clearly the position of political losers: As Friedrich Engels remarked, the bourgeoisie became romantic precisely in those countries where the bourgeois revolution failed, and where the bourgeoisie was therefore unable to appropriate the achievements of the aristocracy. The happy ending in the German bourgeois "loser" novel is thus, as Engels notes, that of monogamous marriage, whereas in the French novel it is that of adultery.[33]

---

30 Sennett, *The Fall of Public Man*, 5.
31 On this see, for example, the precise analysis by André Béjin, "Le mariage extra-conjugal d'aujourd'hui," in *Communications, 35: Sexualités occidentales*, eds Philippe Ariès and André Béjin (Paris: Seuil, 1984), 169–80.
32 Cf. Freud, *Civilization and Its Discontents*, SE 21, 126 ff.
33 Cf. Engels, *Der Ursprung der Familie*, 81.

Lubitsch's insistence on polygamous love as a comedic happy ending, his generous acknowledgment of the surplus that is a consequence of love's becoming real, his care for appearances, and his utopian images of loving brotherhoods and comedy couples can all be taken as a counterbalance to the disequilibrium characteristic of our postmodern era. In teaching us that desire does not stem from intimacy but from our existence as "public men," and that "intimization" will ultimately only prevent love from happening, Lubitsch shows us that in real life comedy is essential to our being not only as passionate lovers, but also as political citizens.

Tatjana Jukić

Garbo Laughs: Revolution and Melancholia in Lubitsch's Ninotchka

Ernst Lubitsch has been credited with saying that there are a thousand ways to point a camera, but really only one. His work too may be seen as one such portal, as it provides a privileged access to Hollywood comedy—David Niven, says James Harvey, called him "the masters' master."[1] The master's appreciation of felicitous positions and openings demands that the scene of analyzing his cinema be set in the same terms. For this reason, I would like to begin by addressing one such position or opening: the moment when Greta Garbo, the icon of the cinematic, enters a Lubitsch film.

It happens in *Ninotchka* (1939). Garbo, cast as Nina Yakushova, the special envoy from Moscow, emerges when the three Soviet trade delegates—Iranoff, Buljanoff, and Kopalski—go to the Paris railway station to see her into the film and into the narrative. As they try to guess what the special envoy might look like, both they and the camera close in on a number of figures before finally closing in on Garbo, when she is literally the only figure left on the platform, shoved to the edge of the frame. But by this time she has already closed in on them, and the film and the narrative, as if organizing—and displacing into herself—the intelligence of the film: as if she is the figure from which the film, and possibly the cinematic itself, receives its intelligence.

Garbo enters the film in its eighteenth minute, well after the story has begun to unfold. Her emergence recalibrates everything that the film up to that point

---

1   James Harvey, *Romantic Comedy in Hollywood from Lubitsch to Sturges* (New York: Da Capo Press, 1998), 7.

wishes to organize in terms of a functional narrative. It is thus not so much that she is for the film the instance of *Nachträglichkeit*; rather, she exposes *Nachträglichkeit* as the structural demand of its first eighteen minutes and hence supplies the evidence that they are somehow flawed—she herself, however, remains strangely exempt from the flaw. As a result, Garbo in Lubitsch is conceived emphatically in terms of education and instruction; she seems bared to crisis and critique.

Which is also what she does from within the story. Ninotchka is sent from Moscow as a special envoy, to put right what the initial trade delegates have got wrong with regard to the politics and economy of state socialism. The original three (Iranoff, Buljanoff, and Kopalski) have come to Paris in order to organize the sale of jewels confiscated from aristocrats by the Soviet government—in this case from the Grand Duchess Swana, now residing in Paris. Swana (Ina Claire) learns that the jewels are up for sale and decides to reclaim them; she orders Count Leon d'Algout, her kept man, to enter into negotiations and trick the delegates into accepting her claim. Leon (Melvyn Douglas) part charms, part convinces them into accepting Swana's terms, encouraging them all the while to enjoy Paris, so different from the harsh life in socialism. Ninotchka arrives in Paris to set the delegates straight and get the deal sorted. Her work, however, hinges on explaining repeatedly why this is necessary: because the sale of the jewels will raise funds vital to Soviet agriculture and help feed the hungry Russian people.

A curious configuration emerges here. The lesson Garbo teaches seems linked inextricably to the economy: she enters the film in order to intervene in what seems to be a problem of lost labor, labor which has become misdirected, errant, divorced from what it set out to achieve. It is the lost labor of the narrative, insofar as Garbo arrives to redo everything that Iranoff, Buljanoff, and Kopalski had been doing in the first place. But it is also the lost labor of the cinematic itself, because it takes Garbo to situate and configure what the film is about, as well as what film generally is about, with the implication that cinema labors in vain without Garbo or what she stands for.

Still, her lesson is not about securing profit or gain. On the contrary, she persists in taking positions where labor is at a remove from economic reason, almost as if the intelligence she brings to the film depends on a careful separation of labor and the market. This is evident already in her insistence that Swana's jewels need to be sold in order to sustain Soviet agriculture and feed the starving people. While it is true that, with its unvaried emphasis on agriculture, Ninotchka's socialism is reminiscent of the physiocrats and early *économistes*, there is nevertheless a

Ninotchka (Greta Garbo) among comrades: Kopalski (Alexander Granach), Buljanoff (Felix Bressart), and Iranoff (Sig Ruman). *Ninotchka*

remove in her reasoning which sabotages any such political economy. What the physiocrats reveal, says Foucault in his lectures on biopolitics, is that "fundamentally the subject of interest is never called upon to relinquish his interest," which is why Foucault proceeds to call it "an egoistic mechanism."[2] Ninotchka, on the other hand, is defined throughout by her relinquishing of self-interest.

Perhaps the finest example of this is the line she delivers upon entering the luxurious Paris hotel where the Soviet delegates are staying, and discovering the cost of the accommodation: "Who am I to cost the Russian people seven cows?" Here it is not merely that sustaining bare life (of others, and hence bare life as such) is premised on relinquishing self-interest; it is also that the self, confronted with bare life, seems conceivable only in terms of cost, as interest and a figure of economy. This of course echoes Foucault's views on biopolitics where they traverse the split between the economic and the governmental. Yet what persists as the governmental in Foucault is cast here as bare life, pointing now to the conditions of the October Revolution and to the residue of the political that *raison d'État* cannot process, not even in state socialism. That this is indeed true of Lubitsch comes to light in a detail later on, when Ninotchka, back in Moscow, meets her boss Razinin, a commissar in charge precisely of yoking the egoistic mechanism of the economy to that of the state. Lubitsch cast Bela Lugosi as Commissar Razinin, so that the image of state socialism is conflated in the film with that of Dracula and vampirism. Lubitsch is right on the mark here, especially considering the Marxist agenda of state socialism, because his Lugosi joke demands that the governmental reason of state socialism be canvassed against Marx's famous comment on capital as vampiric. According to Marx, capital is dead labor which, vampire-like, lives only by sucking on living labor—the more labor it sucks, the more it lives.[3] In this way, what Lubitsch's Lugosi reveals is that the separation of the governmental and the economic reasons depends in fact on the occlusion of labor in its complexity, and that labor, which is constituent to both, is where their separation collapses (and with it any discussion of biopolitics and bare life quarantined to the domain of statism, rights, and the governmental).

It is here also that the pairing off of Lugosi and Garbo shows as symptomatic. The two represent, as it were, different humoral economies. While Lugosi clearly

---

2   Michel Foucault, *The Birth of Biopolitics. Lectures at the Collége de France 1978–1979*, trans. Graham Burchell, ed. Michel Senellart (New York: Palgrave Macmillan, 2008), 275.

3   Karl Marx, *Das Kapital. Kritik der politischen Ökonomie*, in Karl Marx and Friedrich Engels, *Werke*, Band 23 (Berlin: Dietz Verlag, 1962), 247.

stands for the economy of blood, Garbo's Ninotchka stands for the economy of milk—the joke which sustains her throughout the film, from the seven cows, to Leon's lovingly sending her a bottle of goat's milk, to the hilarious joke about the waiter and coffee without milk. While blood implies an economy where loss implies a loss of life (best exemplified perhaps by the narrative conditions of Shakespeare's *The Merchant of Venice*), milk implies an economic scandal of sorts, or even economic non-reason, insofar as its loss implies the maintenance and expansion of life. Of course, given the fact that Lugosi/Razinin, steeped in his particular humoral economy, remains fixed as the index of the Soviet state (and of Stalinism), Garbo/Ninotchka, steeped in hers, indexes the residue of the (bio)political that the Soviet *raison d'État* evidently cannot process. What Garbo/Ninotchka indexes, in other words, is a state of exception, with the implication now that any revolution worthy of its name entails a state of exception; that there is a constituent bond between the state of exception and revolutionary conditions; and that a biopolitical rift persists between communism and socialism. This then raises the question of what constitutes revolution, or whether revolution as the exemplary political event is worthy of its name unless it is enacted in terms of bare life. Which in turn raises the question of bare life itself, vital to recent discussions of rights and biopolitics, because it demands that their perspective be shifted from bare life as it presents itself in the concentration camps and the Gulag (and their related statisms of Nazism and Stalinism) to bare life as it presents itself in revolutions.

Then again, Lubitsch seems to contradict such a reading, as his comedy depends largely upon showing how Ninotchka falls for Leon and all the Paris fineries: in other words, how Ninotchka reestablishes her self-interest or herself in terms of interest. Indeed, the film was publicized under the slogan "Garbo Laughs," which seems to suggest a recovery of interest and self. And yet the story climaxes on a different note entirely. This happens when Swana organizes the theft of the jewels from the hotel safe and confronts Ninotchka with an either-or: she may either win the jewels back by renouncing Leon and returning to Moscow straight away, or keep Leon but lose the jewels. Her decision to take the jewels and renounce Leon demonstrates that she remains true to her relinquishing of self-interest, because she opts once again for the bare life of others (and hence bare life as such) over herself. It thus turns out that the melodramatic climax of the story reflects accurately the terms of her earlier comical line: "Who am I to cost the Russian people seven cows?"

What is more, with this decision Ninotchka collapses into melancholia, so that the narrative climax of the Lubitsch comedy coincides in fact with the resurrection of the iconic unhappy Garbo—the Garbo of melodrama who seldom laughs. Which is where another curious configuration emerges: if the Lubitsch comedy *climaxes* in melancholia, it follows that melancholia is its underlying script. This then is symptomatic where melancholia too presupposes a peculiar economy, aptly profiled by Freud in "Mourning and Melancholia" (1917). According to Freud, mourning is normal and by extension the norm against which to approach the pathology of melancholia or melancholia as pathology. The rift between the two, and consequently the rift between the norm and pathology, takes place in the economy of the ego: while persons in mourning consider the world around them impoverished and therefore find it difficult to invest libidinally in relationships potentially profitable to the ego, in cases of melancholia the ego itself is impoverished and fails to sustain the self to begin with.[4] (A similar configuration surfaces in Walter Benjamin, in *The Origin of German Tragic Drama*. Albeit circumventing any reference to Freud, Benjamin too compares melancholia to mourning. Melancholia, he says, betrays the world for the sake of knowledge, while mourning originates in the allegiance to the world of things.)[5]

What Freud reveals about the self in mourning is precisely what the physiocrats, according to Foucault, reveal about economic reason: that fundamentally the subject of interest is never called upon to relinquish his interest. It would therefore follow that melancholia indicates another type of rationality, one that Foucault associates with the governmental and ultimately with the scope of biopolitics. Yet Freud insists that the same labor and the same affect are at the heart of both mourning and melancholia: it is only that in mourning the ego manages to channel them from the unconscious, where they are taking place, via the preconscious into the conscious, in order to bring them to a close, whereas in melancholia these passages are blocked and the labor of the affect remains stuck in the unconscious. Besides, Freud warns that in melancholia the passages are blocked—and the ego consequently kept in check—because there may be too many causes, but also because the many causes may be working together.[6] This implies that mourning can be designated as successful, as opposed to the

---

4   Why this happens, says Freud, is a question which defies economic terms. See Sigmund Freud, *Das Ich und das Es. Metapsychologische Schriften* (Frankfurt am Main: Fischer, 1992), 175.
5   See Walter Benjamin, *Ursprung des deutschen Trauerspiels* (Frankfurt am Main: Suhrkamp, 1978), 136.
6   Freud, *Das Ich und das Es*, 187.

failure implicit in melancholia, not because the ego in mourning works harder, but because it is faced with less labor. Further, this implies that melancholia, at least as seen by Freud, indicates that there is a constituent pathology to every economy founded on the surplus of labor.[7]

It is once again in the Razinin/Lugosi scene that this position is carried through to its logical consequences. The melancholy Ninotchka presents to the commissar her report on "the materials available for trading," and points out vocally that "we must be extremely careful what goods we take to exchange," adding that she has "already started the survey on our most urgent needs." Of course, her lines read also as a statement on the critical condition of her own libidinal investments, with the implication that the economy in revolution takes place in terms of melancholia and, vice versa, that the libidinal economy of melancholia evokes the revolutionary conditions. Razinin contributes an interesting twist along the same lines when he asks her specifically if her report includes "the products of the far eastern provinces." His comment echoes Ninotchka's original interest in peasantry and agriculture as the field where revolution invokes economic reason only to undercut its calculus. At this particular juncture, however, Razinin's comment demands that an interest in agriculture be equally tied to melancholia: it resonates with the complex configuration of melancholia for classical antiquity and the Middle Ages, when it was associated with Saturn and then with agriculture, so that peasants—along with contemplatives—came to designate its scope.[8] This image is not to be hastily rejected as merely traditional: with its derivation from black bile and its seat in the spleen, melancholia was from its inception associated with food and digestion, but indicated primarily the pathology and the crisis likely to occur in places, seemingly interior, where life reveals itself as depending on an outside that no self can contain or manage. This condition was, as early as classical antiquity, associated with hard labor, the labor of the peasantry, or *labor improbus* as Virgil calls it in the *Georgics*. Of course, if toilsome labor conquers all, as Virgil says, it may well be the kind of labor which conquers the ego too.[9]

---

7   See also Tatjana Jukić, *Revolucija i melankolija. Granice pamćenja hrvatske književnosti* (Zagreb: Naklada Ljevak, 2011), 17.

8   For the long cultural history of melancholia, see Raymond Klibansky, Erwin Panofsky, and Fritz Saxl, *Saturn and Melancholy: Studies in the History of Natural Philosophy, Religion and Art* (New York: Basic Books, 1964).

9   True, when the list of deadly sins was compiled in the Middle Ages, melancholia, associated diversely with *acedia, tristitia, taedium vitae, desidia*, etc., was subsumed under the rubric of sloth. See Giorgio Agamben, *Stanzas: Word and Phantasm in Western Culture*, trans. R. L. Martinez (Minneapolis: University of

Razinin indicates as much when he observes that Ninotchka must have worked on her report day and night and hardly slept for months, to which she replies that she needs very little sleep.[10] When Razinin orders her to stop and turn over her work to someone else (and leave for Constantinople, where Iranoff, Buljanoff, and Kopalski are botching up yet another Soviet trade deal), she implores him not to. "I should hate to interrupt my present work," says Garbo as she fervently clutches her briefcase while the camera switches from a medium shot to a close-up of her unhappy face: "Let me finish my work. I'm in the rhythm of it now. I don't want to go away. I don't want to be sent into that fine atmosphere again. It throws you out of gear. Let me finish my work. I've concentrated everything in it."

The Lugosian Razinin is predictably relentless. He sends her off on a mission to Constantinople regardless, where she reunites with Iranoff, Buljanoff, and Kopalski, and with Leon, presumably never to return to the Soviet Union. This is where the film seems to have reached its happy ending. Yet its conditions call for a closer scrutiny. In her interview with Razinin, Ninotchka begs not to be sent to what she evidently knows is a happy place, because that would interrupt her melancholy labors. The logic which unfolds in her request is particularly cruel: it suggests that, paradoxically, Ninotchka is happier in her present toil than she would be in the fine atmosphere of Paris or Constantinople, because the terrible, critical labor to which she has given her all, the labor which she hopes to bring to a close eventually, is thus interrupted and in effect restaged and reenacted. In other words, what the happy places of Paris and Constantinople promise to Ninotchka is that, instead of finding closure, her labors are premised on reenactment. Indeed, this is precisely what happens to her in Paris: her libidinal investment in Leon backfires into reenacting for her the very terms of the revolutionary crisis. It is thanks to Leon that, once again, she is faced with relinquishing all self-interest for the bare life of others (and therefore bare life as such), and with the *labor improbus* this entails. Not only that: it is thanks to Leon that any confidence in the closure

Minnesota Press, 1993), 3–15, and the introductory chapter in Mladen Dolar, *O skoposti in o nekaterih z njo povezanih rečeh: tema in variacije* (Ljubljana: Društvo za teoretsko psihoanalizo, 2002). While sloth of course denotes deficiency of labor, it remains symptomatic that medieval theologians perceived melancholia precisely in terms of work. Further, one could argue that the sin of sloth, thus contaminated with melancholia, does not condemn merely the lack of labor, but rather that about work which is profitless: which cannot be perceived in terms of economic reason. See Jukić, *Revolucija i melankolija*, 30–1.

10 Incidentally, for Freud, sleeplessness indicates that no energy available for libidinal investment can be channeled from the labor which takes place in the unconscious away to the maintenance of the ego; which then presents itself as an intractable economic problem for the theory of the self in psychoanalysis. See Freud, *Das Ich und das Es*, 183.

and success of these labors is exposed as blindness to the ultimate truth of reenactment (and therefore to the truth of what exactly constitutes *permanent* revolution).
Melancholia in turn shows up as pathological to the self not where some past
libidinal investment persists beyond reason, but where the future is available only
as crisis. The final frames of the film confirm this logic. Symptomatically, the film
does not end with a shot of the reunited lovers. Instead, after the Russians have
opened a restaurant of their own, Kopalski (Alexander Granach) is shown striking
angrily against the management, and hence against himself, in what promises to
be a prelude to revolutionary conditions. Further, in striking against the management of a *restaurant*, Kopalski is striking against the existing management of food
and eating, the very concerns that propelled Ninotchka into the story to begin
with, with milk as her systemic capillary metonym.

This—the awful truth of melancholy reenactment—constitutes the intelligence that Garbo brings to the film when she arrives on the platform of the
Paris railway station and thereby steers the film towards its focus. In turn, this
intelligence defines Garbo as *the* Garbo to begin with: she becomes reducible to
the rationale of the cinematic precisely at that juncture where she relinquishes
all self-interest—where she relinquishes her self. Some of these conditions feature
in Roland Barthes's insightful description of the face of Garbo, in *Mythologies*,
when he says that Garbo's relation to film is of the order of the concept, where
Audrey Hepburn's is that of the event, a development he registers in the cinema
of the 1950s.[11] Barthes elaborates on what characterizes this face-concept: amid
all the snow of the mask-like surface, at once fragile and compact, the eyes alone,
black like some strange pulp, and not at all expressive, are two bruises, slightly
atremble.[12] He may well be compressing, into Garbo, the cultural history of melancholia: from the bizarre black pulp evocative of the black bile of the ancients,
to the dark pulsating bruises evocative of Freud, who compares the complex of
melancholia to a painful wound which attracts to itself all the available libidinal
energies until the ego is left entirely impoverished.[13]

Barthes adumbrates the place that Stanley Cavell will allocate to Garbo in
Contesting Tears. Insofar as, in Cavell, Garbo performs within philosophy or at
least for philosophy, here too her relation to film is of the order of the concept. "It
is in the figure of Garbo," says Cavell, "that the idea of the women's unknownness

---

11   Roland Barthes, *Mythologies* (Paris: Seuil, 1957), 57.
12   Ibid., 66.
13   Freud, *Das Ich und das Es*, 183.

most purely takes on its aspects of the desire of a man for a woman's knowledge, as if to know what she knows may be taken as the answer to the question what a man after all wants of a woman—and does not want after all."[14] Later, he iterates that Garbo is "the greatest, or the most fascinating, cinematic image on film of the unknown woman": "It is as if Garbo has generalized this aptitude beyond human doubting ... so that the sense of failure to know her, of her being beyond us (say visibly absent), is itself the proof of her existence."[15]

Cavell's take on Garbo is interesting here for several reasons. Firstly, his sentences invite a rephrasing in the following terms: that Garbo represents at its purest the desire of philosophy for the knowledge of film, as if to know what film knows may be taken as the answer to the question what philosophy after all wants of film—and does not want after all. Which is where Cavell's take on Garbo comes closest perhaps to Deleuze's thoughts on the concept, when he says that concepts in philosophy have a sphere of influence where they operate in relation to "dramas" and then by means of a certain "cruelty." It follows, says Deleuze, that concepts must have a coherence among themselves, but that coherence must not come from themselves; they must receive it from elsewhere.[16]

Secondly, Cavell situates his unknown woman not only in film but also in the body of psychoanalysis. In the preface to his book he notes "the uncanny origins, at the turn of the nineteenth century into the twentieth, of both the work of psychoanalysis and the work of the art of film in the sufferings of and the threats to women."[17] The unknownness of his woman for philosophy attests therefore to the suffering and the threat that both psychoanalysis and the early cinema register as their point of departure; her unknownness is always also that of unhappiness.

Cavell readily diagnoses this particular unhappiness in terms of hysteria as described by Freud and Breuer: the condition which, whilst giving rise to psychoanalysis, offers itself to its explanation. Indeed, Cavell positions Garbo alongside Freud's and Breuer's case studies, most notably alongside Anna O., and even proposes that Garbo be taken as "an emblem for future argument."[18] The question arises, however, as to whether the specific unhappiness of Garbo on film corresponds instead to that of melancholia: of the condition which presents itself as an

---

14 Stanley Cavell, *Contesting Tears: The Hollywood Melodrama of the Unknown Woman* (Chicago: University of Chicago Press, 1996), 2, 19.
15 Ibid., 106.
16 Gilles Deleuze, *Différence et répétition* (Paris: Presses Universitaires de France, 2003), 3.
17 Cavell, *Contesting Tears*, xiv.
18 Ibid., 105–6.

intractable economic problem to the theory of the self in psychoanalysis. Cavell's own perspective on Garbo is fraught with enough evidence: "I see her *jouissance* as remembering something, but, let me say, remembering it from the future," he says, "as from the perspective of her death."[19] This is why Cavell perceives Garbo "as if she were herself transformed into a mnemonic symbol, a monument of memory," with a further qualification still: "What the monument means to me is that a joyful passion for one's life contains the ability to mourn, the acceptance of transience, of the world as beyond one—say, one's other."[20]

It is here that a passageway opens further into *Ninotchka*, the same passageway that allows Lubitsch's body of work to form the basis for a critical intervention into Cavell's study of film. Cavell's unknown woman is emblematic of a number of melodramas, produced mostly in the 1940s, which he takes up as a genre of their own—the Hollywood melodrama of the unknown woman—in order to analyze ultimately the terms of the possible failure of America as a political and a philosophical project. For that reason *Contesting Tears* reads as a companion piece to *Pursuits of Happiness*, Cavell's 1981 study of a number of Hollywood comedies, produced mostly in the 1930s, which again he takes up as a genre—that of the remarriage comedy—in order to analyze the terms of the success of America as a political and philosophical project. If the unknown woman is emblematic of melodrama, the reverse is true of the comedies Cavell selects for his earlier study, as they all focus on couples. More specifically, they all center on the conversation which secures an ongoing education for both the man and the woman, but primarily for the two of them as they are together, thus securing in fact not merely their contractual bond, but contract as such. Hence Cavell's fascination with the fast-paced conversation of the screwball comedy, which in turn reflects the fascination of the cinema itself with the advent of sound. This is also where America comes in, because Cavell perceives the marital contract which persists in the couple as symptomatic of the health of the community, with America as the project in which the fundamentals of the political are being tested for modernity.

Furthermore, insofar as America is in its very constitution premised on the pursuit of happiness, it is premised on what Cavell, following Ralph Waldo Emerson, phrases as the unattained but attainable self.[21] This, then, is the self which

---

19   Ibid., 106.
20   Ibid., 106–7.
21   See Stanley Cavell, *Pursuits of Happiness: The Hollywood Comedy of Remarriage* (Cambridge MA: Harvard University Press, 1981), 12.

traverses the comedies Cavell analyzes, precisely where the cleft between the un-attained and the attainable is negotiated in terms of conversation, education, and contract, such that all three emerge in Cavell both as constituent to this Emerson-ian self and as occasioning its ineradicable crisis. For Cavell, this evidently boils down to the fundamentals of the political, and consequently to the question of the American Revolution, as when he says, for example, that "happiness is not to be won just by opposing those in power but only, beyond that, by educating them, or their successors. Put otherwise, the achievement of human happiness requires not the perennial and fuller satisfaction of our needs as they stand but the examination and transformation of those needs."[22] Finally, this is why Cavell emphasizes the Hollywood comedy of *remarriage*, such as Preston Sturges's *The Lady Eve* (1941), Hawks's *His Girl Friday* (1940) or Cukor's *The Philadelphia Story* (1940): because, in the final analysis, remarriage—rather than just marriage—al-lows him to isolate in his chosen narratives the force and the appeal of the con-tract itself. Remarriage, in other words, allows Cavell to address what about the contract is constituent to the unattained but attainable self (while occasioning its ineradicable crisis). Also, and not at all insignificantly, remarriage comedies allow Cavell to isolate and address the fantasy behind the contractual.

The Hollywood melodrama of the unknown woman, with its emblematic Garbo, derives for Cavell from the remarriage comedy insofar as it negates its fea-tures, the chief being "the negation of marriage itself."[23] The woman of melodra-ma is subject to education and change, just as the woman in the remarriage com-edy is subject to education and change when she enters into conversation with the man, as part of a couple; but the difference in melodrama is that the educa-tion and change must take place "elsewhere, in the abandoning of that *shared* wit and intelligence and exclusive appreciation."[24] What follows, even though Cavell chooses to leave it implicit at best, is that in this separation from the shared and the contractual his Garboesque heroine is separated also from the conditions constituent to an attainable self. That the separation from the attainable self may be taking place in the same register as Freudian melancholia, with the appropri-ate libidinal economy, can be inferred from the fact that the comedies Cavell is working with, and that his melodrama derives from, are romantic comedies formed around romantic interest and high libidinal stakes. After all, Cavell him-

---

22 Ibid. 4–5.
23 Cavell, *Contesting Tears*, 6.
24 Ibid. (emphasis Cavell's).

self suggests as much when he says that the education of the unknown woman takes place where *exclusive appreciation* is abandoned. He even implies that the melancholia of these melodramas spreads metonymically, as it were, catching up eventually with the philosopher who studies them: "it becomes painful to go on studying them. A compensating profit of instruction must be high for the experience to be justified."[25] He could be echoing Freud here, when Freud describes melancholia as an open wound which draws to itself the available libidinal energy from all sides and commands an extraordinarily high counter-investment.[26]

Ninotchka presents a challenge to Cavell's argument already with Lubitsch's decision to cast Garbo as a comedienne. She works for Cavell from within melodrama, but surfaces in Lubitsch from within comedy, yet in the terms that Cavell assigns to her in melodrama. This reverses for Cavell the order of derivation, signaling that the unknown woman of melodrama, who finds her rationale in Garbo, could be the condition for the comedy he envisions for philosophy, rather than the place of its negation. The crisis that she thus organizes for comedy (the crisis material to self-reflection? education? critique?) comes out succinctly in the advertising slogan, "Garbo Laughs." The fact that Garbo's laughter made it emphatically into the publicity is hardly an indication of comedy pure and simple; rather, it indicates that Garbo takes comedy aback, that she compels comedy to reappraise laughter where laughter is generic to it, or else where laughter is comedy's rationale.[27]

This is evident in the laughter scene itself, which takes place in a Paris restaurant after Leon has demeaned himself and thereby finally succeeded in making Ninotchka laugh. It is not merely that Garbo laughs only once in the film (at other times she smiles, if that); it is that her laughter in this one scene is spastic and convulsive, provoking the idea that all laughter be reassessed in terms of paroxysm, syncope or excess. As Harvey rightly notes, "she howls, she collapses, she chokes—falling across the table, throwing her head back to let the sound out, collapsing across the table again."[28] Harvey documents another symptomatic detail, quoting from Melvyn Douglas, who says in his autobiography "that she managed all this without making a sound that he could hear—on the set. The

25 Ibid., 7.

26 Freud, *Das Ich und das Es*, 183, 188.

27 That this concern informed the project from its beginning can be evinced from a detail duly noted by Harvey: "According to some accounts, the whole project *began* with 'Garbo laughs!': once they had the slogan, they looked for a movie to go with it" (*Romantic Comedy in Hollywood*, 384, emphasis Harvey's).

28 Ibid., 383.

See Garbo laugh. *Ninotchka*

sounds were dubbed in later."[29] What the film registers, in other words, is the separation of sound and spasm in Garbo's laughter, as if signaling a structural disconnection in Garbo between the cinematic image (of silent melodrama) and the cinematic sound (essential to screwball comedy and its conversationalism). Rather than degrading the sound on film, this has the strange effect of calling attention to the rift where sound originates for the cinema: it is almost as if Garbo functions in Lubitsch as a warning to film that hidden in laughter is the surplus labor of paroxysm.

It is in this light that one should reconsider the stakes of the *Ninotchka* publicity: "Garbo Laughs," that is, was conceived as a rejoinder to "Garbo Talks," the slogan used to advertise *Anna Christie* (1930), Garbo's first appearance in a talkie. This indicates that Garbo's breakthrough into laughter was perceived as comparable to her breakthrough into speech, but also, and more importantly, that Garbo's laughter does to comedy what sound did to silent film. (Just as it also indicates that in Lubitsch the Cavellian unknown woman is consistently the proviso of comedy and not the instance of its negation.)

Moreover, the narrative of *Ninotchka* is organized around a couple reenacting their relationship, like in the narratives of Cavell's comedies of remarriage. Indeed, once the process of conversation and education begins during Ninotchka's and Leon's Paris encounter, their relationship gains such a momentum that its

---

29   Quoted in ibid., 384.

reenactment is secured for even after the climactic breach occasioned by Swana's intervention and Ninotchka's subsequent return to Moscow: it is as if the breach is necessary for the film to show that this process allows for no operative closure. (In Lubitsch too, like in Cavell, this process yields an insight into the very the terms of the political.)

Additionally, from first to last the couple's relationship and education are premised on the management of contracts. Leon enters the story in order to intervene, on Swana's behalf, into the contract negotiations between the Russian delegation and the prospective buyers in Paris; Ninotchka enters the story in order to intervene into the contract negotiations about to be closed between the Russian delegation and Leon. Swana and Leon manage a contract to begin with, insofar as he is her kept man; Swana's relationship with Ninotchka too comes out as contractual, when Swana proposes to return the stolen jewels if Ninotchka complies with her request and relinquishes Leon. The fact that Ninotchka does comply with Swana's terms indicates that her management of Leon also takes place as a contract. After all of which it comes as no surprise that the ending is appropriately contractual as well: Ninotchka is sent to Constantinople in order to secure contracts for the Soviet fur trade, because Iranoff, Buljanoff, and Kopalski "are sitting there, those three, for six weeks and haven't sold a piece of fur." True, their failing to sell any fur is a ploy to trick Razinin into sending Ninotchka to Constantinople and back to Leon. Still, it is telling that wishing for a contract is what it takes for the film to end.

It is just as telling that marriage is ostentatiously absent from this world although it abounds in contracts. Swana and Leon are clearly engaged in a long-term sexual relationship with an elaborate economic logic to it, yet all semblance of marriage is dropped in favor of the kept-man script. Ninotchka acquiesces to this script when she trades Leon for jewels; besides, she enters into her relationship with Leon as a vocal proponent of revolutionary free love, where even the likes of Swana suggest too much marital logic, not too little of it. The ending too contains no suggestion that Ninotchka and Leon will be getting married. It is as if the excess of contracts in the film points to the place from which marriage is markedly missing: to where marriage seems to retain a certain residue of pure law which cannot be accessed from within the contractual.

Cavell, by contrast, calls explicitly for marriage if his analysis of comedy, and with it his analysis of America as a political and a philosophical project, is to be viable. He does so nowhere as forcefully perhaps as in an essay on Hitchcock's

North by Northwest (film of 1959), published just after he completed writing *Pursuits of Happiness*. "My ground," he says, "is the thought that while America, or any discovered world, can no longer ratify marriage, the achievement of true marriage might ratify something called America as a place in which to seek it. This is a state secret."[30] Lubitsch, however, carves a niche in marriage allowing for a separation of law from the contractual, where law comes to occupy an empty place, evocative of the place Lacanian psychoanalysis assigns to law. It is as if, thanks to Lubitsch, a Lacanian circumstance in Cavell comes to light, a circumstance which also defines Cavell's view of the political.[31] Of course, insofar as it concerns a state secret, and therefore the secret of the state, it follows that this Lacanian circumstance in Cavell is also his habitat for *raison d'État*.

This means that Cavell fails to address the question he defines as that of America precisely where America is premised on the fact of its revolution. Revolution, that is, may communicate with *raison d'État* but is not accessible from within it, as Lubitsch amply demonstrates in the Garbo/Lugosi scene where the melancholy Garbo performs revolution to the vampiristic Lugosi of state socialism. Hannah Arendt claims that this applies even more readily to America than to the various European revolutionary projects, already where America, with its Jeffersonian accent on the new continent and a new man, renounces the imaginary of the nation-state. Arendt also insists that America and its revolution inspired later revolutions, and structurally so, even if these subsequent efforts failed to maintain, perhaps necessarily so, the standards of their American blueprint.[32] It is here already that Lubitsch's Hollywood comedy—about the melancholia which is constituent to the October Revolution, and about its divorce from state socialism—is a statement above all about America. This position is but a sentence away from yet another pairing of America and the October Revolution, this time in Gilles Deleuze. According to Deleuze, both the Russian and the American political projects hinge on revolutionary communities of sons without fathers, the only genuine threat to such communities being the return of the father (which

---

30 Stanley Cavell, "*North by Northwest*," *Critical Inquiry* 7, no. 4 (Summer 1981), 776.
31 When he proposes a philosophical coming together of comedy and marriage where the latter, it turns out, harbors an irreducible residue of law, Cavell in fact comes close to Alenka Zupančič's claim that shifts and excesses of the symbolic (in Lacanian terms) are formative to comedy: "*Not only are we not infinite, we are not even finite,*" she remarks wittily, and continues: "The stuff that comedies are made of is precisely this hole in finitude." This is "the very generative source" of comedy. See Alenka Zupančič, *The Odd One In: On Comedy* (Cambridge MA: MIT Press, 2008), 53 (emphasis Zupančič's).
32 See Hannah Arendt, *On Revolution* (New York: Penguin, 2006), 14–15.

Deleuze associates with the persecution of the Soviets under Stalinism).[33] Needless to say, the father-figure in Deleuze is implicated from the start in the Oedipal script of psychoanalysis, resonating all the while with the agenda that psychoanalysis ascribes to law.

Lubitsch explores this particular position further in *To Be or Not to Be* (1942), which in many ways reads as a companion piece to *Ninotchka*, just as in Cavell his melodrama book reads as a companion piece to his book on comedy. The conjunction of revolution and the marriage which is conspicuously missing undergoes an inflection here, coming out as a conjunction of Nazism and the marriage which is conspicuously present, now to the point of excess.

In *To Be or Not to Be*, the marriage of two famous Polish actors, Maria and Joseph Tura, persists despite Maria's serial adultery. What is more, it is thanks to her adultery (and to what in her adultery is serial) that the marriage shows up as persistent to begin with. Put differently, in Lubitsch, it takes reenacted adultery to show what marriage is all about, with the implication that marriage takes place where adultery essentially does not matter. In addition, the film contains an interesting visual and narrative meander which further complicates the state of affairs. After the Nazi occupation of Poland, Maria (Carole Lombard) helps the Warsaw resistance movement by supplying them with a photograph of the hateful Nazi spy, Professor Siletsky, and by later agreeing to seduce him into a trap. It turns out, however, that one Siletsky is not enough for the scheme, so Maria's actor husband (Jack Benny) has to step in disguised convincingly as Siletsky. Maria will then end up playing prospective lover to both of them at the Gestapo Headquarters, so that her erotic encounter with her husband comes off as a supplement to her erotic encounter with the hateful enemy, precisely where both husband and enemy are consistent with the photograph she first disseminated.[34] What constitutes the famous Lubitsch touch here is not so much the fact that husband and enemy can both occupy the same elaborate phantasm; rather, it is the assumption that the husband can become his own wife's adulterous lover and cuckold himself in consequence. Once the husband joins up the series of the wife's adulterous lovers, he bares what in marriage is the empty place of the law (baring at the same time law as an empty place). Which is also where the superb logic of Lubitsch's obscenity emerges—their names are Joseph and Maria: because the eponymous couple

---

33   See Gilles Deleuze, *Critique et clinique* (Paris: Minuit, 1993), 113.
34   This of course reflects the moment earlier in the film when the photograph of Hitler proves more convincing than the theatrical presence of the actor in costume who sat for it and from whom it was taken.

in the New Testament point precisely to the position where pure law is accessed in place of adultery.

To Be or Not to Be is in this sense perhaps the most Lacanian of all the Lubitsch films: a proposition all the more convincing in view of the fact that it plays emphatically with and against Shakespeare's *Hamlet*, the specimen story of Lacan's psychoanalysis. Equally interesting is the fact that the politics attached to this configuration is that of Nazism—because in its various narrative derivations it takes Nazism to provide the film with the circumstance that husband and enemy occupy the same elaborate phantasm, and that the husband joins up the series of the wife's adulterous lovers, which then exposes marriage as the relentless empty place of law. In this way the film shows Nazism as constituted around a Lacanian explanation of law, almost as a Lacanian fantasy, in contrast to the political profile of communism in *Ninotchka*. This in turn is reminiscent of yet another comment by Hannah Arendt: that a pedantic legalizing of crime through retroactive legislation was characteristic of Nazism, while Stalinism was characterized by its flair for unremitting confession.[35] Implicit in this is the suggestion that Nazism and Stalinism do not share the same imaginary. Rather, while Nazism emerges as a Lacanian fantasy of law, where law is indifferent to the various economies of the ego, Stalinism surfaces when the revolutionaries are forced to reimagine for themselves a functional ego: because the demand that a political prisoner confess his or her alleged crime time and time again is indicative of a regime which wants to invent the ego responsive to law (and to *raison d'État*) to begin with, only to stumble into the morass of the ego's economy.

Lubitsch amply evidences this distinction. If his individual Nazis appear comical, inept, clumsy, and ultimately conquerable, Hitler included, it is because they cannot but fail to perform to the standard of the fantasy they keep invoking: that of the law which is indifferent to the various economies of the ego.[36] Lubitsch's Soviet commissar, on the other hand, contaminated through Lugosi

---

35   See Hannah Arendt, *The Origins of Totalitarianism* (New York: Harvest Books & Harcourt, 1976), 353. That repeated orders to confess in a detailed and elaborate fashion were routine in the Gulag camps is well recorded, in memoirs and works of literature alike. See for instance Danilo Kiš's *The Tomb for Boris Davidovič* (*Grobnica za Borisa Davidoviča*, 1976).

36   True, Hitler seems to embody this fantasy for the Lubitsch Nazis, because—unlike the rest of them—he is a fanatical vegetarian and a non-smoker: a fact repeatedly mentioned. Lubitsch signals however that Hitler too fails to perform to the very standard he seems to be embodying: early in the film, while panoramic shots are being shown of Warsaw, its inhabitants and its delicatessen, the narrator comments in a voice-over that, even though Hitler is a fanatical vegetarian, he is known to swallow whole countries.

with the cinematic memory of vampires, remains functional in ensuring that the perilous labor of the revolutionaries is kept in check and streamlined from the position where *raison d'État* meets the economy. The same logic applies to the one instance, early in the film, when Ninotchka voices a Stalinist slogan concerning the mass trials in Moscow: they will, she says, create fewer but better Russians. This is in sharp contrast to Ninotchka's habitual references to the famine affecting the Russian people and her reverence for bare life. After all, she does not deliver the "bad" Russians—Iranoff, Buljanoff, and Kopalski—for trial, even though her mission to Paris was to investigate their wrongdoing. Instead, once they are all back to Moscow, she makes sure to divide the eggs they have unevenly saved into four equal meals. What the contrast ultimately reveals is that Stalinism originates where it departs from the revolutionary collective and the revolutionary conditions towards a fantasy of the countable.[37]

This is perhaps where Lubitsch's avid interest in contracts and the contractual calls for a closer scrutiny—because contracts, unlike the law, seem to traverse and negotiate the scope of political economy in its broadest sense, not least where it entails libidinal economy. (It is from here that one could address Foucault's claim: that "the market and the contract function in exactly opposite ways and we have in fact two heterogeneous structures," because the "egoistic mechanism" of the subject of interest "could not be more distant from the dialectic of renunciation, transcendence, and the voluntary bond of the juridical theory of the contract."[38] Foucault's argument, that is, works only to the extent to which it excludes the lesson of psychoanalysis.)

Not surprisingly, the decisive moment to do with contracts in *Ninotchka* coincides with the narrative climax, when the very terms of the story are restacked for reenactment. Swana steals the jewels from the hotel safe in order to force Ninotchka into a contract: she will trade them for Leon, provided Ninotchka accepts her terms. All the other contracts and trade-offs in the film seem to be

37 This is why Lubitsch's two "political" films work as a scene of instruction for Europe too. Europe, to-day, defines itself as a political project based on its having overcome totalitarianism. Totalitarianism in turn offers a position from which Nazism and Stalinism can be addressed together, but often becomes fissureless in the process, as if securing a unified Europe depended on a totalizing gesture performed on totalitarianism itself. As a consequence, in recent European public discourse a number of critical distinctions have been written off as irrelevant—not only that between Nazism and Stalinism, but also those be-tween Stalinism, communism, and socialism, which are often homogenized and addressed inadequately as "communism."
38 Foucault, *The Birth of Biopolitics*, 275–6.

leading to this one and climaxing in it, bursting open for analysis. Its terms, however, betray a peculiar logic: by stealing the confiscated jewels Swana is in fact stealing what she legally claims was hers to begin with. Further, she proposes to trade them for Leon, although she has already abundantly paid for him, paid to him, and has thus bound him contractually as her kept man. This reveals that contracts operate where they curtail not only the law but also the logic which sustains their own conditions. By accepting the proposition, Ninotchka reveals in turn that Leon is somehow hers to trade off—that she sustains their relationship in terms of peculiar coldness and cruelty. I have already suggested that this moment is climactic for Ninotchka insofar as it reenacts for her the revolution as premised on melancholia (just as the comedy reaches its climax when it resurrects the iconic unhappy Garbo outside of melodrama and the law of genre).[39] But this moment is also climactic because it reveals that Ninotchka's and Leon's relationship, the central narrative interest of the film, has registered no progress at some fundamental level, since Ninotchka is as cruel and cold to him at this critical juncture as she was when she first met him—possibly even more so.

Indeed, Leon is the one to pursue her after her return to Russia. He lays siege to the Soviet embassy in Paris and keeps writing letters to Moscow. The ploy to trick Razinin into sending Ninotchka to Constantinople has his handwriting all over it. Yet what he finally secures as a happy ending is merely a likely reenactment of the Paris scenario, the moment Ninotchka is provoked to relinquish self-interest (for the bare life of others, and therefore bare life as such). What he secures, in other words, is Ninotchka's contract on him. Still, this may very well be the condition on which his sentimental education can take place: on entering into his relationship with Ninotchka he changes so much that he is brought to reconsider the very structure of self-interest. At first comfortable with his arrangement with Swana, he is now eager to invest libidinally in a relationship where gain is, as it were, premised on prescheduled pain. Swana is the first to take note of his transformation, describing it mockingly but aptly as a regeneration.[40]

---

39 A similar proposition informs Sturges's *Sullivan's Travels* (1941), which likewise climaxes when comedy is shown to relate to unhappiness more critically than drama.

40 In consequence, when Swana enters into a contract with Ninotchka, she proposes to buy off what she cannot possess; once again, this suggests that contracts operate where they curtail the very logic that sustains their conditions. This particular contract in *Ninotchka* corresponds to the climax of Lubitsch's *Trouble in Paradise* (1932). Lily and Gaston, two sexy thieving lovers and con artists, agree to rob Mariette, a rich widow (Miriam Hopkins, Herbert Marshall, and Kay Francis, in that order). Gaston, however, falls for the suave and melancholy Mariette whom he was meant to seduce. At the end, he is shown honoring

Accordingly, if Ninotchka—inseparable for the film from Garbo—sketches for Lubitsch the scope of melancholia, Leon inflects her sphere of influence in terms of masochism. His masochism is of a markedly Deleuzian disposition. In his 1967 essay on Sacher-Masoch, Deleuze critiques masochism as described in psychoanalysis, around the Oedipal model. He argues against the explanation which perceives the masochist as the Freudian child who is being beaten and reduces the dominatrix to a mere vehicle for the fantasy of paternal authority. Instead, says Deleuze, the phantasmatic script of masochism relies on the abolition of fatherhood and law, or more precisely on the abolition of fatherhood where it is inseparable from law. It is not a child but a father who is being beaten, says Deleuze. This is made possible thanks to the contract which the masochist arranges with a complex female figure. While law is in principle timeless and applies to all, contract is limited temporally and applies only to the interested parties. The contract facilitates the transfer of paternal authority onto the woman, so that she may act as a cruel, cold, commanding Oedipal mother, while also remaining active as a primitive, uterine, sensuous Venus, suggestive of promiscuity, even prostitution. As a result, the woman who guarantees the contract essential to masochism is defined by Deleuze as a zone of resonance between the punishing Oedipal mother and the uterine Venus. Defined as resonance, she comes out as an oral mother, a complex tripartite female figure irreducible to any one of her functions. (The oral mother, says Deleuze, is the core of the masochist's fantasy.) In this way she displaces the issue of incest and organizes parthenogenesis for the masochist: a process of regeneration in which the father plays no role.[41]

---

his initial agreement with Lily, but to the excess of making Mariette party to the contract, so that Mariette freely hands over all the items Lily wants from her, Gaston included. But Lily, it turns out, is bargaining for what she cannot possess, namely Gaston: this comes out in the very final frames of the film, when Lily is shown embracing Gaston but clasping just as eagerly a little extra something she has stolen from Mariette, a little more than she agreed to, as if compensating for the loss she cannot be brought to acknowledge. The little extra item is a bejeweled purse, which the two had originally stolen from Mariette for Gaston to return and thus win Mariette's confidence. By stealing it again Lily is reenacting for the story the very terms she wants to cancel, because the purse contains the promise of Gaston's return to Mariette. The final frames suggest that the film itself cherishes the same phantasm: Lily and Gaston are huddled up in a car, with the purse in Lily's lap. Symptomatically, their arrangement accurately reflects the image Gaston invented for Mariette when he first returned the purse and she asked him where he had found it: he found it in a dark little niche, he says, next to the figure of Venus. It is as if *Trouble in Paradise* ends on the note on which *Ninotchka* climaxes, so that *Ninotchka* operates in many ways as an extension and an execution of the narrative—and libidinal—terms of *Trouble in Paradise*.

41 See Gilles Deleuze, *Présentation de Sacher-Masoch. Le Froid et le Cruel* (Paris: Minuit, 1967), 60–7.

Of particular relevance here is the fact that Deleuze also analyzes masochism alongside the conditions of the political, presenting both masochism and revolution as premised on the fantasy of sons without fathers, or else on a radical abolition of fatherhood. True, he remains sensitive to what is specifically Austrian-Hungarian about the phantasmatic makeup of masochism; still, it is equally true that Austria-Hungary, structurally implicated in the fantasy of masochism, remains for Deleuze a passageway to the very conditions of the revolutionary and the collective.[42]

It is at this juncture that, in Lubitsch, Garbo functions as a scene of instruction: she traverses the film as its critical nucleus from the first frame in which she appears to the core of the masochist fantasy, until the film itself emerges as a massive zone of resonance between these two points. And she is clearly one such scene to Melvyn Douglas's Leon, and the core of his fantasy. Ninotchka appeals to him where she is cold and cruel, and where the sexual exploits in her stories coincide with extreme punishment. Recall the anecdote about the Polish lancer: he was her lover, she recounts (her lancer!, a sexual joke quite in Lubitsch's line), but she coldly killed him all the same. Furthermore, her promiscuity resides precisely in her coldness and cruelty, the lancer story being a case in point. It is not only that the lancer becomes part and parcel of her belief in revolutionary free love; she also recounts the story to Leon as means of foreplay, appealing to an aspect crucial to his sexual fantasy.

According to Deleuze, the coldness in this fantasy serves to keep pagan sensuality at bay and secure the kind of latency necessary to parthenogenesis. What survives in the cold, says Deleuze, is not sensuality but rather a suprasensual sentimentality, shackled in ice and protected by fur (hence Venus in furs in the eponymous Sacher-Masoch novel).[43] Suprasensual sentimentality can then be taken as an accurate description of Garbo, not only in Lubitsch but for the cinema as such, especially in contrast to the accentuated sensuality of its more routine stars. Furthermore, the fantasy Deleuze thus sketches offers a position from which to approach one of the wittiest and most absorbing lines in the film—when on arriving in Paris she is offered courtly niceties and help with her luggage, to which she coldly replies "Don't make an issue of my womanhood!" Indeed, in her stern

---

42 A similar affinity should be noted in Lubitsch. "His fondness for obscure Hungarian plays of the well-made school was a widespread Hollywood joke," says Harvey: "'I have a special weakness,' he once told an interviewer, 'for the Continental type of thing, works like Molnár's'" (*Romantic Comedy in Hollywood*, 7).

43 See Deleuze, *Présentation de Sacher-Masoch*, 51–2.

Ninotchka (Greta Garbo) and Leon (Melvyn Douglas) after the fall. *Ninotchka*

socialist outfit she seems stripped of all the vestiges of Hollywood womanhood, only to expose the excess which survives shackled in Russian ice. In other words, "Don't make an issue of my womanhood!" calls attention to womanhood lingering where it has been ousted, and therefore to too much womanhood, not too little of it—an excess now formative to masochism.

Garbo exits the film in the same vein, appropriately shrouded in a Deleuzian fantasy: she arrives in Constantinople and back to Leon wearing a fur hat and a fur-collar coat. Her exit is that of a veritable Venus in furs, afresh from the freezing Moscow winter, emanating suprasensual sentimentality.[44] Moreover, Garbo's costume—the lines of her fur hat, the way it defines the contours of her face for a close-up—corresponds rather precisely to that of her entrance in *Anna Karenina* (1935), so that a recurring Russian winter fantasy is secured. (Since Garbo's railway entrance in *Anna Karenina* is also the promise of her railway suicide exit, the Russian winter fantasy that this scene reenacts in *Ninotchka* also harbors the promise of extreme cruelty. Not to mention the fact that Garbo has already entered *Ninotchka* on the same note, i.e., via the railway, so that a comprehensive correspondence with *Anna Karenina* is established.) True, the fur is in contrast to her earlier, more austere Soviet garb; yet both surface in *Ninotchka* from within the same phantasm of Russia and the same fantasy of cruelty.[45]

The fur theme also stretches metonymically to the Lugosi/Razinin sequence, immediately preceding her mission to Constantinople, because she is sent there (and to the ending of the story) in order to advance the Soviet fur trade. Fur therefore comes to her logically as it were; what Hollywood perceives in the register of sensuous luxury surfaces here simultaneously in a different register altogether, that of the Soviet economy, more specifically, of "the products of the forest and provinces" that Ninotchka is in charge of to begin with. The ending, that is, shrouds her once again in the fantasy of Russian agriculture, inseparable here from hunting. Hunting in turn is integral to the fantasy of masochism. In describing the imaginary of Sacher-Masoch's novels, Deleuze claims that three types of rite interact so as to produce this imaginary: hunting rites, agricultural rites, and rites of regeneration and rebirth. Ultimately, they all converge in the woman who

---

44 The Lugosi/Razinin sequence, immediately preceding Ninotchka's Constantinople scenes, opens with an establishing shot of Moscow under snow.

45 That this is the phantasmatic core of the Lubitsch imaginary can be evidenced from the fact that *Anna Karenina* continues to appear in Lubitsch's films of the 1940s: in both *The Shop Around the Corner* (1940) and *To Be or Not to Be* Tolstoy's novel is used as a code-holder, a container of ciphers, a secret sign for the initiated.

secures the masochist contract, because, ideally, she hunts the bear or the wolf; she presides over an agrarian collective or organizes it; and she ensures that the man undergoes the process of regeneration.[46]

The peculiar political economy of melancholia thus converges in Lubitsch's Garbo with the fantasy of masochism. The film is permeated with appropriate references: the studious association of Garbo with furs and hunting is reciprocated by a comprehensive network of references to milk and to Ninotchka's peasant upbringing. On the one hand, the peculiar political economy thus assembled around Garbo preserves the logic of the October Revolution against what in Stalinism can be perceived as counter-revolutionary. (Indeed, Deleuze perceives Stalinism in terms of counter-revolution.) On the other hand, Garbo is here also the phantasmatic core of Deleuzian masochism, specifically where she invokes agrarian collectives and the political economy they entail; after all, Deleuze himself qualifies the agricultural element of the masochist fantasy as "agrarian communism."[47] There is yet another aspect to these agrarian collectives which Deleuze singles out as symptomatic and which is as symptomatic of Lubitsch: the communities fantasized in this way are Slavic. They displace into the Slavic imaginary interactions constituent to masochism. Ninotchka is an obvious case in point, with her October Revolution, Russian people, and her name itself inflected the Russian way. But the same is true of the Lubitsch imaginary as such, with its Ruritanian kingdoms of the early musicals; its Razinin, Iranoff, Buljanoff, and Kopalski; with its Novak and Kralik, its Matuschek and Pirovitch in *The Shop Around the Corner*; its Siletsky, Sobinski, Bronski, Lubiński, Kubinski, Łomiński, Rożański, Poznański, Masłowski … and its Warsaw of *To Be or Not to Be*; its Belinski in *Cluny Brown* (1946)—all of them finally reverberating in Lubitsch's own name and the Slavic logic of its suffixation.[48]

---

46 See Deleuze, *Présentation de Sacher-Masoch*, 94.

47 Ibid., 96.

48 A note is required here about the inflection that this imaginary registers in *To Be or Not to Be*. Like *Ninotchka*, this film too depends on a Slavic collective strongly calibrated in terms of food and eating. Unlike *Ninotchka*, however, where food indexes the tension between the logic of the revolution and the *raison d'État* of state socialism, food in *To Be or Not to Be* traces throughout the scope of original prohibition as somehow formative for the Nazi imaginary. People in *Ninotchka* are hungry and starving; people in *To Be or Not to Be* are forbidden to eat. Lubitsch's Hitler is a strict vegetarian; but given to eating whole countries, he is exposed primarily as a cannibal—his primary transgression is that of cannibalism. The joke attached to him throughout the film is that he will be remembered as cheese, but the joke is suppressed as alarmingly transgressive. *Hamlet*, on the other hand, whose production is formative to the film's story, is readily associated with ham (bad actor), but no sooner than ham is exposed as prohibited meat: what you are, says a Jewish actor to one such ham, I would not eat. *Hamlet* in consequence is implicated from the

For Deleuze, this matters to the overall scheme of masochism where the woman, configured in this fashion, brings about the man's collapse from the scope he envisions for the law straight down into the workings of the ritual—because the masochist, claims Deleuze, is propelled into the contract with the woman by his wish to refine the terms of the contract into law. His contract with her, in other words, is based on his fantasy of pure, Lacanian law. (Deleuze explicitly quotes Lacan as his source here.) By thus obliquely accessing the law and conforming to its every demand, the masochist manages to derive enjoyment precisely in the position where the law inhibits it.[49]

There seem to be two problems with the Deleuzian model, however, both evidenced in *Ninotchka*. The first concerns the very imagination of the law here. It is clear that the Lacanian vision of law is attractive to Deleuze where it promises the relinquishing of self- interest. Its promise, in other words, is political, and the one which comes close to Foucault's vision of the juridical and of sovereignty, in his lectures on biopolitics. It remains unclear though why the masochist, if this be his fantasy, would want the woman to begin with, as his devoted commitment to law is such that, paradoxically enough, it should render him quite self-sufficient in this sphere where selves are abandoned. (One can easily imagine him contracting himself for a spectacle of, say, auto-flagellation.)

The second problem proceeds from the first and can be discerned in a remark Deleuze makes in his short essay on masochism in *Critique et clinique*: the contract with the woman is essential to masochism, he says, but how it is rooted in masochism remains a mystery.[50] Thus attached to mystery, the contract in Deleuze remains divorced from the purity of logic that the law promises and that Deleuze's analysis seems to promise as well; rather, it behaves like a dream in Freud, when Freud says that all dreams have navels—the points impervious to access where analysis halts.[51] This in turn suggests that the masochist's unmiti-

---

start in the logic of the original prohibition where law resides, but now as hamlet, literally the little ham, contaminated for the film and the law with the pound of flesh it cannot shed. This pound of flesh surfaces ultimately in the film's systemic references to *The Merchant of Venice*, so that Shakespeare seems to subsist for Lubitsch in a position where *Hamlet* cannot be properly understood outside of a comparative analysis with *The Merchant of Venice*. This in turn calls for a critical reassessment of Lacanian psychoanalysis where *Hamlet* is its specimen story.

49   See Deleuze, *Présentation de Sacher-Masoch*, 88. This fantasy is also where Deleuze locates the humor of masochism, or the comedy integral to masochism. Which means that Deleuze situates comedy in the Lacanian aspect of his model of masochism; this in turn aligns him with Zupančič's perspective on comedy.

50   See Deleuze, *Critique et clinique*, 71.

51   See Sigmund Freud, *Die Traumdeutung* (Frankfurt am Main: Fischer, 2009), 125.

gated loyalty to law can be accessed not in the register that psychoanalysis (and Deleuze, for that matter) ascribes to law, but in the register that psychoanalysis ascribes to the phantasmatic. Put differently, what transpires in masochism is in fact the position where pure law emerges as fantasy. Of course, insofar as the ideation of pure law is constitutive to psychoanalysis, the script of masochism could well be describing the inner workings of psychoanalysis itself, especially that of Freud in the 1920s and later, and that of Lacan.

Ninotchka's study of Garbo offers instruction on this particular point: situating in Garbo the intelligence of the cinema, it focuses on the figure wherein the masochist contract mysteriously resides, but now as the figure of intelligence. In consequence, the mystery is somewhat dispelled when her specific intelligence is canvassed against the masochist script attached to Leon/Douglas. Indeed, what she promises to this script is the relinquishing of self-interest that the law calls for; it is only that the relinquishing now takes place in the register of melancholia. A curious little correspondence in Deleuze shows that this could well be the case, even though Deleuze is not the one to acknowledge it: in 1967 he keeps describing masochism in terms of cruelty, whereas in 1968, in a passing remark in *Difference and Repetition*, he attributes cruelty to melancholia, saying that melancholia is "cruelty in cruelty," insupportable to the self.[52] Defined as cruelty in cruelty, melancholia seems to be delineating the very terms of the masochist contract, suggesting that the woman's melancholia is the mysterious linchpin which keeps it in place. It is as if the melancholy woman, cruel to the self to begin with, cannot but secure cruelty to what the masochist shapes into a fantasy of law. Which is once again where this woman provides an insight into the logic of the revolution, just as her relationship with the masochist provides an insight into the character of the relationship of revolution and *raison d'État*. This in turn generates another footnote on Foucault's view of biopolitics, because a trajectory comes to light whereby the question of rights and bare life shifts from the scope of sovereignty and the governmental to that of revolution.

The way in which *Ninotchka* adds to Deleuze's model of masochism suggests also a footnote on Cavell. His two film books—one about the Hollywood comedy of remarriage, the other about the Hollywood melodrama of the unknown woman—now read as a massive comparative analysis of masochism *cum* melancholia, where the comedy book surveys the fantasy formative of masochism, while the

---

52 Deleuze, *Différence et répétition*, 198.

book on melodrama focuses on the unknown woman as its mysterious linchpin. Indeed, Cavell's emphasis on the woman's *unknownness* echoes Deleuze's remark that the contract with the woman is essential to masochism, but how it is rooted in masochism remains a *mystery*.

Similarly, the men in the remarriage comedies depend for their education on scripts uncannily reminiscent of Deleuzian masochism. What Cavell describes as woman's equality with man in these films often transpires as the woman's strictness and austerity, even as coldness, as for instance with Katharine Hepburn's Tracy Lord in *The Philadelphia Story*. (Barbara Stanwyck is no less harsh to Henry Fonda in *The Lady Eve*. And the remarriage romance of Rosalind Russell and Cary Grant in *His Girl Friday* is negotiated literally in terms of a capital punishment narrative.) Theirs is also always the scandal if not of promiscuity then of its threat: these women shift between men all too effortlessly. Finally, they all climax for comedy as incessant talkers; theirs is the climax of orality; they are the Hollywood oral mothers. Cavell is hardly insensitive to these attributes or to the fact that they keep undermining the green political world of his America: it shows when he insists that Tracy Lord's moral superiority is a flaw, although he himself explicitly suppresses the invocation of sexuality in romantic comedy, which cannot but contaminate it, in favor of friendship. *Ninotchka* with its Garbo is thus critical where it brings the two Cavell genres together: it exposes the comedy of it as masochism while exposing the unknownness of the Cavell woman as the intelligence of melancholia.

This of course calls for further analysis of the crisis implicit in the pursuit of happiness, and of the various intersections of philosophy and psychoanalysis in which this crisis has been addressed. Even so, the complex barely glimpsed here demands that Lubitsch's cinema be taken not merely as their platform, but as an active scene of their instruction. His truly is the masters' master's lesson.

MLADEN DOLAR

To Be or Not to Be?
No, Thank You

Let me state from the outset that in my view *To Be or Not to Be* (1942) is one of the best movies ever made in the whole of cinema history. I've never been part of the *Sight & Sound* periodical polls, but if I ever had a say, *To Be or Not to Be* would be my first candidate for number one. As it is, it finished a pitiable 144th in the last poll, which no doubt shows the sad state of the spirit of the times—a state the present volume has the ambition to change. No doubt the low ranking is also due to the general deprecation of comedy (one never finds comedies high up on these lists) that began, tellingly, with the loss of the second book of Aristotle's *Poetics*, a contingent loss that can be seen as emblematic for the entire tradition, where comedy largely featured if not quite as the missing half of spirit, then as its limping leg. It was always invariably seen as the younger, less glamorous and more superficial sister of tragedy, entertaining but not serious, a minor genre never entitled to a rank of honor. No doubt it speaks volumes for the glory of Hegel that he was the only one among philosophers in the entire tradition to place comedy in the highest position, above tragedy, seeing in it, in its very superficiality, the best proponent of the profound and the sublime. The "depth of Spirit," he says in the *Phenomenology*, is "only as deep as it dares to spread out and lose itself in its exposition [*Auslegung*],"[1] and what forms the spirit of comedy is the daring, the courage of the surface, and the loss of spirit in either its depth or its height or both. Berlin is the place of the short-circuit where from Hegel to Lubitsch *il n'y a qu'un pas*.

---

[1] G. W. F. Hegel, *Phenomenology of Spirit*, trans. A. V. Miller (Oxford: Oxford University Press, 1977), 6.

Lubitsch seems to be the best-kept secret in cinema history, but like all true secrets it's *le secret de Polichinelle* of cinema history—all true secrets are public secrets, displayed for the public eye for everyone to see. All cinema people, critics, historians, theoreticians, would readily agree that Lubitsch was one of the most important directors of the classical Hollywood era, and one would also quickly find a general consensus that he was one of the greatest directors of film comedy ever.[2] Yet, and this is a big yet, one is then astounded by the fact that he seems to be so poorly present in the minds of the general audience such that one is hard put, in different countries and milieus, to find anyone who has actually seen any of his movies, as if there were a collective amnesia around this man who was, in his time, surrounded by fame and one of the most instantly recognizable movie icons. And, an even a bigger "yet," one is surprised by the relative lack of critical literature on Lubitsch, given the extent of the cinema studies industry around the globe—compare this to the avalanche of literature on, say, Hitchcock, Welles, or Lynch, although Lubitsch is in all respects their match. The fans are scarce, but their scarcity is amply counterbalanced by their enthusiasm, devotion, and determination. We who are fans are truly fans, we are starting to organize congresses of the "Lubitsch International," the coming out of the underground activists, with the ambition that the public secret finally be made public.

To Be or Not to Be is the best-known Lubitsch movie, but I must nevertheless say something about its background and historical conditions. This is necessary not merely for shedding some light on its framework, but for inherent reasons, since its particular anchorage in its historic moment is also what makes this film unique in cinema history. There was an unease surrounding its production and its reception, an unease having to do with the fact that this is a comedy about fascism, blatantly disregarding all political correctness, and, what is more, a comedy about fascism made at the time of its steep and sinister rise, confronting its disastrous historical and political reality at the time, as it happened, rather than from the distanced privilege of hindsight.

One has to mention that the idea for the script stemmed from Lubitsch himself, exceptionally and for once, since he usually took the cue for his plots from

---

2   The filmmakers know *To Be or Not to Be* by heart, "frame by frame, dialogue by dialogue," maintains Georg Seeßlen, yet enjoy the film each time as a new revelation. "It is almost as impossible to step into the same river twice as to see in *To Be or Not to Be* the same film twice." Georg Seeßlen, "Vom Verlust des Paradieses der Schwäche und der Sinnenfreude," in *Sein oder Nichtsein*, Programmheft, Deutsches Theater Berlin, 2009, 53.

successful novels, stories, or plays, although at times entirely reworking them. *To Be or Not to Be* was his own brainchild, although this is the one movie where he is not credited for the script. This was the one time in his life that he was obsessed with his own original vision, but he was no screenplay writer, so he entrusted the script to Edwin Justus Mayer, which was a great stroke of luck, providing one of the most inspiring and happy moments in scriptwriting history. It has been said a number of times that this is possibly one of the best scenarios in film history, a masterpiece of plotting where everything fits, where all elements are repeated and reused later to produce ever new effects, all elements are mirrored, echoed, turned upside-down, twisted and double-twisted, eventually creating a snowball effect. I will come back to this—to the particular use of repetition as a comic device which in the whole history of comedy as a genre has hardly ever been used with such a fortunate hand. I must here just point out one simple and central case, to which I will return: that there are two very famous Shakespeare monologues—Hamlet's, and Shylock's from *The Merchant of Venice*—both of which are repeated three times in the movie, each time acquiring a new effect of the novelty of the same.

The most crucial fact about this film and its impact is spelled out simply by the date of its production: it was shot in November–December 1941, and the opening night was March 6, 1942. One must pause to ponder seriously over this simple fact. What did the world look like in December 1941? This was two years into the war, which had begun with the attack on Poland in September 1939, and the subsequent occupation of Warsaw. So the movie, in its opening half hour, starts precisely on this threshold, at the emblematic and symbolic origin of the war, in Warsaw. During the two years between the beginning of the war and the production of the film, Hitler had managed to occupy practically all of Europe (except for Great Britain). In some places there were puppet or friendly regimes, while a couple of countries stayed "neutral." In December '41, Hitler's troops were marching on Moscow and at that point it seemed that victory over Russia was within easy reach. Mussolini had captured parts of south-eastern Europe and of Africa; Japan took hold, over the years, of large slices of China and most of south-eastern Asia. During the shooting of *To Be or Not to Be*, on December 6, 1941, the Japanese attacked Pearl Harbor, provoking the US into entering the war. Between the end of shooting and the opening night, the Wannsee conference took place, in February '42, at which the plan for the holocaust was conceived. In other words, this was the moment of the great triumph of fascism—two years into the war Hitler has effectively won. At the time there was no prospect of a viable counter-strategy and revolt, no hope of bringing him down, no serious opponent to stand up to him, no organized force or army. Stalingrad and El Alamein, the two turning points of World War II, were than two years away, D-Day almost three. There was no hope, no serious opposing force one could stake on.

I am listing these well-known historical facts to highlight one simple point: December '41, when *To Be or Not to Be* was being shot, was arguably the blackest moment in the whole of European history. Nothing can quite match it in the past 3,000 years, with regard to its scale and global catastrophe. "The man with the little moustache," as he is referred to in the movie, has pulled off an incredible feat in just two years, dragging the world into the darkest pit. How can one deal with such a situation? Lubitsch's answer to this hopeless predicament, the answer given by this movie, is: now, precisely, is the moment for comedy. Comedy is the best answer to the hour of greatest despair, the bleakest moment, the biggest catastrophe humanity has ever faced. This is the time for arguably the best comedy ever. There is an ethical stance of comedy involved here, which is what makes this film absolutely unique, unmatched in the history of cinema. No other film has quite this stance and courage, this sweeping cheek in face of the greatest calamity. It is the funniest comedy in the hour of greatest despair, the most dearly needed comedy ever. It's the response to the most dramatic historical occasion imaginable that makes it unique.

I must point out that the two perhaps best films about fascism are both comedies: Charlie Chaplin's *The Great Dictator* is the only match for *To Be or Not to Be*. Its shooting started in September '39, a couple of weeks into the war, and was finished six months later, being released in October 1940.[3] Both films were made in the heat of troubled times, and their courageous stance gives them an incomparable ring of truth that puts them into a category apart from everything else. They were made without retrospective knowledge, as acts of immediate engagement, and prior to anti-Nazi propaganda movies produced to bolster the support of audiences for the Allied war effort (cf. Hitchcock's *Lifeboat*, 1944). There is a certain innocence about them both: "Both these films, and this constitutes their persistent cultural and moral value, don't stand up against fascism in the name

---

3 The anecdote has it that Chaplin got the idea for the movie when he watched, together with René Clair, *Triumph des Willens* by Leni Riefenstahl (1935). Clair was horrified (as reported by none other than Buñuel); he believed in its persuasive power and thought it should never be shown in the West for fear of mass conversions by the force of its propaganda. Chaplin, on the contrary, laughed and thought it was already almost a comedy, it just needed a little push, and he took its staging as the model for many elements in his own film.

of a nation, an idea, a strategy, a social order. They speak against it in the name of humanity."[4] But there they importantly differ: what is the humanity in the name of which they speak? I'll come back to this.

I began with the claim that *To Be or Not to Be* is arguably the best film ever made. My first argument in support of this is simple and, I think, compelling: all it takes is to spell out the film's take on its own historic moment in order to remind us of the incredible gesture of making a movie like this at that moment. Or rather, not a movie like this, but *this* movie, for there is hardly anything like it. Pinning it to its particular dramatic circumstances does not amount to seeing it as historically dated or conditioned by a particular conjuncture, but rather to pointing out that its instant and universal appeal stems from its being fully rooted and immersed in this bleak moment with all its despair. Hegel's claim for the superiority of comedy may here find its exemplary instance.

It is perhaps not surprising that, given the circumstances, the film didn't go down well at the time: there was a lot of unease and perplexity, and the reviews were mostly negative. "This is not the time to poke fun!" Thus, the English critic C. A. Lejeune in May 1942:

> To my mind, a farce set against the agonies of bombed Warsaw, is in the poorest of tastes, especially as the film makes no attempt to ignore them … rather indulging, now and then, on a personally conducted tour of the ruins … Perhaps we in England are too close to the real thing to take a detached view … At any rate I feel convinced that this is a film we could never have made in this country and much though I covet the Lubitsch technique for our studios, I am very glad we couldn't.[5]

Another critic, Dilys Powell:

> The Lubitsch marital comedy is funny. The Hitler joke is funny. But is the joke funny? Is the background of terror in Poland funny, with its constant reminders of the frightful reality? Hitler in Ruritania, yes, but the Gestapo in Poland, no … I find myself wondering how America just now would take a brilliant bit of farce about Pearl Harbor.[6]

---

4   Seeßlen, "Vom Verlust des Paradieses," 10.
5   Quoted in Peter Barnes, *To Be or Not to Be* (London: BFI, 2002), 46.
6   Quoted in ibid., 47.

But much to her credit, the same critic retracted and covered herself with ashes 45 years later in the *Sunday Times Magazine* in 1987:

> It was easy to misjudge this comedy when it was first shown forty years ago … the disapproval reckoned without the Poles themselves: those who escaped from Poland liked the movie. Ernst Lubitsch who … wrote and produced and directed the film had been right all along…[7]

This points to a fact that already caused some consternation at the time: those who should have been the most offended and furious, those who were the closest to "the real thing," namely, the Poles who formed a large expatriate community in London at the time—they loved it. The immediate victims enthusiastically espoused the film and thought that this was the best thing that could happen to them in their bleakest hour. They immediately grasped the point that it takes a comedy to deal with despair, and that moral indignation is a luxury afforded only to more distant observers.

Positive reviews were very few, but we can single out one that appeared in *BFI Bulletin* in 1942, signed with the initials D. E. B.:

> This film is no thoughtless excursion into the doubtful humours of war. Some people indeed may think the agony of Poland altogether an improper subject for comedy … These strutting fools marching into a beautiful historic city are not to be feared, only to be infinitely despised. Lubitsch proceeds to despise them with every inch of his film and he achieves his purpose. Many more serious films make us half unwillingly admire Nazi efficiency and fanaticism, this apparent comedy barbs its shafts with subtle poison; we see a machine which can be broken and men who can be human and stupid, as well as brutal.[8]

This early critic put his finger on something absolutely essential. There is a key message in this movie and it is very simple: Nazis can be defeated. And not only are they beatable, they can actually be beaten by conceited, second-rate, self-aggrandizing actors, who are just as stupid as the Nazis. The message of the comedy is one of empowerment, of instilling power into the powerless, a refusal of powerlessness. Nazis are just like us, stupid and conceited, they are no incarnation of diabolical evil and a perfect unfailing scary machine, they are just as incompetent

---

7   Quoted in ibid., 47–8.
8   Quoted in ibid., 49–50.

The Polski theater lands in England: Bronski (Tom Dugan) as "Hitler" (above). The troupe (below).
To Be or Not to Be

and foolish as we are, driven by the same conceit and vanity. This was the big draw-back of the more serious films, then and since: to have fallen prey to an unwitting admiration for these diabolical monsters that one secretly envies, trading with an unconscious fascination, the awe of the inhuman, the greatness of a crime that one secretly covets, the tremor of horror and awe.

Chaplin himself was not exempt from this: he presents the Nazis, in the final speech, as "machine men, with machine minds and machine hearts," evoking the clichéd image of perfect machinery, and in maximum opposition to this he launches an appeal to true humanity, love, and brotherhood. Compare this to the incompetence of Colonel Ehrhardt blaming every blunder on the proverbial Schultz. One could call this "the Schultz theory of fascism." But comedy doesn't oppose this fascination with the inhuman and the machine-like with an appeal to heartfelt humanity; quite the contrary, comedy rather tends to find the mechanical and the inhuman, as it were, in the human heart itself. It is the comedy of that in the human which is not reducible to humanity, of that in life which is not reducible to life. Setting up the monstrous machine Other on the one side and the truly human feeling on the other is not the set-up of comedy. It is as if Chaplin, in the final speech of *The Great Dictator*, forgets the mechanisms that have been driving his comedy up to then. If, in this last scene, he speaks in the name of humanity, for real and without comedy, for Lubitsch, by contrast, humanity wholly coincides with theatricality, appearances, machine-like behavior, breakdowns of the machine which are inherent to it, that is, with mechanisms which were actually shared by and permeated both sides. It is on the basis of this shared comic "machine humanity" that the political decision has to be taken—and the film takes it.[9] The bottom line is not, as it is in Chaplin, "we are all human," but rather "there is the inhuman in humanity"—which doesn't allow for the universalizing "we are all inhuman." Comedy dwells on singular points that form series and repetitions, but that don't quite allow for universality.

How to find resources of power out of weakness, helplessness, and incapacity? Only comedy can do this. James Harvey put it well: "The Nazis here are not defeated by our ridiculing them—but by our knowing them: being able to imitate

---

9   "Nazis and their opponents originate at the same time from a totally different and one and the same world; they use, and this is so important for Lubitsch, (almost) the same things, (almost) the same words, (almost) the same forms. But precisely this vicinity all the more sharpens the question of the decision." Seeßlen, "Vom Verlust des Paradieses," 61.

and predict and finally understand them ... This comedy about power is also a refusal of powerlessness."[10] An essential trait of comedy is its indiscriminate aim. It cuts both ways, it cuts all ways, it pokes fun at everyone without discrimination. *The Great Dictator* ridicules Hitler, but in the same breath it ridicules Jews who are far from innocent victims, it doesn't spare anyone. With Lubitsch, the Nazis are ridiculous, but so are the actors, in their self-promotion, delusions, and vanity. "The Nazis in this film *are* like ordinary people. They are also monsters."[11] This closeness between ordinary people and monsters is the stuff of comedy. Pursuing this logic one could say: we are monsters, and monsters are ordinary people like us. Comedy knows no boundaries, and only if it can poke fun at everyone, without exception, is it really comedy.[12] To be sure, the capacity to poke fun at Us just as much as at Them is in itself not a sufficient prerequisite, for the adoption of an ironic distance towards our own demeanor can easily function as the leeway one needs in order to espouse and inhabit a certain social slot (a point that Slavoj Žižek has often insisted on). This is why irony, including self-irony, and comedy stand at opposite ends—to put it in a nutshell: irony is always about being clever (including and especially self-irony), whereas comedy is about being a sucker. Given the choice, one should always opt for being the sucker. But then again, one is not given the choice, and this is what makes the comedy of it. *N'est pas sucker qui veut.*—The essential point is that this indiscriminateness doesn't relativize the message of the film but enhances it. As Harvey put it, this is the least cynical comedy ever made.

Comedy doesn't offer relief, and Lubitsch was adamantly aware of it: "I was tired of the two established, recognized recipes, drama with comedy relief, and comedy with dramatic relief. I made up my mind to make a picture with no attempt to relieve anybody from anything, at any time..."[13] This is one of the greatest lines on comedy ever written, and one must take one's hat off to its author. Let me remind you that Lubitsch began his career in theater before World War I, and not in any theater, but with the Max Reinhardt theater group in Berlin, one of the best and most prestigious theaters at the time, the ideal place for an apprenticeship. He started as a stage hand, then as an extra (referred to as the spear-carrier in

---

10   James Harvey, *Romantic Comedy in Hollywood from Lubitsch to Sturges* (New York: Knopf, 1987), 492–3.

11   Ibid., 494.

12   "The view is equally mercilessly precise not only regarding the opponent, but of the subject of the revolt. For Lubitsch power is not dangerous and comical in the wrong hands, but in itself." Seeßlen, "Vom Verlust des Paradieses," 57.

13   Quoted in Barnes, *To Be or Not to Be*, 55.

the movie), before being given some small speaking roles, including the second gravedigger in *Hamlet* and also Lancelot Gobbo, Shylock's servant, in *The Merchant of Venice*—so he witnessed the two great monologues from that side-view, "looking awry." The scene with the gravediggers is notoriously perhaps the most famous scene of comic relief in history, providing the respite, the contrast, the side perspective, the volume, for the true tragedy, the grand drama. I would say that what is at stake in the movie is "the second gravedigger's theory of Hamlet"—it takes as comic relief not the gravediggers' scene, but the "to be or not to be" soliloquy itself, in the genre of the gravediggers' scene, and, indeed, takes the whole of Hamlet as a massive comic relief. Which means: there is no comic relief, no relief at all, no recess that might let you off the hook for a time in order to confront something else, just relentless comic relief without relief. Barnes makes this point well:

> I believe what really shocked contemporary critics was … that Lubitsch was not going to be serious about a serious subject. They could not see he and his writer were being serious by being funny. As in all the best comedy, the seriousness is in the comedy, not outside it … Comedians are at their most serious … when they are at their funniest. In the end, I believe, the only thing in the theatre that has the ring of truth is comedy. Great comedy isn't there to help to make the serious stuff easy to swallow. Comedy is the serious stuff. A work isn't great despite the comedy. It's great because of the comedy.[14]

The whole film was seen as highly problematic at the time, but there was one line which was particularly controversial. Colonel Ehrhardt, the head of the Gestapo, makes the following comment about "the great, great Polish actor Joseph Tura": "What he did to Shakespeare, we are doing now to Poland." During the preview people laughed at everything else, but there was stone silence after this line. Pressure was put on Lubitsch to cut it—including from his wife and Billy Wilder. Lubitsch got very angry and was adamant to keep it in—it seemed to him that this was a key line on which everything depended. Why the unease and commotion at this particular line? The problem was that the rejoinder comes from the mouth of a Gestapo chief, making it appear that Nazis also have a sense of humor, even a lot of wit, and that they ridicule us just as we ridicule them. "This was the sort of joke we told about our victories over them. To suggest that they might tell the same

---

14 Ibid., 51–2.

sort of joke, on the same sort of occasion—about us—was shocking, and not what people were used to. This is just the sort of distinction, however—between Them and Us—that Lubitsch was incapable of making."[15] Nazis, with all their egomania and stupidity, can actually be just as witty as us, and disturbingly close. ("We do the concentrating and Poles do the camping," another immortal line, was much easier to swallow, since it is said by Jack Benny while impersonating a Nazi and so could be read as us parodying Nazi brutality. The joke may seem far more sinister now, for it was made before Wannsee and the subsequent camps, which actually happened to be in Poland.)

***

The title of the movie was subject to controversy as the studio, United Artists, deemed that it was not commercial enough and furthermore created a false impression by taking a reference from high-brow culture. Lubitsch, when pressed, jokingly suggested the title *The Censor Forbids* as an alternative, but the whole cast protested fiercely and threatened to pull out—everybody thought that the title was essential. The title is a question, the most famous question in world history. And indeed the historic moment was such that it raised the question "to be or not to be" for bloody real, and indeed the film is about staging *Hamlet*, among other things.

What's in a question? There is something abysmal in this, for one already asks about the question in the form of a question, and the form itself is full of pitfalls. The question of the question is best treated in a book by Aron Ronald Bodenheimer, *Warum? Von der Obszönität des Fragens*.[16] The thesis of the book is simple and radical: there is something wrong, indeed obscene, with the very form of the question, with the question as such. The question always places the interlocutor in a subjected position, the position of a culprit—one is guilty already by being asked a question, whatever one answers. A minimal scene of domination is always at stake. There is no way to answer a question—the very exactitude of the answer is already a subterfuge, an escape, and therein lies the obscenity involved in questioning. One is always exposed by a question: structurally it brings forth guilt, an admission of something that should have remained hidden, an intimacy, a hidden enjoyment, a guilty pleasure, a lack of responsibility and vigilance,

---

15 Harvey, *Romantic Comedy in Hollywood*, 492.
16 Aron Ronald Bodenheimer, *Warum? Von der Obszönität des Fragens* (Ditzingen: Reclam, 1984); incredibly, there are no translations.

something that has no coverage and no sufficient reason, something one cannot account for. One cannot justify oneself, one can never answer a question at the point at which the question was aiming. In being exposed to a question one is always potentially debunked as an impostor. The question always tips the balance of power, allotting the position of power to the questioner and dooming the one questioned to structural impotence.[17] In a word, there is no proper answer to the question "why?," featuring in the title of Bodenheimer's book. By asking why, by the very form of this question, one brings forth the lack of sufficient reason.[18]

But if the question is something in principle obscene and problematic, what should one do? Drop questions altogether? Bodenheimer, much to his credit, doesn't shy away from drawing this extreme conclusion: one should learn to behave *fragefrei*, without questions, questionfree, questionless (*"die Forderung nach einer neuen—fragefreien—Art von Umgang,"* "the demand for a new—question-free—mode of interaction"[19]).

"To be or not to be" is a strange kind of question, for a number of reasons. For a start, it has no question mark, neither in the play nor in the title of the movie, but instead of the question mark there comes the assertion: "that is the question." It is a question that conspicuously and ostentatiously presents itself as a question, it firmly asserts its being a question, it is not merely posing a question, but reflexively enacting its own questionness. It is the question *par excellence*, the question to finish all questions, the quintessence of questioning, and staged as such. If one addresses this question to someone, as if asking for advice, then it makes no sense, for what could one possibly answer—to be? not to be? Is there a sufficient reason for either? "Why?" is looming in it, so that the moment one asks it no reason can measure up to the question and vouch for an answer. The question is a trap; there is no way out of the question. The mousetrap scene which (almost) immediately

---

17 To take just one of Bodenheimer's examples: "Father, why is the sky blue?" Whatever one answers, the question exposes father's impotence. And as Bodenheimer adds: the worst kinds of fathers would be in this respect an astrophysicist or a psychoanalyst, providing a factual explanation, either in terms of cosmology or of the Oedipal frame of posing such a question. Which leads us to the paradigmatic Freudian question: "Father, don't you see that I am burning?"

18 As an aside, there is perhaps something to be gained by dividing philosophies into two camps: philosophies of questions (Socrates, Descartes, Kant, Heidegger—cf. Derrida, "Heidegger et la question") and philosophies of answers (Spinoza, Hegel, Lacan). The common line that the history of philosophy is the history of questions, not of answers—the line shared by the unlikely companions Heidegger and Althusser—could be opposed by the view of philosophy as a history of answers in search of questions. Just like comedy.

19 Bodenheimer, *Warum? Von der Obszönität des Fragens*, 287.

follows is preceded by the private mousetrap in the monologue, where Hamlet is himself caught by his own cunning, a self-laid trap.

What would be an appropriate answer to Hamlet's question? What does the very form of his question imply, the question addressed to himself? The form of the question implies the answer, and there is ultimately only one answer to the question, once one has asked it: not to be. Bodenheimer puts it brilliantly:

> Even someone who has never seen this drama, someone who attends its performance for the first time in his life, knows by the end of this monologue: the answer is "not to be"—this man cannot bring together this being with his life's role [*dieser Mann kann dieses Sein mit dieser Lebensrolle nicht vereinbaren*]. Whatever else will happen—and many terrible things will happen until it comes to it—one surmises: the self-questioning has found its answer.[20]

Hamlet's question has found its answer in the very form of the question; once he has come to the point of asking this question at all, it is already too late. Having asked, he is done for, his fate is sealed.

What does comedy do with the question? *To Be or Not to Be* provides the brilliant answer: walk out on it. Three times there is Hamlet's monologue, and each time a guy walks out on it. Walk out on the question. To be or not to be? Sorry, I have to see my mistress. Comedy consists of answers, not of questions: the comedy of unexpected answers popping up in unlikely places, coming from another quarter than the direction aimed at by the question. The answer to the question refuses the terms of the question and walks out, thereby answering not in the terms of the alternative, which seems to be exhaustive and exclusive—to be or not to be?—covering all possible entities and eventualities, squeezing them into the straightjacket of two clear-cut options. And this is the moment of comedy: to produce an interloper, an intruder who blurs the lines, who refuses the question asked, and who instead provides an answer that nobody asked for. One has to get out of place, out of the allotted spot in the second row where the question has placed us, thus interrupting the circle of question and answer. If posing the question in these terms already implied the necessary answer "not to be," then the only way to choose "to be" is to choose an out-of-place being with no place in this alternative, neither to be nor not to be. To choose being is precisely not to choose the being of "to be" in the proposed alternative with "not to be," but to choose

---

20   Ibid., 241.

something which has no firm being, without thereby falling into "not to be," a pop-up being, or more appropriately a stand-up being, as in "stand-up comedy," popping up in the second row, not quite reducible to the (rather stupid) lover nor to any particular being.

There is a triple viewpoint repeated three times: the point of view of the wife who has deviously plotted a blow at her husband—not only having a lover, but ruining his moment of actor's glory, staging her private revenge; the point of view of the hapless husband-Hamlet, who sees the intrusion as the response of the audience to his acting, and desperately tries to counteract it; and the point of view of the lover who doesn't care about existential questions or literature (he can drop tons of dynamite, but the finer points of Shakespearean exegesis seem to be lost on him), but takes this as his exit cue. The point of view of comedy is none of these three, or rather encompasses all three in one and the same move, at the intersection of their impossible relation.[21]

Once one has seen *To Be or Not to Be*, one can never see the Hamlet monologue in the same way—there is a moment when it appears as its own caricature. One feels the pressing urge to walk out and rejoin one's lover. To be or not to be? No, thank you.

Jack Benny, who played the role of Joseph Tura and Hamlet—and it was the role of his lifetime, as one interpreter put it: "the most unlikely Hamlet in history"—Jack Benny was not primarily an actor, but an entertainer, a stand-up comedian, a showman. His radio show *The Jack Benny Program* ran for twenty odd years, from 1932 to 1955, and was one of the most popular, to be surpassed only by his TV show, 1950–65, hosting virtually all the greatest stars of the time. In one of his famous gags a mugger holds him up in a deserted street: "Your money or your life." When he doesn't stir, the mugger becomes impatient and aggressive, repeating an ever more threatening "Your money or your life, buddy." After an infinitely long pause Benny says: "Hmmm ... I am thinking it over."[22] Here there is something of the same strategy of dodging the question and displacing its frame, of trying to sidestep the seemingly exhaustive alternative, which actually has the form of "to be or not to be." It might be a quick summary of Hamlet's monologue: "To be

---

21 If there is a "why" question implied in "to be or not to be," pointing at the impossibility of justifying being, of substantiating it with a sufficient reason, then comedy essentially replaces the "why" question with the "how" question. How does this function? How does the question function? How does the guy function who asks this question? How does being function? Or more appropriately, instead of asking "why" it displays the "how" without asking, but by providing an answer.

22 Quoted in Barnes, *To Be or Not to Be*, 23.

or not to be? Hmmm … I am thinking it over." One cannot but be reminded of Lacan, who uses this example, "your money or your life," to demonstrate his *vel* of alienation. He presents it as the forced choice: one is forced to choose one alternative, life, but at the price of it being stripped of money, curtailed. Comedy—this is perhaps one way of describing its procedure—doesn't accept the choice as it is presented, counteracts its forced character, opting for the impossible intersection of the two which takes the form of an excess or an intruder, a quirk, something not quite covered by the alternative "either being or non-being," "either life or money," but which emerges at their interstice. It stands up, like the spectator in the second row, or rather springs up, and then persists, keeps springing up with clockwork regularity at precisely the same spot. Comedy hinges on this curtailed part which on either side of the choice was doomed to fall out—something that neither is nor is not, a partial object.[23]

***

Finally, we must consider the question of doubling as essential to comedy, and by extension the double and its repetition. Comedy thrives on doubles.[24] Some of the oldest blueprints for comedy, established by a few ancient authors and then endlessly embroidered on in the great tradition, literally involve doubles: think of *Maenechmi*, the play by Plautus, which entirely revolves around the career of two twins, exact doubles, whose identity is inevitably and constantly mixed up and produces a total *imbroglio*, a comedy of errors—and indeed Shakespeare's remake of the Plautus play is appropriately called just that, *The Comedy of Errors*. One person is taken for another on the good grounds that he looks exactly the same, thus the zero point of one of the major resources of comedy, the mistaken identity. One could say: *it is in the nature of identity to be mistaken for identity.* There is a mistake involved in every identity that the mistaken identity only makes appear. Or think of Plautus' *Amphitruo* (remade by Molière, Kleist, Giraudoux, etc.), where the god Jupiter can only seduce the faithful Alcmene by assuming the spitting image of her husband Amphytrion, while the god's helper Mercury assumes the image of Amphytrion's servant Sosias (the proper name that inevitably

---

23   Should one say that comedy espouses separation, the second move paired with alienation in Lacan, as the
      answer to the *vel* of alienation?
24   For more on this, see Mladen Dolar, "Comedy and Its Double," in Robert Pfaller (ed.), *Stop that Comedy!
      On the Subtle Hegemony of the Tragic in Our Culture* (Vienna: Sonderzahl, 2005), 181–209.

turned into a generic name in French, *sosie*, a double). Or think, at the other end, of Vladimir and Estragon.

Pascal brought it to the gist, to the minimal: "Two similar faces, neither of which causes laughter in particular, together cause laughter by their resemblance. [*Deux visages semblables, dont aucun ne fait rire en particulier, font rire ensemble par leur ressemblance.*]"[25] The beauty or austere elegance of this line is that it tries to pin the comical down to its very minimum, to the mere mechanism of doubling. It brings it to this core: *one is not funny, two is funny*, but provided that two is the replication of one, its imitation, its likeness, its mimetic double, its similar twin. What happens between one and two to produce the comical effect? Not between one and two, for it is like a crack in the midst of the same. Two different faces are not funny, two similar ones are. So, ultimately, this is neither a two nor two ones, but a split one, where both parts can neither be counted for two nor made one. The comical object emerges in their very split. With the doubling, it is as if reality loses its footing, becoming entangled in a web of appearances and replicas; but this doesn't mean that everything is merely appearance, rather that the appearance is never just an appearance: there is a real in the doubling and in the appearance. And this real is spelled out in repetition, in the insistence of the same, but of the split same.

No comedy puts this to more spectacular use than *To Be or Not to Be*. The object appears between two copies, in the in-between. The film starts with the question of how to impersonate Hitler, a problem that one could call "Hitler and his double." Hitler appears as redoubled in the very first scene—between the actor impersonating Hitler and the picture of Hitler on the wall (which turns out to be a picture of the actor posing as the real Hitler, the actor as the Hitler-impersonator redoubling himself). What makes a persuasive double of Hitler? What is the trait by which Hitler is Hitler? It can only appear between two doubles. Chaplin also used this in grand ways: Hitler and the Jewish barber are one and the same person (just as in other Chaplin's films: the millionaire is the double of the tramp in *City Lights* (1931), Monsieur Verdoux is redoubled into the mass murderer and the philanthropist, the ideal family man).

This is a theater comedy, set in a theater company, a comedy of the theater's relation to reality, redoubling both theater and reality, redoubling their split. Theater (supposedly) redoubles reality as its diminished model, and this comedy

---

25 Pascal, *Pensées*, eds Philippe Sellier and Gérard Ferreyrolles (Paris: Le livre de poche, 2000), fragment 47, 58.

takes this redoubling as its lever and its source. One crucial point that the entire movie insists on can be simply put: theater precedes reality. The double precedes what it is supposed to be the double of. Staging comes first, then reality catches up with it, but it can only catch up with it as staged. In the first scene we have the actor impersonating Hitler on the streets of Warsaw, rehearsing, trying out his outfit, thus repeating in advance, as it were, the real Hitler marching into Warsaw. Hitler is first "the man with a little moustache" staged on the streets of Warsaw and his arrival is already a replica, he cannot but appear as an impersonator of himself. Then there is the play the company is rehearsing, called *Gestapo*, prefiguring pretty much what was to come. In the two scenes with Colonel Ehrhardt and Professor Siletsky which stand at the heart of the film, first there is the fake Colonel Ehrhardt, impersonated by Joseph Tura–Jack Benny, with "the concentration camp Ehrhardt" gag, then the real one, who appears as the replica of his impersonator, his own caricature, dismantled in advance, using the same gag that the actor has foreseen ("I thought you would react that way," says Benny in an aside, congratulating himself on the foresight), unable to do otherwise than helplessly follow the anticipated script. Acting anticipates the original. In the first scene of the Hamlet monologue, we have the same device in miniature and I suppose at its best, featuring a prompter who has to help the actor with the most famous line in history, the only line for which nobody would need a prompter. The prompter whispering "to be or not to be," one of the great highlights of the movie, functions like a preemptive strike at the title question, preempting its first appearance, stealing the show, making it appear as the text repeated from the prompt, the existential question if there ever was one as the replica of the prompter, a line that one first has to be told or reminded of, thus ruining its aura and the unique authenticity of the most famous and fateful scene in theater history, and reputedly the most profound. All it takes is a prompter, by definition a quintessential but invisible and inaudible theater hand. What would theater be without a prompter? Without this preemptive device that strikes at the heart of the stage and the supposed immediacy of presence? No Hamlet without a prompter; but showing this missing half of Hamlet inevitably turns him into a figure of comedy, a figure of contrivance at the heart of the existential drama.

There is a thesis in this film, which also spells out the bottom line of comedy: repetition comes first. Double comes first. It foreshadows the original. It presents a reflective turn of comedy procedures, reversing them, or displaying the reversal at their core. The Lubitsch conference in Ljubljana was held under the title

"First as Comedy, Then as Farce," which could be taken as a slogan, calqued on Marx's famous line: "Hegel remarks somewhere that all great world-historic facts and personages appear, so to speak, twice. He forgot to add: the first time as tragedy, the second time as farce." There is, by the way, a most curious circumstance that this quotation, one of the most well-known lines by Marx, from the beginning of *The Eighteenth Brumaire*, is actually itself a repetition, taken almost verbatim from Engels's letter to Marx written on December 3, 1851 (the day after the coup), Marx for once plagiarizing Engels, repeating his great line on repetition.[26] It looks like Marx needed a prompter to write one of his most notorious lines, a bit like Benny needing a prompter for "to be or not to be." If one looks for the source in Hegel, let me quote a single sentence from his *Philosophy of History*: "Through repetition, what at the beginning seemed to be merely accidental and possible, becomes actual and established." Hegel gives two examples: "Napoleon was defeated twice, and twice the Bourbons were driven out."[27]

We could, in a simplified manner, provisionally propose three takes on repetition. First the Hegelian one: what at first appearance seemed accidental, taking place by chance, becomes through repetition a rule, gains its symbolic sanction and is thus taken for actuality, a chance event is elevated to the symbolic. The mission of repetition here is to turn chance into necessity, a haphazard one-time appearance into regularity. (Could one say: first as *tyche*, then as *automaton*?) The second version is Marx's: Hegel forgot to add that the second time may well be a farce. What seemed to be serious the first time, a landmark pertaining to the logic and the necessary progress of history, is struck by a farcical character the second time round. The first time it seemed necessary, the second time it is an empty repetition parading as necessity, but in fact displaying necessity as a mirage, not symbolically sanctioning the first occurrence, but preventing the repetition of the first from producing something new. The farcical repetition is repetition against the power of the repetition, it prevents repetition, and this is what turns it into a farce—it cannot repeat its historical model and is thus doomed to fail, no matter how much havoc it can cause. Third, there is repetition with the Lubitsch touch:

---

26 "It really seems as though old Hegel, in the guise of the World Spirit, were directing history from the grave and, with the greatest conscientiousness, causing everything to be re-enacted twice over, once as grand tragedy and the second time as rotten farce, Caussidière for Danton, L. Blanc for Robespierre, Barthélemy for Saint-Just, Flocon for Carnot, and the moon-calf together with the first available dozen debt-encumbered lieutenants for the little corporal and his band of marshals. Thus the 18th Brumaire would already be upon us" (Engels, MEGA, III. Abt., Bd. 4, 260).
27 G.W.F. Hegel, *Theorie Werkausgabe*, Vol. 12 (Frankfurt am Main: Suhrkamp, 1970), 380.

here the first time preempts the second time, stages it in advance as comedy, thus undermining the necessity and the historic fatality of the second time. It starts with comedy which anticipates the tragedy, so when the tragic moment arrives it is already struck with farce, as a farcical repetition of something already staged, repeating comedy as a farce, despite the bloodiest and harshest historical reality. The staging and redoubling undermine reality, even of the harshest kind, making it appear as contrived, as a reenactment of theater, a double of itself. It takes away its natural self-evidence, dismantles its glue, its aura and its fatality. But this doesn't lead to cynicism or the universality of appearance—there is a real at stake that one can only get to through redoubling and that one can affect by these means. This is why it leads to the empowerment of the powerless and can work so efficiently with such a terrible thing as fascism. It demotes its power, undoes its diabolical nature, displays its contrivance; it shows how it can be deluded and how comic actors, professional impersonators (and not the best at that), can deploy the theatrical craft of appearance and delusion to take the victory.

To create the comic double and the replica of the bloodiest, the most serious, the most fateful event in European history is to make a political statement of the most far-reaching proportions. To make a theatrical double of this, and to put it to maximum use, is the best possible way to practice the principle of comedy. There is no comedy quite like it.

ELISABETH BRONFEN

Lubitsch's War: Comedy as Political Ploy in To Be or Not to Be

The traumatic history of war can always only be grasped as a belated representation that references a Real it can never fully touch. War is something we *anticipate*
or something we *reflect on*, while those caught up in the fog and noise of actual battle or actual occupation lack the visual and emotional distance necessary
for narrative management.[1] Paul Fussell, himself a US veteran of the European
campaign, has fruitfully reconceived Freud's distinction between a civilian and
a wartime self so as to explain how for both him and his war buddies surviving
the horror of war was predicated on imaginary theatricalization. "If killing and
avoiding being killed are the ultimate melodramatic actions, then military training is very largely training in melodrama," he recalls. To conceive of oneself as
an actor in a grotesque situation allowed the soldier to do things his civilian self
would not have been capable of. Fussell adds: "Seeing warfare as theater provides
a psychic escape for the participant: with a sufficient sense of theater, he can
perform his duties without implicating his 'real' self and without impairing his
innermost conviction that the world is still a rational place."[2] Playing the role
of soldier allows for a suppression of civilian judgment that is tantamount to
relinquishing a critical distance towards one's actions. Furthermore, there can
be no true-to-life war film, as Samuel Fuller has noted, and not only because the
enormous noise and fog of battle makes the coherent orientation necessary for

---

1   See Elisabeth Bronfen, *Specters of War: Hollywood's Engagement with Military Conflict* (New Brunswick:
     Rutgers University Press, 2012).
2   Paul Fussell, *The Great War and Modern Memory* (Oxford: Oxford University Press, 1975), 192.

cinematic depiction impossible. Any claim to authenticity would also require that real bullets be shot from behind the film screen. It would need to draw the audience viscerally into the world depicted on screen.[3]

Thus, when it comes to war's cinematic re-imagination by Hollywood entertainment films, both what is *in front* and what is *behind* the screen is problematized. On the one hand, the issue of reference is foregrounded, with the knowledge of actual death hovering around the edges of the film frame. On the other hand, the movement of troops and those sustaining the war effort on screen serves to mobilize the audience in front of the screen as well. As the will for victory, transported by the actors, spills over to an audience only too willing to identify with this passion, any neat distinction between playing and watching is also self-consciously blurred. As I argue in *Specters of War*, the most compelling war films are, therefore, cinematic re-figurations that acknowledge how representing the Real of War is always an *approximation*. If, however, the most forceful way for mobilizing film viewers is by self-consciously pointing to the mediality of cinema itself, the rhetorical and technical diversion this strategy deploys thrives on what can pointedly be called the *affective effect* of cinema's re-imagination of history.[4] While a suspicion regarding the deployment of carnivalesque humor or satire as means for an intervention in war propaganda is justified, the resilient force of Lubitsch's precise comic dramaturgy calls upon one to rethink this position.

The following essay will revisit *To Be or Not to Be* (1942) in the context of the spectacular Hollywood war effort that began in 1941 after the attack on Pearl Harbor, forging an unprecedented bond between the Pentagon and the entertainment business that would last throughout World War II. Special about Lubitsch's own war effort, however, is the fact that he chooses a genre mix, splicing together the tone of sophisticated comedies such as *My Man Godfrey* (1936) or *Nothing Sacred* (1937) (films with which his female star Carole Lombard had come to be identified), with standard anti-fascist thriller narratives. To offer an additional patina of high pathos, he also brings together Shakespeare's grand tragedy *Hamlet* with the disturbing *Comical History of the Merchant of Venice, or Otherwise Called the Jew of Venice*.

---

3   See Samuel Fuller, *A Third Face: My Tale of Writing, Fighting, and Filmmaking* (New York: Applause Theater and Film Books, 2002).

4   See also Robert Burgoyne, *Film Nation: Hollywood Looks at US History*, Revised Edition (Minneapolis: University of Minnesota Press, 2010).

The Opening

Three outrageous scenic moments sustain the rhetorical use of comedy as a means of addressing political tyranny in the first six minutes of the film. Seminal for the appeal made to the audience is that while, on the diegetic level of the film, we are in Warsaw in August of 1939, which is to say in a Europe that is still at peace, the scenes unfolding on screen are located on a set in Hollywood. The year of the film's release is 1942, a historical moment with not only Europe but also the US at war. The framing sets the tone for the dramaturgic ploy of a play within a play. Initially a male voice-over explains, "at the moment, life in Warsaw is going on as normally as ever," while we see people leisurely window-shopping, sitting in street cafés or moving busily along one of the main streets of Poland's capital. Then the narrator's voice becomes excited as he explains, "but suddenly, something seems to have happened. Are those Poles seeing a ghost?" Now pedestrians and drivers are shown arrested in their movements, staring in shocked awe at something we do not yet see. To underscore the suspense, the narrator adds, "Everybody seems to be staring in one direction. People seem to be frightened, even terrified. Some flabbergasted," while the camera captures their astonishment in close-up shots. As and more people flock to the one place everyone seems to be staring at, the narrator calls out: "Can it be true? It must be true. No doubt." The camera pans rapidly across the shop window of J. Masłowski's delicatessen store, and the voice-over finally explains the mystery: "The man with the little moustache, Adolf Hitler." Then, as the narrator continues with his ruminations by adding, "Adolf Hitler in Warsaw when the two countries are still at peace…," a man looking like the Führer separates himself from the crowd of staring people that has formed behind him and, briefly scanning his audience, begins to walk unconcerned up and down in front of the shop window, with the onlookers forming a semi-circle around him.

Warsaw in *To Be or Not to Be* is, thus, marked from the start as an urban stage, located outside but comparable to the stage of the Polski theater where, as we discover a few moments later, everything began. The excited tone of the voice-over, recalling wartime propaganda shorts the Hollywood audience would have been familiar with after the attack on Pearl Harbor on December 6, 1941, gives an urgency to this first audacious moment by splicing fictionality with documentary. The voice draws us emphatically into a scene in which Hitler appears in the midst of a crowd of Poles, to whom his unexpected presence is like the emergence of a ghost. Given the film title's explicit reference to Shakespeare's *Hamlet*, we are implicitly propelled to the parapets of a castle in Elsinore, where everyone is awaiting the invading army of Fortinbras, the adversary of the melancholic Danish Prince. In Lubitsch's film, however, the specter of a terrifying ruler is not returning from his transitory abode in Purgatory, as Hamlet's father does in order to call upon his son to avenge his death and liberate his soul. Rather, the leader has come from the belligerent neighboring country of Germany. This Hitler is installed as an actor, furthermore, not only because he is the object of the crowd he draws but also because the distance they keep to him produces a stage in front of the shop window. Transforming the leader of the NSDAP, of whom everyone is afraid, into an actor debunks his authority even while establishing it.

The second audacious moment splices together a break-down in theatrical illusion with political satire. The narrator goes on to ask, "How did he get here? What happened," only to add, "Well, it all started in the General Headquarters of the Gestapo in Berlin." Seamlessly the camera moves to a set that could be taken for a Hollywood version of this infamous site of torture in an anti-fascist propaganda feature film such as Sherman Scott's *Beast of Berlin* (1939), until the actor Bronski (Tom Dugan), playing the Führer, enters saying "Heil myself." Only once the producer of the play, Dobosh (Charles Halton), gets up in outrage, protesting "that's not in the script," do we recognize that we are on stage in the Polski theater. This battle, we soon realize, is not over geographical territory but over the issue of what genre is appropriate for political propaganda. Bronski insists that even if his joke is not in the script it will "get a laugh," and a fellow actor, Greenberg (Felix Bressart), comes to his rescue. Against the producer's insistence that he isn't interested in hearing any support for Bronski's improvisation, the only actor in the troop who is marked as being Jewish, in turn, insists on giving his reaction (if not his opinion), by supporting the dramaturgic value of laughter. A laugh, he maintains, "is nothing to be sneezed at." Dobosh, however, valiantly maintains that they are putting on a "serious play, a realistic drama. It is a document of Nazi Germany." By turning down Greenberg's intervention and reminding him that he was hired not as a writer but as an actor, the producer/director insists on the unequivocal authority of a script which is not to be tampered with.

Two things are worth taking note of here. In the course of the film narrative, taking liberties with the script is what several of the actors will be compelled to do, because a change in circumstances will force them to deviate from all preset lines of dialogue. Indeed, the happy ending of *To Be or Not to Be* is predicated on skillful improvisation as well as a clever reiteration of classic passages from

Shakespearean texts. Also installed is a running joke having to do with what *will* and what *will not* get a laugh. This brings into play the question of who is to be the butt of the joke—the actor himself, the Führer whom he is debunking, or the audience taken by surprise. But it also draws attention to a troubled relation between political appeal and comedy as a genre, in which those who embody unquestionable authority are shown to be playing a role in relation to symbolic interpellation. By adding the line "Heil myself," Bronski's performance of Hitler is one of an actor aware of politics as theater.

The third audacious moment is one Lubitsch would probably not have gotten away with by the end of the '40s and introduces Carole Lombard as Maria Tura, the lady star in this theatrical troupe. While the men are still arguing over the right of an actor to change the script, she suddenly walks on stage wearing a tight, shimmering, silk evening gown. When Dobosh asks her whether this is what she will be wearing for her scene in the concentration camp, she defends her outrageous choice of costume by imagining for the outraged director the tremendous effect it will have, given the contrast between her gorgeous appearance and the grim reality of camp life. "Think of me being flogged in the darkness," she exclaims with relish, "I scream, the lights go on and the audience discovers me on the floor in this gorgeous dress." Once more Greenberg, the spirit of comic relief who will not be kept away, insists that this dramaturgic ploy would garner "a terrific laugh." Against the serious-minded Dobosh, who will be relegated to the sideline once the Nazis actually arrive in Warsaw, Greenberg, together with Maria Tura, will prove to have the better artistic sense after all. At this point in the film narrative, however, the problem of what is effective political critique—documentary realism or satire—is resolved with Bronski ostentatiously leaving the stage. He insists that he knows he looks like Hitler and that he is going to prove it right now by going out on the street in his costume and make-up to see what happens. He is, of course, almost immediately recognized by a young girl who sees through the masquerade. She cautiously pushes through the bemused crowd and approaches Bronski, smiling as she asks for his autograph.

Given that this sequence serves as an introduction to Lubitsch's comedy, the point to bear in mind is that we are called upon from the start to ask what Bronski's sudden departure from the theater and move to a street in Warsaw implies. The emotional and political effect which actors, taking part in an anti-fascist play, will have, is clearly decided not on the stage but on the streets of this city, which is itself installed as a stage. Decisive for this effect, furthermore, is how long a given performer (in this case Bronski) can pull off the theatrical illusion in a situation in which the line between theater and reality has become blurred. If the young girl is alone in seeing through the trick, she does so because she is a fan of the actor. Everyone else sees only the costume. This inaugural sequence thus allows Lubitsch to comment on Hollywood's star machinery and our willingness to be duped by celebrity performances. On the extradiegetic level, addressed to the audience sitting in the movie theater, this scene, however, also draws attention to the fact that the authority of Hitler as the leader of the Nazi Party is contingent on the plausibility of his performance. Pitting political theater (the documentary play *Gestapo* which this Polish troop is rehearsing) against the theatrical politics which the presence of Bronski's Hitler on the streets of Warsaw anticipates, involves a surplus that troubles all safe distinctions between artistic veracity and the audacious debunking of the authenticity the realism of documentary makes a claim to. Subverting the explicit anti-fascist message doesn't make it less politically forceful but rather more effective.

Excess is at issue when an actor says "Heil myself," or when an actress inappropriately chooses a glamour dress for her concentration camp costume out of vanity, or when a fan undoes the power of theatrical illusion and breaks the invisible wall between audience and stage by walking up to the actor so as to ask for his autograph. And if it is this excess that makes us laugh, comedy wins the first round against Dobosh's serious-minded directorial taste, setting a dialectical game in motion. It is, thus, appropriate to take our cue from the way Greenberg counters the seriousness of his director/producer by arguing that an audacious dramatic gesture will, if nothing else, "get a laugh," so as to interrogate more closely the political space of theater in *To Be or Not to Be*. Representing the resilient spirit of the comic in the face of catastrophe, Greenberg serves as its reflection and correction, and in so doing reveals the ethical dimension to be found in the rhetoric of repetition all comedy is predicated on.

War as Vanishing Point of Theatrical Performance

One must, thus, take note of how the Real of War which the Nazi occupation brings to Poland is bookended by theater. The first scene revolves around the anti-fascist play, *Gestapo*, and the discussion among the producer and his cast as to the value of comedy for political critique. Then, just before the Blitzkrieg sets in, the producer Dobosh is forced to censor his theatrical troupe and exchange a play he fears might displease Hitler for a Shakespearean tragedy. *Hamlet*, however, is also

Polski theater's rehearsal: Maria Tura's (Carole Lombard's) style for the concentration camp.
To Be or Not to Be

a play about war, in which, in the final act, Fortinbras, who has been on a bloody campaign in Poland, finally overruns the castle in Elsinore, only to discover that everyone but Horatio is dead. Once the Polski theater is indefinitely shut down by Nazi censorship, occupied Warsaw itself becomes the decisive stage. There, this staunch troupe of actors will play an improvised version of *Gestapo* in the Real, even while they will draw on another Shakespearean text, *The Merchant of Venice*, for the final deployment of theater as subversive weapon. Only at the very end do we return, once more, to *Hamlet*, now performed at a different location, in the land of Shakespeare himself.

How, then, does Lubitsch enact this seminal transition from the theater to the streets of Warsaw as stage, a move anticipated by Bronski's defiant act. First we see an advertisement poster. The announcement of a change in program, as well as the title of the play that will be performed that night, *Hamlet*, only barely covers the much larger poster for the play *Gestapo*, which the director of the Polski theater has been compelled to censor. Then, as the first of several comic repetitions, the pilot Lieutenant Stanislav Sobinski (Robert Stack) walks out on Joseph Tura's (Jack Benny) performance of the monologue "To be or not to be," engendering the latter's outrage at what he considers to be a foul conspiracy against him as an artist and a man. This battle of the sexes is soon, however, interrupted (even if only barely appeased) by the declaration of war, which the members of the Polski theater read about in the evening paper backstage. For the duration of Warsaw's occupation, Nazi crimes put all personal grievances on hold. Joseph, who storms into his wife's dressing room, is successfully stopped in the middle of his tirade against his rival, first by his fellow actors, who inform him that they are at war, and then by the air alarm, forcing everyone to leave the theater.

With the front line running through Poland, the theatrical troupe comes together, united in its battle against this mutual enemy. The need to act against the occupying forces serves unequivocally as their shared cause. The point of Lubitsch's comic spirit is, however, first and foremost to mobilize the American audience to identify with this cause as well; to recognize it as their own, even though they are geographically far away from the European theater of war. In the cellar during this first bomb raid of Warsaw, Joseph is the one to first address the fact that political reality has caught up with all theater. In response to his comment, "Well anyway, we don't have to worry about the Nazi play anymore," the actor Rawitch (Lionel Atwill) notes, "the Nazis themselves are putting the show on, and a much bigger one." The mise-en-scène places Carole Lombard and Jack

Benny in the center of the actors and stage hands, sitting on or huddling around the spiral staircase. Visually they form the nucleus in a troupe that is just about to be re-united for a next round of theatricals. They may have lost their theater stage but not their audience. The mise-en-scène places us where the Polish theater audience, watching Joseph Tura as Hamlet, was shown to sit in the previous scene.

As peacetime turns into wartime, these actors transform the world outside the theater into their new stage, mirroring and commenting on the global theater of war the film references. By moving beyond the confines of the Polski theater, they draw their audience—regardless how far geographically it is distanced from them—into their comedy. Noteworthy is the fact that Maria has the last word. She draws yet a further analogy between them and the military forces that have just invaded Warsaw by bleakly noting "there's no censor to stop them." Implicitly, as the theater troupe takes to the streets, there will also be no censor to stop her and her friends. That the Nazi occupation is to be understood as theater is something Lubitsch underscores in the scene that comes immediately after the air raid. We see stock footage of a bombed building collapsing in a rear projection behind the ruins of the burning Warsaw storefronts of the opening scene, all clearly marked as a Hollywood stage set. So as to underscore the theatricality, we hear a melancholic song played by string instruments but no diegetic sound that might reference the actual destruction of a city. The male voice-over recalls the opening sequence, yet raised to a different pitch, it now melodramatically declares that "the curtain has fallen on the Polish drama."

While this commentary continues, we see Greenburg and Bronski walking amongst the props of destruction, the rubble of the bombed city. Once more the camera isolates the poster on the door of the Polski theater, advertising *Hamlet*, only it, too, has been partially torn off. At this point, the narrator's voice stops and Bressart begins to speak, reiterating what Lombard has said in the cellar during the first air raid: "there was no censor to stop them." He is thus positioned as the actor to articulate the double voicing so seminal to Lubitsch's mise-en-scène. What we are shown on screen is not the Real of War, but the effects of destruction the occupying forces have left. We see this collateral damage, furthermore, both as stock footage and as a stage set referencing this stock footage. The actual battle taking place in Europe is what lies behind the theatrical scene that unfolds on screen. The horrible catastrophe thus obliquely invoked is what extends the film screen out towards us, the audience, affectively drawing us into its movement. The Nazi troops that march across the screen as this transitional sequence comes to an end, are doing so for two sets of spectators—the actors Greenberg and Bronski on screen and the audience in front of the screen.

The rhetorical point regarding the manner in which Lubitsch thus references his cinematic medium is that it renders the Real of War implicitly present, the ground and vanishing point for the comedy of errors about to begin anew. In contrast to the play *Gestapo* which this troupe had wanted to put on in the Polski theater, their improvisation will have only contingency as its censoring agent. The extreme stylization of the transitional sequence serves more as a shield than a cover up. It obliquely points to the horrific catastrophe it can not directly represent. The second version of *Gestapo*, in which, along with Polish actors playing Nazis, real German Nazis take parts (albeit unwittingly), is a genre splice. We return to the gender battle typical for the sophisticated comedy of the '30s and '40s, with a husband and wife using witty conversation to determine, as Stanley Cavell has argued, the terms of marriage as a trope for the meet and happy relation between the nation and its subjects.[5] Even while Maria is playing cat and mouse with her jealous husband Joseph, she takes on the additional role of female spy, using her seductive allure to prevent a real Nazi spy, Professor Siletsky (Stanley Ridges), from delivering the material he has gathered about the Polish underground to the Commander of the Occupation and through him to Berlin. Important for the double voicing the political force of *To Be or Not to Be* is predicated on is thus the way the comedy of errors performed by the Turas and their troupe overwrites the Real of War explicitly invoked in the scene of transition, even while transcoding such anti-fascist propaganda films as *Casablanca*, which came out the same year. At issue is a multiply terraced screening over of the Real of War, implicitly making reference to what it cannot screen directly.

Throughout the comedy of errors that makes up most of *To Be or Not to Be*, the false beard of Professor Siletsky, the Nazi spy pretending to work for British intelligence, keeps popping up so as to gesture towards the comic medium itself. At first it is merely an attitude. The pilot Sobinski, having joined the RAF, immediately becomes suspicious of this older man when he discovers that he has never heard of Maria Tura. Because Sobinski is an ardent fan, he is able to convince the British secret service that no one could have lived in Warsaw in the last few years without having run into this female celebrity. Not knowing her is what proves Siletsky to

---

5   See Stanley Cavell, *Pursuits of Happiness: The Hollywood Comedy of Remarriage* (Cambridge MA: Harvard University Press, 1981). It is interesting to note that one year earlier, Carole Lombard had played such a part in *Mr. and Mrs. Smith*, the only comedy of remarriage Alfred Hitchcock ever made.

be offering a false identity of himself, even if his beard is real. Once he has returned to Poland, Sobinski immediately involves Maria in the political theater they must play out in the Real, setting in motion a comedy that gets more complicated with every turn, because the contingency of the events forces them to improvise. In the case of Maria's husband, this causes him to dangerously abandon his role several times when his vanity as an actor or his own jealousy as a husband are at issue. He will not content himself by letting his wife take the lead, as she plays a seductive woman who shows herself to be willing to become a collaborator for the luxury the Nazi brass can offer her. Tura's own ambition as an actor prompts him to design for himself the major role in the repetition of the documentary drama *Gestapo* which they are now putting on in the back room of the Polski theater, disguised to look like the real Gestapo Headquarters in Warsaw.

Tura, having convinced the other actors to kidnap Siletsky so as to steal his documents, finds himself in a theatrical impasse when he discovers that there are copies of these dangerous papers in the professor's trunk in his hotel suite. In the dramatic resolution the film comes up with, the reference to *Hamlet* is again double voiced. In contrast to the mouse trap in Shakespeare's tragedy, clandestine knowledge is not to be brought to light. Rather the secret information about the Polish underground is meant to disappear in darkness forever. Yet the killing happens on stage and places Siletsky in the position of Polonius. As the curtain rises, the actors, who have all rushed into the dark, empty theater in pursuit of the Nazi spy, see him facing his killer. For a brief moment he stands upright, holding his left hand to the wound in his lower body. All the men watch silently in suspense from the bottom of the stage. Then, raising his right hand in the infamous Nazi salute, but without uttering a word, his bleeding body collapses on the floor. In this condensed representation theatrical means are used to spotlight a real political enemy even while turning him into the perfect embodiment of a melodramatic villain. If his dying on stage serves as a reprieve, the lap dissolve which seamlessly moves from an image of the corpse to the suitcase containing the secret documents anticipates a new round of danger but also a new round of comic errors.

The narrative must thus return once more to the issue of false beards. To up the ante not only on Bronski playing Hitler, but also on his wife doing her version of Mata Hari, Joseph adopts two competing roles. Having initially played the Nazi Colonel Ehrhardt during the rehearsals for *Gestapo*, he now decides to take on the guise of the Nazi spy he has watched die on stage. To do so, however, he needs the dead man's beard. In the decisive scene of disclosure, one of his fellow actors, dressed as a Nazi officer, pulls off the false beard in front of the astonished eyes of the real Colonel Ehrhardt, who had fallen into the mouse trap and been successfully duped by Tura's performance. A sleight of hand, in turn, helps Joseph out of what looks like a hopeless situation. Having found the corpse of the real Siletsky, the Commander of the Gestapo has placed the dead man on a chair in the room next to his office. He then ushers the Polish actor (who is pretending to be this man) into the same room, waiting in the adjourning room to see how he would respond to their counter-trap. Tura, however, proves his own artistic wit by shaving off the beard of his model and re-attaching it with glue.

This ruse proves to be a game with truth and illusion worthy of Shakespeare's Danish prince. To prove that he is, in fact, the real Siletsky, Tura will compel the Nazi Commandant to pull at the beard of the corpse, thus offering ocular proof that the latter (and not he) is the counterfeit. Since logic forbids one to believe that there could be two false beards, Tura's assumed identity as Siletsky cannot be questioned. The appearance of his actor friends, seeking to save him from the hands of the Gestapo, and as such pitting their improvisation against his, undoes the logic, proving that in this carnivalesque world a false beard is not always a false beard. With the Nazis positioned as the duped audience of these theatricals (while we are in the know), the comic repetition sustains the subversive appeal to political action.

Greenberg's Shylock

The culmination of this comedy of errors on the stage of occupied Poland occurs when Dobosh's troupe, having produced an impasse owing to their exaggerated improvisation, is compelled to restage a second play, *Murder in the Opera*, in the Real. If their performance of *Hamlet* over-wrote that of *Gestapo*, it is now Greenberg's Shylock who overwrites everything, above all Joseph Tura's ham performance of Hamlet's monologue. The precision of Lubitsch's comic pathos sustains the three different moments when Felix Bressart speaks parts but never all of Shylock's famous monologue. Indeed, if this play within a play serves to critically reflect on any ludic appropriation of the designation Jew, the allusion to Shakespeare's text also brings with it a decisive shift in tone. Bressart/Greenberg's Shylock serves as a sober counterpoint to the carnivalesque impersonation of Nazis on the part of Joseph Tura (both as spy and as commanding officer) and Bronski (as Hitler at the beginning and the end of the film). His claim, as a Jew, to humanity speaks not only to the urgency of their theatrical play but also marks those moments when acting takes on the authority of an ethical appeal.

The first time Greenberg intones Shylock is backstage during a performance of *Hamlet*, just after Bronski has been chastised by Dobosh for adding lines to the script. Greenberg tries to calm him down by reiterating that he knows his improvisation would have gotten a laugh. He assures his friend that "they can't keep real talent down forever." His insistence that they, as subsidiary actors, simply need to wait for their time to get the big part they deserve, works with a quasi-comic innocence. With childlike glee, Greenberg imagines what it would be like for him to play the Rialto scene and turns to Bronski to assure him, "Shakespeare must have thought of me when he wrote this. It's me." Identifying completely with this role, he begins his recitation: "Have I not eyes? Have I not hands, organs, senses, dimensions, affections, passions." The medium close-up shows us not only the silent film pathos with which Bressart delivers the famous lines, "if you prick us, do we not bleed? If you tickle us, do we not laugh? If you poison us, do we not die?" In a reverse shot we also see Bronski, first frozen into admiration, then breaking the illusion by adding, "you'd move them to tears."

There is a note of self-irony in the air because the pathos of the performance is offset by the setting. They are not only behind the stage but also wearing the costumes of a different Shakespeare play. Furthermore, the personal emotion Greenberg gives to his recital, proving that he is, indeed, made for the part, is immediately undercut again as he moves to joking about himself. In response to Bronski's praise, he falls back out of his role and replies, "Instead, I have to carry a spear." Seamlessly the two subsidiary actors have once more moved the tone to farce, complaining about the lowly roles they are forced to play. Then, repeating the beginning of the film with a difference, the script once more returns to Bronski's improvisation of Hitler and the spirit of comedy. Still deep in conversation, he assures Greenberg that he would love to drop the other lead actor, Rawitch, as bad a ham as Joseph Tura, right in the center of the stage, and his friend replies, "that would get a terrific laugh." The shift in tone surprises even themselves.

The second declamation of Shylock follows upon the Blitzkrieg and the closing of the Polski theater. Now, the two subsidiary characters are shoveling snow outside the theater building and Greenberg reduces his recitation to a few lines: "If you prick us, do we not bleed? If you tickle us, do we not laugh? If you poison us, do we not die?" His performance is no longer a sign of his pleasurable identification with this theatrical role but rather an identification of the plight of the Polish people with the suppression of a Venetian Jew, standing in for all of Europe's Jewry. The tone is now one of nostalgia, and yet, typical for the double voicing so seminal to this film, is also a shift back into the comic. Bronski repeats his praise, only now he says, "What a Shylock you would have been." While the possibility of celebrity is now spoken in the past tense, Greenberg's response once more breaks the tragic pathos. With a touch of exaggerated histrionics he again recalls (now also in the past tense), "All I had to do was to carry a spear." As the camera moves back, Bronski nods in agreement with this shared memory: "I wonder if we'll ever carry a spear again." This invocation of the past also serves an ideological purpose. It seeks to imagine a future based on the success of the current war effort taking place on screen but also one Lubitsch's own film self-consciously seeks itself to support. The scene segues into images of the Polish underground committing acts of sabotage, while the male voice-over, in contrast to the tempered voices of these two actors, is invigorated by anti-fascist furor. By including documentary stock footage of the RAF flying formations in a darkened sky, before moving the narrative to the Polish pilots in England, the nostalgic melodrama of Greenberg and his friend bleeds into the buoyancy of war-effort propaganda.

When Greenberg recites Shylock for the last time, we find urgency re-inscribed in the lighthearted sadness of both previous scenes. Significantly, Dobosh, the producer who was overly serious at the beginning of the film, is now rehabilitated. He has again taken charge after the improvisations of his unruly troupe and their tampering with the script have gotten them all into dire straights. Having gathered together to figure out how to escape from Warsaw now that the Nazi command is onto their theatrical tricks, he is the one who comes up with the idea that they might revive the play *Murder in the Opera*. His sobriety, as he explains to them what they will be asked to play, is a synthesis between histrionic buoyancy and nostalgic sadness. Calmly, he anticipates the possibility of failure even as it is from this possibility that he draws his affective power. His assertion that the play might flop again, but that "we have to take the chance to get out of here" can be read as a coded message to the American audience in 1942 regarding the uncertainty of the outcome of the call to arms they have just embarked upon.

As Dobosh addresses Greenberg, who has assumed the pose of the melancholic, sitting apart from the other actors, the Jew willingly responds to his interpellation. Even at the acme of despair he maintains his spirit of comic relief. To Dobosh's suggestion, "if we can manage that Greenberg suddenly pops up among all those Nazis," he replies with his standard line: "it will get a tremendous laugh." The difference in repetition so seminal to comedy now adds a tone of gravity to mark the distance this troupe (and with it the film narrative) has covered since the audacious wit of the inaugural scene of *To Be or Not to Be*. This time, Dobosh's negation is sustained by compelling sincerity. Shaking his head, he counters Greenberg's suggestion by asserting, "No it won't." The comic ethos of Lubitsch resides in the fact that we are given both a lighthearted argument over the legitimacy of improvisation (with which the film began) and a producer's sober anticipation of a theatrical effect on which not only their lives but the survival of the Polish underground depend. Dobosh's appeal to Greenberg, "You've always wanted to play an important part. If you don't play it right, we're all lost, and if you do play it right, I still can't guarantee anything" is ominous and urgent. And it is an appeal that moves from the diegetic to the extradiegetic level of the film, appealing as much to the audience in front of the screen as to the actors on screen.

Reciting Shylock for the third time, Greenberg is re-energized both because he is finally able to do what he has been dreaming about and because, in realizing his narcissistic fantasy, he will be the one to make the difference. In the foyer behind the royal box in the opera house he once more recites Shylock for Bronski, only now the two actors are surrounded not only by their friends but also by real Nazis, taken in by the theatrical illusion. Pretending to be an assassin, asking what Hitler wants of Poland, he launches into a longer version of Shakespeare's monologue, with a medium shot focused on his outraged face as he declaims one last time, "If you prick us, do we not bleed? If you tickle us, do we not laugh? If you poison us, do we not die?" Only this time he adds the line, "if you wrong us, shall we not revenge?," at which point Tura (once more in the guise of a Nazi colonel) has him arrested by two of their fellow actors and led away to his alleged headquarters, while he convinces the bedazzled Nazis that he needs an escort to take himself and the Führer to the airport immediately. This time round Bronski remains completely silent, perfectly aligned with his role as Hitler.

After his fulminant performance, Greenberg, in turn, disappears from the screen. For a brief moment this subsidiary character has outplayed the "famous Polish actor" who, as the real Colonel Ehrhardt (Sig Ruman) had claimed, does to *Hamlet* what the Nazis are doing to Poland. Then the film narrative returns to Joseph Tura with his melodramatic excess. En route to the airport, he proudly discusses with Bronski how Greenberg had always wanted to play Shylock. The question whether they will ever return to the Polski theater prompts yet another histrionic pose, even while recalling the nostalgic pathos of the scene between Greenberg and Bronski, shoveling snow in front of the theater. Then a bomb explodes and melancholia transforms into euphoria as the two Polish actors realize that the underground is still alive. If the point of staging Shylock in the foyer of the Warsaw opera was meant to subvert fascist politics with political theater, Lubitsch subverts this political pathos with another turn to the comic. While his two actors embark on the fantasy that a monument will be erected to them for having saved the underground, Bronski's discovery that Tura has lost his moustache makes the grandiose again ridiculous. In despair, the two vainglory heroes are reduced to looking for the false moustache in the upholstery of the car.

How might we evaluate these three citations? The question of appropriating a text which in Shakespeare's comedy involves accepting the injurious interpellation Venetian society attaches to the Jew is complex. Not only does an actor, who up to this point had primarily carried props on stage, become the lead actor in a scene where he challenges another actor, performing the part of Hitler. Not only is this a scene on which everyone's survival depends. Bressart is explicitly used for the part as a Jewish émigré actor in Hollywood, playing the one markedly Jewish member of the Polski theater, appropriating the role of the vengeful Jew so contested in the Shakespearean oeuvre. In this tautology he also plays the part against the grain. The politics of this theatrical space are such that while some actors are performing Nazis, he performs theater's most infamous Jew. Yet while the former masquerade thrives on the rhetorical gesture of satire, the latter is sustained by the dignity of ethical legitimacy. Lubitsch's Shylock is not the avenging figure of Shakespeare who seeks to redress the social prejudice he has suffered under, but rather an instance of salvation to whom the film makes such a forceful tribute, not least because Joseph Tura's vanity does not include him in the statue he imagines for himself while driving to the airport. This re-figured Shylock is the character we have unequivocal sympathy for, while Jack Benny's performance of Hamlet is self-consciously satiric. The joke, in part, consists in the visual discrepancy between the high tragedy of Shakespeare's character and Joseph Tura's hamming up Hamlet.

When Greenberg finally gets to deliver his performance of Shylock, having rehearsed it twice before, Bressart's performance is so engaging not only because, at this moment, the theatrical role and the real actor embodying it for the camera coincide, but also because this convergence dovetails with the ethico-political

Greenberg (Felix Bressart) as Shylock: "If you tickle us, do we not laugh?" *To Be or Not to Be*

attitude of the film *To Be or Not to Be*. Bressart as Greenberg as Shylock references Lubitsch himself, appealing—in the name of displaced European Jewry—to the American film audience, then as now. We never actually see him perform the part on stage. We are only given indications that this is something that might happen in the future, implicitly when the Nazi occupation of Poland will have ceased. If Lubitsch understood his comedy as part of Hollywood's war effort, the final rhetorical ploy consists in turning an identification with the anti-Semitic stereotype of the Jew lusting for revenge into the right of the free world to retaliate against fascism. The bond Lubitsch's Shylock insists on—that is the ideological point of the film—is the pound of flesh the American forces, along with their allies, would be compelled to stake in their battle against the Nazis. In contrast to the court scene in Shakespeare's play, the contract which Lubitsch forges with his audience is precisely not concerned with *not* shedding a drop of blood. In 1942, America could only guess the extent of the bloodshed their recent entrance into the war would ultimately cost. Yet decisive in the appeal Greenberg *qua* Lubitsch makes, when their Shylock insists that the Jews/the Poles will also bleed if one pricks them, is simply the unequivocal legitimacy of a claim for an equally unambivalent political action.

Maria Has the Last Word

Tracking the comic ethos of Lubitsch also means taking note of the fact that the film does not end with the successful flight of this troupe of actors from Poland. Instead, once they are safely installed in their airplane, en route to the British Isles, we are presented with a title card giving Scotland as the location of the next scene, followed by stock documentary footage of the resilient British anti-aircraft fire. This visual reference to the Battle of Britain functions as a chiasmic closure to the footage of bombed buildings in Warsaw in the transition sequence. Most poignant in these final sequences, however, is the manner in which, because Maria has the last word, we are also called upon to remember the earlier scene in the cellar, following the first air raid over Warsaw, and her comment regarding censorship.

As the film once more turns from anti-fascist adventure narrative to sophisticated romantic comedy, the battle of the sexes opens up again in all its force, exposing the gender antagonism which the presence of enemy occupation of Warsaw had tentatively put on hold. Having arrived in Scotland, Maria sheds her role of glamorous seductress and instead plays the part of the demure, subservient wife. When the journalists suggest that her husband "played the real hero in this amazing play," she does not contradict them. Instead, in response to their question as to what he would desire most, she slyly confesses: "He wants to play Hamlet." Almost shyly, her husband adds that they are, after all, in the country of Shakespeare, and once more she interrupts him, repeating that he wants to play Hamlet. Only apparently does she accept the subsidiary role he is assigning to her, claiming after the event that the contribution of the other actors to their amazing play with the Gestapo in Warsaw was very minor. The lap dissolve from Lombard's radiant and Benny's smug smile leads to the interior of a British theater. Joseph Tura once more appears on stage to deliver his monologue. For a brief moment he hesitates until his gaze can fix on Sobinski. We, literate in the logic of comedy, can only expect a repetition of the previous two scenes and so are surprised by the unexpected twist Lubitsch comes up with. The minute Tura beings to say "to be or not to be," a man does get up and leave the room, yet it is a perfect stranger.

The inclusion of this decisive difference leaves our ham literally speechless. All he can do is stare in horror at the off-space beyond the stage. Lubitsch won't even give him a close-up. For a few moments the camera remains with a frontal image of the actor, who has not only once again been interrupted in his most glamorous performance but also knows that at this very moment his wife is betraying him. Then the screen turns black. Maria is the final victor in this battle of the sexes, again deployed to screen out the real battle for Europe. She is once more pitting her seduction against her husband's vanity, and Lubitsch underscores her power by allowing his heroine to act from the off-space of the screen. Alone on stage, Joseph Tura may believe he commands the attention of his audience, but from behind the stage Maria is able to draw his attention, as well as ours, to her clandestine act of revenge. The last image may be his but she has the last word because, by virtue of the directions she has given to her lover, her husband will not be able to finish his monologue. We laugh at his helpless rage and can imagine her laughing with us, invisible to our gaze in her dressing room. This is, of course, our fantasy, since we don't see her in her triumph: a lighthearted counter-point to Greenberg's sinister disappearance from the screen.

The comic turn serves to introduce a final troubling rhetorical gesture. Who, we are left to ask ourselves, is in charge of this romantic game? The vain actor who continually ups the ante on his wife or the clever actress who can successfully entrap her husband because she knows jealousy to be his weakness? Maria has learned something from Greenberg's performance of Shylock. Power goes not to the ham in the center of the stage, but to the one who, as an agent of interruption, draws attention to him or herself. With his dignified performance of Shylock, Greenberg refigures the generic war comedy by introducing into an adventurous comedy of errors the urgency to act in the name of preserving human rights. His absence from the end of the film makes this claim resound with immense force. Maria Tura's intervention also uses the force of the screen's off-space, of which we know that it triggers our imagination in a far more effective manner than anything shown on screen. Like Greenberg's silent disappearance, her insistence that her husband wants to play Hamlet tarries with us even after the screen has turned dark. Putting theater so suddenly on hold, her subterfuge continues to hold us. If nothing else, it spells trouble.

GREGOR MODER

The Beard, the Bust, and the Plumed Helmet

In what is perhaps one of the best sequences in *To Be or Not to Be* (1942), the central role is played by a fake beard. The Polish actor Joseph Tura enters Gestapo headquarters in occupied Warsaw, posing as the informant Professor Siletsky. What Tura doesn't know is that the Gestapo have already found the real Siletsky's dead body and that he is walking into a trap. What is more, Tura's fake beard, worn to impersonate the informant, seems to be malfunctioning, so he has had to take a *second* fake beard as a replacement. But, as is typical in comedies, all these setbacks turn out to be advantages. The head of the Gestapo, Colonel Ehrhardt, is playing a game of cat and mouse with Tura: he showers the impostor with excessive pleasantries and formalities and then asks him to wait in the next room—where the dead body of the real Siletsky has been placed in an armchair. Shocked at first, Tura quickly recovers. He takes out the spare fake beard in his pocket, finds a razor in the washroom next door, and works out a plan. After a while, he politely calls the Germans in. When Ehrhardt and his aides enter the room, he and Tura continue their game of excessive politeness. Nevertheless, everything looks very bad for the Pole: the dead man's suit was made in London, which is where the real Siletsky had just arrived from, his wrist watch is set to London time, etc. But before the Colonel can triumphantly expose Tura as the impostor, the hero goads him into pulling at the dead man's beard—which, to everybody's surprise, comes away in his hand. Though the film does not show it, it becomes apparent that Tura has used his short time alone with the body, the razor, and the fake beard to great effect—in this elliptic procedure we witness the classic

Siletsky (Jack Benny) about to pull
Siletsky's (Stanley Ridges's) beard.
To Be or Not to Be

Lubitsch touch. The dead body is assumed fake and Colonel Ehrhardt begins to apologize dramatically, promising Tura everything he demands, just to get him out of Warsaw. At this point, however another twist in the plot takes place. Having learned that Tura is walking into a trap, his colleagues from the Polski theater have decided to act quickly and save him. So, just as our hero is escaping with victory in his grasp, his fellow actors enter the Colonel's office, posing as officers of Hitler's personal guard. In front of Ehrhardt's bewildered eyes, they pull Tura's fake beard off, denounce him as an impostor, arrest him, and march him out of the Gestapo headquarters.

There are many comic principles at work in this sequence. The most obvious is perhaps the popular motif of doubles and mistaken identities, which is here wonderfully complicated.[1] Then there is the stark contrast between the deadly seriousness of the situation on the one hand, and the gentlemanly behavior of Tura and Colonel Ehrhardt on the other—a contrast that is also a very typical comic device. The writing is simply excellent, using clever repetitions rather than inventing new lines of dialogue; in their previous scene, Tura had suggested to the Colonel that Captain Schultz was "shifting responsibility" for a failure back onto the Colonel, and now Ehrhardt repeats the same line directly to Schultz. In fact, Captain Schultz gets blamed for everything from this point onwards,

---

1   Mladen Dolar goes so far as to suggest that the entire film is based on this mechanism of doubles and repetitions. See his "Comedy and Its Double," in Robert Pfaller (ed.), *Stop That Comedy! On the Subtle Hegemony of the Tragic in Our Culture* (Vienna: Sonderzahl, 2005), 181–209.

Colonel Ehrhardt (Sig Ruman) politely refuses to pull Siletsky's (Jack Benny's) beard.
To Be or Not to Be

and the angry cry "Schultz!" becomes a running gag for expressions of Colonel Ehrhardt's incompetence.

Robert Pfaller describes yet another principle at work here in terms of the paradigm of success. Tragedies are based on the formula of failure, writes Pfaller, but comedies are based on success, on too much success even.[2] In this sequence, the success of a trivial prop—the fake beard—is even an explicit topic of the conversation. The Nazis ridicule the idea that the impostor could have worn a fake beard, and insist that he must have carefully observed Professor Siletsky for a long time before he was able to grow the exact same beard. This makes the effect of finding a false beard on the dead body even more devastating for the Colonel. And when Tura's colleagues burst into the room masquerading as Hitler's guard, the pompous actor posing as the commanding officer shouts at the poor Colonel, delivering the stunning line: "Here's a man with a beard, and you didn't even pull it!"—As if comedy were perfectly aware of its mechanism of success, such that one should always, upon seeing a beard, assume that it is a fake.

But I want to draw attention to another comic principle used masterfully here, namely the *status game* played between the protagonists, the Polish actor

---

2   "The predominant paradigm of comedy is that of success." Robert Pfaller, "Comedy and Materialism," in Pfaller (ed.), *Stop that Comedy!*, 253. One example of this excess is precisely the success of the Polish actors: not only does Tura manage to convince the Nazis that the real Siletsky's dead body is actually an impostor's body, but his colleagues from the theater also successfully—albeit counter-productively—save him from the clutches of the Gestapo.

Joseph Tura and the Gestapo Colonel Ehrhardt. Tura starts off with a very low status, since he has just walked into a trap, while the Colonel lavishly displays his high status, showering him with excessive politeness. The fact that Tura believes he has the upper hand, that he is successfully deceiving the Colonel, only reduces his status even further. When Tura begins to understand the situation and takes matters into his own hands, a radical change in status occurs. Even though the polite exchange of compliments never ceases, Tura is now leading the game, and it is the Colonel who is now walking blindly into a trap. When the fake beard is discovered on the body, it is the Colonel who must apologize, and Tura who has the opportunity to be cocky and excessively benevolent, practically begging the Colonel to try pulling off his own beard.

Status games are a popular mechanism for generating comic situations. A very clear example occurs in another World War II film, Chaplin's *The Great Dictator* (1940), when the Nazi dictator Hynkel meets the fascist dictator Napaloni. Following the advice of his Minister of Propaganda, Garbitsch, Hynkel tries to act superior by playing rather silly games like making Napaloni wait outside his office and offering him a lower seat so that he will have to physically look up to Hynkel. The sequence ends with a surrealist clown scene in which the two dictators, both sitting on barber's chairs, keep raising them in order to be able to speak to the other from a higher position. The chairs rise higher and higher, far beyond any realistic height, almost to the roof, until Hynkel's chair malfunctions and collapses back to its lowest position. In Chaplin's film, the status game begins in a reasonable, mundane framework but then spins out of control into a fantastical clownish finale. In the fake beard scene in *To Be or Not to Be*, however, the status game is played completely differently, with elegance and finesse. First of all, the players raise their status by negation, i.e. through humility and excessive politeness towards their opponent. Secondly, they both arrange a sequence of events so that their opponent will become the creator of his own downfall. Tura, especially, plays this game very cleverly, lowering his own status by examining the dead body and noting all the details that look very bad for him, while at the same time provoking the Colonel into losing his calm and pulling off the fake beard himself, precisely at that moment when Ehrhardt should have triumphantly unmasked Tura as the impostor.

Let us now focus on the object at the centre of this cleverly played status game—the fake beard itself. Clearly it functions as a prop enabling the comic mechanism of mistaken identity, a comedy of errors. But there is more to it than just that, for the beard embodies a mechanism of its own. It serves as an object that has the power either to grant the utmost authority or to take it away in an instant. It is, so to speak, an authoritarian object. It functions as the microphone functions for the speaker, or the scepter for the king—by taking hold of the microphone, or by displaying the scepter for all to see, one immediately gets everyone's attention and is recognized as an authority that must be listened to. This is an aspect of the fake beard that cannot be reduced to the comic procedure of mistaken identity—a procedure that this comedy indeed uses quite a lot. There is something about this specific object, something that captures the general atmosphere of the film. It is an authoritarian object for an authoritarian comedy. In comedy, generally speaking, a wife may pose as her husband's lover and surprise him on their date; a man may dress as a woman to hide from the Mafia; and yes, a Pole may put on a fake beard and pose as a Nazi informant. But in this sequence from *To Be or Not to Be*, the imposture carries the specific meaning of an usurpation of authority. The status game played by Tura and the Colonel hinges on the question of the beard. The contention of the film is, of course, that authority as such functions as an usurpation of authority: Authority is always staged and performed.

The finer point to be made here is that the fake beard is the object that makes this usurpation possible precisely insofar as it is a fake beard and not an authentic one. Perhaps we should even go as far as to say that the authentic organic beard can function as a symbol of masculinity and authority only on condition that it is potentially fake. What I am trying to suggest is that a fake beard is not just a later copy of an earlier authentic beard; rather, the fake beard is somehow primordial to the authentic beard. In other words: just as with language in Derrida's famous thesis, so too with beards. Derrida criticized the spontaneous assumption that writing is secondary to the spoken word. We naturally assume that it is a privilege to listen to someone speak in their immediate presence, when we can hear the voice, the inclinations, the passions, and where there is always the possibility of an interruption—at least in comparison to the necessarily impoverished transcript of the speech, within whose temporality one cannot talk about an interruption in the proper sense at all. Writing appears as secondary to speech not only in the temporal sense, but specifically at the level of the idea, because writing necessarily involves a delay, a mediation. Derrida criticized this assumption as being that of a logocentric metaphysics of the presence, and claimed that the necessary delay or mediation typical of writing is in fact precisely what constitutes language as such, including spoken language. Writing can therefore be considered primordial to "natural" speech in the sense that it is an "institution" in itself.[3]—In this precise sense, then, I am proposing the idea of the primacy of the fake beard over the authentic one: it is the potential fakeness of the beard that makes the beard an authoritarian object; the fakeness is its precondition. This is why I claim that the organic beard can function as an authoritarian object—that is, as an object that holds authority—only if it is in itself something that could be fake.

We can call the fake beard a negative object. Negative in the sense that it is not so important for its physical, affirmative characteristics, but rather because it can easily be detached and re-attached, and because it doesn't belong to any specific chin. It is a fake *beard*, but it could also be a fake *moustache*. Could not the same function be fulfilled by fake glasses, a fake hat, etc., just as well? The difference is that the beard and the moustache are organically linked to the body, while glasses and hats are not. When glasses, hats, gloves, walking canes, or any other such object carry the symbolic weight of the authoritarian object, they are in themselves something fake, something forged. They function as additions. When someone assumes authority with the help of such accessories, this undoubtedly involves an element of usurpation or forgery, whether those objects are made from genuine materials or not. Such objects are even more obviously negative objects; they represent or manifest without anything authentic that could count as their foundation.

In *The Great Dictator* we can find many negative authoritarian objects used by Hynkel—albeit unsuccessfully—to demonstrate his superiority over Napaloni. The most interesting among them is Hynkel's bust, with its head larger than life by a factor of at least two. The bust is carefully positioned by Garbitsch on Hynkel's desk so that it will glare at Napaloni during their conversation. It seems that

---

3   Derrida writes: "Now from the moment that one considers the totality of determined signs, spoken, and *a fortiori* written, as unmotivated institutions, one must exclude any relationship of natural subordination, any natural hierarchy among signifiers or orders of signifiers. If 'writing' signifies inscription and especially the durable institution of a sign (and that is the only irreducible kernel of the concept of writing), writing in general covers the entire field of linguistic signs. In that field a certain sort of instituted signifiers may then appear, 'graphic' in the narrow and derivative sense of the word, ordered by a certain relationship with other instituted — hence 'written,' even if they are 'phonic' — signifiers. The very idea of institution — hence of the arbitrariness of the sign — is unthinkable before the possibility of writing and outside of its horizon. Quite simply, that is, outside of the horizon itself, outside the world as space of inscription, as the opening to the emission and to the spatial distribution of signs, to the *regulated play* of their differences, even if they are 'phonic.'" Jacques Derrida, *Of Grammatology*, trans. Gayatri Spivak (Baltimore: Johns Hopkins University Press, 1997), 44.

Who's the real Hitler (Tom Dugan)?
To Be or Not to Be

the negative object, the symbol, wields more power than its original; this confirms our initial thesis that its negativity (or fakeness) is the condition of its potency. There is a very similar and perhaps even more effective example at the beginning of *To Be or Not to Be*. The theater director is very dissatisfied with the appearance of the minor actor playing Hitler. When the others ask him what exactly it is that he finds so unconvincing, the director points to the stage where a photo-portrait of Hitler overlooks the set of Gestapo Headquarters and exclaims: "That's it! That is what Hitler looks like!" But it turns out that the photograph was taken of the very actor representing Hitler. There is more in the portrait than in the person being portrayed—this is the fundamental claim of the negative object.[4]

Objects like the fake beard obviously exhibit something phallic in the psychoanalytic sense of the term. Jacques Lacan even explicitly linked the phallus to this comic operation in his discussion of Jean Genet's *The Balcony*. Genet's comedy takes place in a brothel where clients can dress up as authority figures: as a judge, a bishop, a general. Nobody, however, dresses up as the chief of police. Lacan offers an explanation: in a time of open revolution, it is only the power of police, the ultimate law of the fist, which counts. The chief of police, usurping the power

---

4   See also Alenka Zupančič's commentary on this sequence where she points out that the mysterious charisma of the Leader apparently emerges in the minimal difference between the actor representing Hitler and the photograph of the same actor. In this short circuit of representation, where the universal is self-referential, what is represented becomes concrete. Alenka Zupančič, *The Odd One In: On Comedy* (Cambridge MA: MIT Press, 2008), 36.

of the dictator, even goes so far as to propose that the new symbol of his power be a phallus. At that precise moment one of the workers in the brothel announces that, finally, a client has demanded to know what is required to resemble the chief of police. She then tears the wig off the chief's head, and "castrates" him by informing him that he was the only one who believed that no one knew he wore a wig.[5] Tura's fake beard, then, functions precisely as does the chief's wig: as a phallic object.

It is not only that these objects resemble male sexual characteristics such as the penis or facial hair. In fact, what makes the fake beard phallic is precisely its fakeness. In psychoanalysis the concept of the phallus indeed demands that it be part of the organism, but it is an independent part. One could say that, for Lacan, the phallus is the signifier of castration. But this does not mean that the phallus is a castrated penis, an organ freed from its body; on the contrary, the phallus only functions insofar as it is grown with the body. The connection between castration and the phallus therefore resides rather in the fact that the phallus is grown with the organism in a paradoxical, retroactive manner; as if the phallus was first something independent and only later organically grew with the body. The curious logic of this concept is principally the same as in Derrida's idea that writing is somehow primordial in language in general. We spontaneously assume that the organic characteristics of masculinity are something immediate, and that they can be considered phallic only in a later, mediated interpretation. But in truth— which is to say, on the level of the concept—it is the other way around; masculinity is something organic only because it has become phallic, only because it has phallicized, or, to put it another way, it is organic only insofar as it is phallic. We can say, in accordance with Derrida's critique, that the assumption that the phallus is something secondary is the typical assumption of the metaphysics of presence. And this is precisely why the fake beard is a phallic object: as long as it is nothing but a spare lump of hair in the actor's pocket it is truly only that—a lump of hair; only when it gets attached to the actor's chin does it start functioning as a phallus.

Insofar as the phallus is the signifier of castration, we could describe the negativity of phallic objects in general as the negativity of a cut or break. This determination can help distinguish it from other conceptions of negativity, especially

<hr>

5   See Jacques Lacan, *Seminar V: Formations of the Unconscious* (London: Karnac, 2002), Seminar of March 5, 1958.

from the negativity of torsion or loop which can also function as a generator of comic effects. However, these distinctions deserve their own proper analysis.[6]

But why is the fake beard comic, why is it a comic accessory? Certainly because it is phallic—but does this imply that a phallic object is in itself an object of comedy? If we take another look at the examples from *The Great Dictator*, we can see that the comedy of the authoritarian objects arises from their grandiosity coupled with their failure. It seems that what is comic is precisely the gap between what the object is supposed to signal and what it actually signals. Hynkel's attempts to display his superiority over Napaloni fail miserably, one by one. Napaloni's slightly vulgar and loud appearance is simply overwhelming; the bust, for instance, fails because Napaloni uses it to brush the ash from his cigar. But the idea that comedy emerges from the gap between the desired and the actual effect of the objects on Napaloni needs reworking, since the failure is inscribed in their fundamental structure. When Garbitsch explains his plan to Hynkel, the mere mention of the bust on the desk makes the dictator wince in terror, as if he was unaware of its presence before. This detail is brilliant. It demonstrates that Hynkel's bust is indeed terrifying, but precisely to the one who should perhaps be the least terrified of it at all—Hynkel himself. In this case the excess of the symbol of authority and power is necessarily and originally coupled with its failure. A dictator who is terrified by their own bust, by their own symbol of political power, can only be a comical dictator.

With the fake beard in the Lubitsch film, the relationships are not so unequivocal. Chaplin's film ridicules the fascination of a people with their leader, and it is therefore natural that its authoritarian objects are comical in themselves. This kind of comedy is less abundant in *To Be or Not to Be*.[7] One of the reasons the film was received with mixed feelings at the time of its release was precisely that it ridiculed Poles at least as much as it did the Germans. In the film, the latter are no more pompous, self-indulgent, foolish, or arrogant than the former. We could even say that Joseph Tura is a typical hot shot (in the guise of Professor Siletsky he keeps asking the Germans if they know of the "great, great Polish actor Joseph Tura") and that his wife Maria Tura is a typical diva (with all the lovers and

---

6   For an introductory work on the distinction between the comedy of torsion and the comedy of the cut or break, see Gregor Moder, "Comedy and Negativity," *Stasis* 1, no. 1 (2012).

7   An example is the plane scene where the Polish actor posing as Hitler—the same minor actor who failed to satisfy the director's vision of Hitler at the beginning of the film—orders the German pilots to immediately jump from the plane without a parachute, which they do without hesitation.

intrigues that come with the office). However, the rule that makes characters that take themselves too seriously immediately comical also applies to the world of *To Be or Not to Be*. In the history of comedy, there is a comical type whose performance is concentrated precisely on the exaggeration destined to fail; he is called *Miles Gloriousus* after the play by Titus Maccius Plautus, and was represented by Capitano in commedia dell'arte. We could say that this type specializes in phallic comedy; and we can imagine him with a plumed helmet. Capitano's characteristics are shared by Hynkel, the *great* dictator, by Napaloni, who actually wears a plumed helmet, but also by many actors of the Polski theater.[8]

The fake beard in the Lubitsch film certainly performs the function of a Capitano accessory—especially at the moment when Tura persuades Ehrhardt to pull it—but it has other comic functions as well, such as those of comic travesty (concealment and discovery). It seems that it is precisely the elegant conflation of two comic principles in one object that makes this sequence truly brilliant. Napaloni's plumed helmet does not conceal anything, it rather blows up or enlarges, it is nothing but a phallic prop. We could say the same about Hynkel's props and devices, with the exception of the bust: the fact that the "original" is, if only for a moment, terrified of it, signals that it has alienated itself as a prop and has become independent, threatening to take over the substance of their shared identity—as if Hynkel is merely a copy, an exaggeration of his bust, and not the other way around.

We can thus make out three comical uses of the phallus that differ from one another in some detail. First, the comedy of Napaloni's plumed helmet; second, the comedy of Tura's fake beard; third, the comedy of Hynkel's bust. The plumed helmet and the bust function as a pair in *The Great Dictator*, but they can nevertheless serve us to distinguish certain moments of the concept of the phallus in psychoanalysis. The plumed helmet is phallic in the sense that it is a symbol of power and authority, independent of its carrier. However, it is clear that with Napaloni there is no question of the retroactive grown-ness of the object with the carrier, since he is indivisibly one with the plume. Napaloni functions in the film as the plume itself, that is to say, as the ideal dictator. If this is the phallus then this phallus has not yet phallicized. Perhaps we could call it the naive or the immediate phallus; or, with a Hegelian name, the identity phallus. With Napaloni,

---

8 And if we go back to Lacan's account of Genet's *The Balcony*, where the chief of police keeps asking the proprietress of the brothel whether any client has asked for the uniform of the chief of police, we can explain the comic effect of this persistent questioning as precisely a Capitano routine.

there is no tension between the office and the person; he is a completely calm and undisturbed phallic unity. Strictly speaking, this is not phallic at all, but a myth of the phallus at best. This is exactly why it works so well in combination with Hynkel; Napaloni is what Hynkel wants to be but fails. But if the plumed helmet is too attached to its carrier to truly act as an instance of the phallus, then Hynkel's bust is too detached and too much independent from its carrier. The bust does not seem to be retroactively grown with Hynkel, but rather acts as his doppelganger, as his horrifying double, threatening to replace him. If the plumed helmet has not yet become phallic and is immediately unified with its carrier, then the bust is no longer phallic and has already detached itself from the carrier. It would seem that, in the end, it is only Tura's false beard that is phallic in the strict psychoanalytic meaning of the term.

The phallus can fulfill the comic function as fully phallicized, as a pre-phallic identity, or as a completely detached phallus. But—to return to our question—is it comical in itself? The phallus produces effects in real life just as well as in comedy; it therefore seems almost natural to assume that it is comical only in the special cases of theater, film, or performance. But at the same time, the phallus is eminently and emphatically a device of presentation, performance, and appearances. A ceremonial event such as the inauguration of a prince, a knighting, a promotion, a ribbon-cutting or a foundation-laying ceremony, or a procession with a monstrance, always involves a phallic element—and this goes to some extent also for weddings, funerals, and other rites of passage or initiations. And if we consider the king's scepter as the paradigmatic phallic object, then it seems reasonable to conclude that there is no phallus save for a phallus that is displayed for all to see. From this perspective, ceremonial events are certainly close to comedy (and to tragedy), since they include an element of exaggeration.

Anca Parvulescu has analyzed the unusual case of Kafka's laughter in the presence of the president of the Worker's Insurance Agency where he worked. The occasion was, as Kafka explains in a letter to Felice Bauer, like a meeting with the Emperor; the president's speech was as pompous as his words were meaningless. During the speech, Kafka began laughing uncontrollably at one of the president's little jokes that was meant, at best, to induce only a friendly smile.[9] Let us leave aside the question of psychology which may play a trick on us in moments of

---

9   Anca Parvulescu, "Kafka's Laughter" (manuscript); published in Slovenian as "Kafkov smeh," *Problemi* 50, nos. 5–6 (2012), 84.

great emotional stress, faced with events of immense symbolic importance where our role is limited to few minimal gestures and a simple "I do" or "I accept." Here I will focus only on the president's pompousness, on his exaggeration, or, if I may be allowed to use this term, on his theatricality. This example clearly points to the proximity of the comic and the phallic, in that both are inclined to staging.

As an aside, let me warn against a possible misunderstanding about the relationship between the comic and the phallic. Since the phallus is a matter of authority and power, it may seem that the role of comedy, in general, is to reveal the empty space covered by phallus: if in our mundane lives we recognize people with plumes or stripes as legitimate authorities, then in comedies we laugh at them as we discover that there is only a plume and no authority, only a stripe and no power. But there are at least two mistakes in this reasoning. Firstly, in mundane life the phallic objects are no less comical than in comedies. The president of the Agency is a real person who could also be a fictitious character on stage; in fact, any person representing universality is a potentially comical character. Jokes adore police officers, bishops, presidents. Moreover, jokes and comic genres in general prefer types to individuals, that is to say, they prefer incarnations of universality: the naive beauty, the jealous husband, the stingy old man, etc.[10] Hence, secondly, the stake of comedy cannot be the unmasking of the phallus as groundless or contingent. Strictly speaking, the phallus only exists as something theatrical and therefore groundless; moreover, it is always presented precisely as such, i.e., as something to be displayed and as something that exists in its displaying. A comedy that would limit itself to "unmasking" phallic objects or phallic rituals would therefore only further establish their universal power. Taking up the terminology proposed by Alenka Zupančič we can label such an approach as "false" comedy.[11] What we laugh at in the process of "unmasking" is the contingency of the carrier with regard to the universality of the phallic function it carries, while the phallic universality itself remains beyond question, indeed is even fortified by such a negation (in the Hegelian sense) of the carrier.

---

10 Henri Bergson proposed that we can recognize the well-known distinction between tragedy as the genre of individuality and comedy as the genre of universality even in the titles of the plays: "many comedies have a common noun as their title: l'Avare, le Joueur, etc. Were you asked to think of a play capable of being called le Jaloux, for instance, you would find that Sganarelle or George Dandin would occur to your mind, but not Othello: le Jaloux could only be the title of a comedy." Henri Bergson, *Laughter: An Essay on the Meaning of the Comic* (Rockville: Arc Manor, 2008 [1900]), 15. See also Zupančič, *The Odd One In*, 37.
11 Zupančič, *The Odd One In*, 30–1.

We misunderstand the phallic comedy if we see it as laughter in the face of authority, because theatricality and performance are a constitutive part of the process of phallic authority. However, the link between the phallus and comedy remains too general in this account. The relationship between the beard, the bust, and the plumed helmet can perhaps help us determine this link in more detail. Even though ceremonies include the exaggeration of a performance, they are not comic in themselves, just as the plumed helmet is not. If we find Napaloni comical, it is probably due to the stereotypical image of the Italian soldier as the braggart, as the Capitano. The properly comic dictator is, as was discussed above, Hynkel. He tries to impress his ideal, Napaloni, failing spectacularly time and time again. And even when he is alone in his office, dancing his famous dance with a large balloon painted in the image of the political map of the World, we could say that his aim is to impress his ideal, even though in that scene his ideal is himself as "Caesar, the emperor of the World." His failure in that scene is just as spectacular as it is unsurprising: the balloon, of course, bursts in the most dramatic way.

The example of the comic dictator as a dictator destined to fail is misleading insofar as it implies that comedy is a genre of failure. Of course, comedy loves characters endowed with some very obvious and at the same time very banal flaw; moreover, comedy exploits with great success situations in which the comic hero spectacularly fails at some utterly mundane task. But to say that the phallus is comic precisely insofar as it fails would lead us back to what Alenka Zupančič calls the false or conservative comedy. Failure itself is not a condition, and far less a guarantee, of the comic; in fact, comedies often employ a refined procedure wherein the hero's actions are performed badly and produce unwanted effects, and yet it is precisely these effects that, in the end, lead to a successful resolution.[12] Tura's fake beard is a perfect example of a phallic object that produces comic effects both in the case of success—recall Tura's cocky gesture of offering his beard to Colonel Ehrhardt for inspection—and in the case of failure—when Tura is unmasked by his colleagues in their bold attempt to save him from the Gestapo, which effectively ruins his own plan. The first example is a case of success produced by a failure, while the second presents a failure produced through too much success.

<hr />

12   One must recall here the master of this procedure, Peter Sellers: as the clueless Inspector Jacques Clouseau in *The Pink Panther* film series (1963–); as Hrundi V. Bakshi in *The Party* (1968); and perhaps even as Chance in *Being There* (1979).

In conclusion, there are three points we can make about the comic effects of the phallus. Firstly, even though the phallus is in itself something that belongs to theater, it is not in itself comic. Secondly, the phallus can become an object of ridicule, if its groundlessness is revealed; but this only fortifies it in its phallic function. And thirdly, the phallus is comic in the full meaning of the term when it is entirely consumed in something contingent—for instance in a fake beard— when it is revealed as phallicized. Robert Pfaller is correct in claiming that "comedy is representative of materialism in theater":[13] the universal or the spiritual is revealed as something completely immanent to the material order, and has no proper terrain outside of it.

---

13 Pfaller, "Comedy and Materialism," 251.

Alenka Zupančič

Squirrels to the Nuts, or, How Many Does it Take to Not Give up on Your Desire?

Cluny Brown was made in 1946, and was Lubitsch's last film. It is perhaps also the strangest. It is definitely the strangest romantic comedy ever made, and we'll return to this point later. But let us first stop at the title.

It is rather rare for titles of comedies to consist solely of a personal name, whereas this is a common practice with tragedies.[1] If tragedies focus on exceptional individuals and their likewise exceptional destinies which are somehow encapsulated in their name, comedies prefer generic names, names of types and situations, or plays on words. It would be hard to imagine having universal or generic names as titles of tragedies—to change, for example, *Antigone* into *The (Untamed) Shrew*, *Othello* into *The Jealous Husband*, or *Romeo and Juliet* perhaps straight into *Love's Labour Lost*. This shift itself entails something of a comedy, something that escapes the veil of dignity and respect carried by proper names. Proper names always function as a veil—of what? Of something "improper," of something that is not supposed to be there.

There are exceptions, however, to be found on both sides. On the side of tragedy, the most striking example is perhaps Paul Claudel's *Humiliated Father*, which actually sounds like a prototype comedy title. This is not unrelated to the specificity of the Claudelian tragedy, which could be described as tragedy beyond tragedy. But it is also non-negligible that this tragedy nevertheless revolves in the orbit

---

1   I am here briefly resuming the argument I developed in more detail in *The Odd One In: On Comedy* (Cambridge MA: MIT Press, 2008).

of a very strong family name, since it is part of the so-called Coûfontaine trilogy. On the side of comedy, there are also notable exceptions—most recently, Sacha Baron Cohen with his *Borat* (2006) and *Brüno* (2009). In Lubitsch, we have two: *Ninotchka* (1939) and *Cluny Brown*. It is rather obvious, however, that such names function differently than they do in tragedies, as if they were a different *kind* of name. Quickly put, we could say that in most cases they are not so much names of individuals as they are general names for some characteristic or peculiarity of these (and other) individuals. On the other hand, they can also be names for some particular excess, for something "improper" that escapes the cover of the proper name. They are names for what slides away from (proper) names, for precisely that which can never become the point of a subject's identification. They are, in short, names for the "object" in the Lacanian sense of the term.

In this context it is very interesting to look at what Lacan says about this difference between tragedy and comedy in *Seminar VI* (*Desire and Its Interpretation*—in which he develops his famous interpretation of *Hamlet*). He starts by focusing on a particular aspect of the structure of desire, namely

> the correlation that binds the object and the subject, and on account of which the object has precisely [the] function of signifying the point where the subject cannot name himself, and where modesty [*pudeur*] is the royal form of what, in symptoms, is converted into shame and disgust. Contrary to accepted belief, comedy is what we have of the most profound in the access to the mechanism of the stage, because it allows to human being the spectral decomposition of its standing in the world. Comedy is beyond that modesty. Tragedy ends with the name of the hero, it ends with the hero's total identification. *Hamlet* is Hamlet, he is this name. It is even because his father was already Hamlet that finally everything resolves here, namely that Hamlet is abolished in this desire for ever … But comedy is a very curious desire trap, which is why whenever a desire trap operates, we are in comedy. This is the desire as it appears where one does not expect it. Ridiculous father, hypocritical saint, a virtuous man falling prey to adultery, this is the stuff of comedy. To be sure, there needs to be an element on account of which the desire is not admitted to. It is masked and unmasked, scorned, sometimes punished, but this is only for the sake of the form, because in true comedies the punishment doesn't even touch the wings of the crow of desire, which runs off absolutely intact … In comedy, desire is unmasked, but not refuted.[2]

---

2   Jacques Lacan, (unpublished) lecture from June 3, 1959.

A lot of things could be said about this remarkable passage, but we will focus on just one point here. Namely, what does it mean to say that comedy is "beyond this modesty," that is, beyond the modesty that veils, screens off, something that disturbs our perception of reality and of ourselves as part of this reality? The answer is not as simple as it may seem. It doesn't mean that comedy ignores modesty and disgust and "shows it all," for in that case there would be nothing to prevent us from simply leaving the theater in the affect of disgust. It is thus important to note that whenever troubling or disgusting objects appear in a comedy (as they often do), they appear, for example, as *objects of somebody's desire* or fascination. And this produces a fundamental comical schism, a spectral decomposition that distributes the otherwise linearly superimposed elements so that they can be seen at the same time. This is also the way in which comedy skillfully measures out the right amount of disgust, or shame (or, on a more fundamental level, of anxiety), hence keeping it within the game, and along with it the object in its non-fantasmatic dimension. A fantasmatic object (object of fantasy), on the other hand, could be defined as an object that screens off or veils this object which disrupts all possible identification. In this precise sense, a fantasmatic object is not an object that is not really there, rather, it is an object that helps us believe that something else (some other, disturbing object) is not really there.

In this respect we can indeed see comedy as a machine for measuring out anxiety, administering it in very precise, "just" dosages. This link between comedy and anxiety (for example in the form of the uncanny), especially their often surprising proximity, pointed out by many authors, raises of course the question of their relationship. Instead of seeing comedy as a kind of counter-entity in relation to anxiety, we could perhaps define it precisely as the artistic skill or technique of measuring out anxiety; a technique for keeping the "impossible" object within the scope of desire. Comedy does not appear against the background of anxiety, in the sense of being a relief from it; rather, it is something that *works with* anxiety (or, on a different level, with disgust): we get to laugh at the troubling object, and not simply at, or because of, its successful elimination (which would be a "relief"). "Comic relief" is not to be confused with comedy proper, which has its own inner tension and dialectics.

This is the other, objective facet of what Lacan means when he says that in comedy "desire appears where one does not expect it." There is certainly a movement of unmasking, of tearing off the veil, at work in comedy. Yet if, at the same time, to unmask is not to refute, it is because what is unmasked finds its support in an unexpected appearance of desire, which can then itself begin to function as the principal comic object in the structure of comedy.

Cluny Brown is, among other things, also a showcase for this dynamics of comedy which often moves very close to its own limit or edge. Summaries of the movie like to describe Cluny (Jennifer Jones) as "spontaneous," as a "free spirit, who lives in the moment." Yet this somehow misses the point. Cluny decidedly lacks what one could call the *pathos* of a "free spirit, living in the moment"—the *pathos* encapsulated, for example, in the maxim *Carpe diem!*, "Seize the day!" She certainly doesn't know or see herself as a "free spirit." She is impulsive, and particularly subject to one impulse: fixing the pipes. Whenever there is congestion, a sink that won't drain, a "pipe problem," anything to do with plumbing, her passion takes over and makes her act—inappropriately, out of place, as well as against her best interest. As she herself most succinctly puts it: "You know what plumbing does to me. I just can't keep my hands off it."

And one has to admit that for a love story, a "romantic comedy," the female character has a very strange, bizarre, unromantic passion. It is not, for example, that she wants to be a journalist, a pilot or involved in some other glamorous "male" profession—a configuration often encountered in comedies. Fixing the clogged pipes and relieving the drains—which, moreover, is for her a matter not of ambition, but of uncontrollable passion—does not belong to this category. Her passion is somehow at odds with the very genre in which it appears, a "romantic comedy," where people are supposed to marry at the end. As she again puts it most concisely: "Men just don't marry plumbers." And she finds this out the hard way.

Associated with different kinds of "pipe problems" and their fixing is, of course, the obvious sexual innuendo, and the movie makes a well measured use of it. But what is crucial and most interesting is that these naughty sexual connotations do not so much underline as actually soften and mediate the uncomfortable directness of Cluny's bizarre passion for plumbing. Already, the scene in which Cluny appears for the first time is an excellent example of this.

We are in London and Mr. Ames is giving a Sunday party to which he has invited the cream of society. When his sink gets clogged during the preparations, he desperately tries to get hold of a plumber, but with no success.[3] He also calls Cluny's uncle, who is a plumber but spends his Sundays visiting his late wife's

---

3   In accordance with the proverbial experience thus phrased by Woody Allen: "Not only is there no God, but just try finding a plumber on weekends."

Cluny Brown (Jennifer Jones) and her object. *Cluny Brown*

grave. Mr. Ames sounds so desperate that Cluny, who lives with her uncle, decides to go there on her own and try to fix the clogged sink herself. When she takes a look at it, full of dirty water with the half-rotten remains of food floating in it, she is completely taken in by the sight. Looking at the disgusting sink with the utmost admiration, excitement and joy, she exclaims: "Oh my, what a congestion! It's more stocked up than you sounded. I never thought it'd be as good as this!"

We could say that without the sexual connotations relating it to the more commonplace and familiar framework of desire, the scene would be close to uncomfortable, unpleasant. In other words: Cluny's desire certainly appears where one does not expect it. This desire is unmasked, but not refuted. Her delighted gaze helps us keep our gaze on the disgusting sink. But we can further say that her bizarre desire might have itself become an object of disgust and refutation, were it not intercepted in the movie by another desire, that of Professor Belinski (Charles Boyer) who finds Cluny and her weird passion irresistible. Belinski happens to be in Ames' apartment when Cluny shows up to "relieve the drain," and is fascinated by the scene he witnesses. We'll return to this scene a bit later, but let us first outline the story of the movie.

It takes place in pre-war England (1938/39). Cluny is an orphan. As we've already seen, she lives with her uncle who is a plumber, through whom she has most likely come into contact with the object of her passion. Her impulsive character causes her uncle many worries, and he keeps telling her that she ought to be aware of her place: "Cluny Brown, you don't know your place. Cluny Brown, this is not your place. Cluny Brown, you ought to learn your place." When—in the first scene of the movie, described above—Cluny unclogs the sink at Mr. Ames' apartment, she is so overjoyed at her success that she drinks a couple of cocktails offered to her and falls asleep on the couch. The uncle, arriving shortly after, finds her in this state and refuses to believe Ames' and Belinski's assurances that "nothing happened." He decides that Cluny has to leave London, and sends her to serve as a maid to an aristocratic couple living on a country estate. She is to learn her place there. Belinski, who has stayed at Ames' party after the incident, is recognized by two "politically awakened" young men as a famous Czech "freedom fighter" who has fled Hitler and come to hide out in England. One of the young men arranges for Belinski to stay for a while at his parents' country estate—which turns out to be the very estate to which Cluny has been sent by her uncle. So they meet again there, but, in spite of Belinski's efforts, the romantic aspect of their story is put on hold as Cluny becomes involved in another, quite different, love story.

The main plot of the movie consists of two love stories: one that excludes the impossible object, and one that includes it; one in which love follows a fantasy scenario, and one that involves a different kind of love (a genuine "comic love"). The first is Cluny's relationship with the local pharmacist, Mr. Wilson, whom she falls in love with soon after coming to serve at the country estate. It is enough for the pharmacist to express an interest in (marrying) her, for her to fall fully and genuinely in love. Here, we are clearly on the side of love as fulfillment of a fantasy scenario. The movie shows us this most clearly and skillfully—we could speak of the "ravishing of Cluny Brown," to paraphrase the title of one of Marguerite Duras' famous novels.

In following this love story the movie plays adeptly upon a striking discrepancy between the rather plain reality and Cluny's rapture. Everything related to the pharmacist is extremely boring, suffocating, prejudiced, and rigid. And yet Cluny is *genuinely* swept off her feet by the prospect of finally having a place, finding a home, and finding a mother that she never had. (The pharmacist lives with his mother, and the movie is almost worth seeing for the character of the mother alone, although she only appears twice. If we've always wanted to see how Mrs. Bates—Anthony Perkins' mother from *Psycho* (1960)—looked when she was alive, then this is our chance.)

There is a very powerful scene that takes place when Cluny is invited to the pharmacist's home for the first time, to meet his mother. Again, the whole setting is extremely creepy. The mother doesn't say a single word, but only keeps emitting strange coughing sounds. The pharmacist turns out even more boring and painfully moralistic than expected. (Indeed, as much as Lubitsch shows some indulgence towards the aristocrats in their arrogant stupidity, he has absolutely none for this average, middle-class setting.) And yet, Cluny is shown as being genuinely happy. The scene reaches its climax in a sequence which manages to capture and preserve the whole radical ambiguity of the configuration, without turning it into a simple "comedy." The pharmacist undertakes to play a song on the harmonium. The harmonium is out of tune, the pharmacist plays awfully, and the song is terrible. The mother falls asleep and starts snoring. At the same time, we get a series of close-ups of Cluny listening and watching all this with an expression of rapture, of genuine happiness. Crucially, the scene does not simply play upon the comic contrast between the plain reality and Cluny's idyllic perception of it. Her rapture doesn't simply make us laugh (even if we might be tempted to)—in the way the scene is shot, in the way the camera

Cluny's rapture (Jennifer Jones).
Cluny Brown

actually *supports* Cluny in her rapture, instead of simply revealing her unrealistic perception of the reality, there is something extremely interesting, something which cannot be "laughed off," something that remains in the air, irreducible as it is to any description of positive reality.

Let us now look at how Cluny's idyllic setting nevertheless breaks down—here we are dealing with a textbook example of what fantasy is and how it tends to collapse.

What is really ingenious in the way Lubitsch films this break down is that we can clearly see that the fantasy does not come to be broken subjectively (it is not that Cluny suddenly realizes how awful Mr. Wilson and his mother really are). Rather, the fantasy comes to be broken *objectively*; and this is because—as Lubitsch rightfully suggests—it is also propped up by something objective or object-related. What the fantasy screens-off is not simply the real in the sense of objective reality (at no point does the movie suggest that Cluny has finally become aware of the reality "such as it really is"), but rather some Real of the subject herself, in this case the "unbecoming," out-of-place passion of Cluny Brown. And the fantasy scenario breaks down when this passion unexpectedly reappears at the very peak of her fantasy.

This happens during a small dinner party that Mr. Wilson has organized to celebrate his mother's birthday, and to announce his engagement to Cluny to his friends. In the middle of the dinner, strange loud noises start coming from the bathroom—there is obviously something wrong with the plumbing (and the sounds are also of the kind to suggest, well, gastric problems…). Cluny's passion is instantly awakened; for a few moments she desperately fights the impulse which is obviously too strong for her, then jumps up, proudly announcing that while she may not be the best of cooks, whoever will marry her will not need to worry about his plumbing… Upon which she runs into the bathroom, from where we hear more loud noises (rattling, banging…), until the sounds stop and Cluny returns triumphantly, accompanied by a young boy (the son of one of the visiting couples) who has been watching Cluny work with great admiration. Among Mr. Wilson, his mother, and the rest of the guests the mood is very different—full of silent indignation and embarrassment. Cluny has acted in an utterly improper and unbecoming way, and has thus "humiliated" Wilson and his mother; the guests look at them with pity, wondering if the mother's weak heart will be able to bear this. Coughing loudly, the mother retreats to her room, at which point the guests suddenly "realize" that it is very late. They leave, without so much as a look at Cluny. Cluny stands there utterly confused, not sure what she's done wrong, with her sleeves rolled up and slightly tousled hear. Wilson says sharply, "I wish I haven't seen what I saw," and tells her to make herself presentable. The scene remains heavily uncomfortable to its very end, and Cluny's dreams are obviously over.

So, the Thing happens, appears. And since there is absolutely no support for it in the configuration of people gathered there (except for the little boy who admires Cluny—a hint at infantile sexuality as "polymorphous perversion"?), it appears as an object of disgust. People turn away and leave, and Cluny is forced to realize a couple of things. She realizes that her fantasy is absolutely incompatible with this Thing—and we'll see later how she tries to rationalize this incompatibility in a desperate attempt to save her fantasy. Although we learn later that Mr. Wilson has decided to give her another chance, it is clear that the rapture is over for Cluny, and that if she were nevertheless to "find her place" alongside Mr. Wilson, it would be without the genuine happiness that has existed for her up to this point. If she is to stay on the side of the fantasy, she has to compromise (her desire), yet the paradox and the lesson we learn here is the following: It is not that she can keep her fantasy only at the expense of sacrificing her unusual desire, it is that by doing this, she loses both. In the given circumstances, a compromise is not about having one thing, and giving up another, it rather leads to having neither the one nor the other. To compromise, in this case, is to live with a crushed fantasy. The moment we get the impression that we have to compromise, it's usually already too late (the fantasy for which we think we have to make the sacrifice is already broken). The either/or, the mutual exclusion of the fantasy and of the unacceptable Thing, does not in itself require any sacrifices. And this is because fantasy as such *is already* a successful and fully operative mode of screening the Thing off, it is already the very form of "sacrificing" it. The feeling that we have to compromise and make sacrifices for our fantasy only appears when the latter is already broken. Which is precisely why, at this point, it is already too late and whatever we do now will only make things worse—no sacrifice will be enough.

It is not that we ever get to choose between fantasy and following some other non-fantasmatic object. Whenever fantasy appears, the choice has already been made, and is fully effective. The fantasy is not on display for us to choose it or not. And we are perfectly happy, in spite of what may be the obvious flaws in the situation, which we genuinely don't experience as such. The problem begins when the fantasy scenario starts cracking, breaking down, and we think we can mend it. "If only I did this or that"—such is the formula of this kind of fantasy-mending. It is only here that a choice appears for the first time—a possible alternative to desperately trying to keep the fantasy scenario alive. In this case, the alternative is plumbing ("follow the call of the plumbing," which is like a libidinal compound of Cluny' out-of-placeness). The possible (other) choice for Cluny would thus be to leave with the uninvited surprise-guest that has crashed the party of (her) fantasy. To recognize it as her most joyful, albeit inhuman partner. But how? How is this possible?

This brings us to the other love story in *Cluny Brown*. The chief male protagonist, Professor Adam Belinski, is a Czech refugee. This status of his is of crucial importance in the structure of the movie. Like Cluny, the Professor has no place of his own, he doesn't belong anywhere, his address is "general delivery," and he seems to like it. He isn't looking for a place in life; he is a philosopher (acquainted with psychoanalysis), and it looks like "general delivery" is somewhat in tune with his idea of freedom, which seems to be also the elected object of his studies and concerns. When Belinski and Cluny first meet during the opening sequences of the movie (in Mr. Ames' apartment), he is very fascinated by the fact that she "doesn't seem to be inhibited," as he puts it. Their encounter is of a very different order to the one that binds Cluny to the pharmacist. They "hit it off" immediately, in the midst of Cluny's plumbing activities. He is absolutely taken in by Cluny's weird passion and immediately provides her with something that later proves to be much more solid and reliable than a "place of one's own":

"Relieving the drain": Adam Belinski (Charles Boyer, on the left) provides Cluny (Jennifer Jones, on the right) with the formula at Mr. Ames's apartment (Reginald Gardiner, in the middle). *Cluny Brown*

namely a phrase, a *formula* (a "matheme"), that encapsulates the unexpectedness of her desire. The formula is: "squirrels to the nuts."

While crouched under the sink which she is trying to repair, Cluny joyfully tells Professor Belinski how sometimes things just come over her, and she follows these impulses. She also tells him about how her uncle is constantly reminding her that "she ought to learn her place." Belinski helps her come to the conclusion that since her uncle never tells her what this place actually is, he obviously doesn't know himself. He goes on to say that our place is where we feel happy, and then illustrates his point with the following example: "In Hyde park, for instance, some people like to feed nuts to the squirrels. But if it makes you happy to feed squirrels to the nuts, who am I to say 'nuts to the squirrels!'?"

Cluny is very impressed by this rendering of the nature of her desire, and asks him to say it again. But before he is through repeating it, we hear the loud noise of the drain being relieved. It sounds like a consummation of their encounter, right there, under the sink and the astonished eyes of Mr. Ames. Considering that their conversation bears some resemblance to a psychoanalytic session, the whole thing could also be taken as a sublime rendering of what the "talking cure" is supposedly meant to achieve. To the well-known descriptions "talking cure" and "chimney sweeping" (both referring to the psychoanalytic practice), we could perhaps add a third, derived from plumbing: "relieving the drain." Cluny does the talking and the plumbing, whereas Belinski provides her with a formula of her being-towards-plumbing, if we can be allowed this comic paraphrase of Heidegger's famous being-towards-death.

So there it is: *squirrels to the nuts*. This becomes a kind of codeword between them. It is the very form and substance of their bond, the thing that binds them in the Real so to speak. It is not so much emotions, or fantasy, as this phrase that binds them. For the rest of the movie, almost until its end, their relationship will remain at this: There is a strong and obvious complicity between them, and they enjoy each other's company; the desire is there as well, although in Cluny's case it is disavowed on account of his "not being her type" (the type to provide her with a place in life, we may suppose), whereas he seems to be reluctant to make a more definite move not only because of Cluny's infatuation with Wilson, but also because of his not being exactly the marrying type, as the expression goes.

So, the bond between them is maintained by this formula which is repeated three more times in the movie (once in its reversed, "normal" form). The third and last time it occurs at the critical moment in Cluny's story with the pharmacist, discussed earlier. This is the moment when Cluny is about to give up on her strange desire for plumbing and instead set about mending the fantasy. Meanwhile, Belinski is about to return to London, having come to the conclusion that his efforts with Cluny are in vain, since she has eyes only for Mr. Wilson. He doesn't know how badly the previous evening had turned out for Cluny (when her plumbing passion erupted in the midst of Wilson's party). Before Belinski leaves for the train station, he asks the housekeeper to give Cluny his farewell gift (silk stockings), and a message. He wishes her every happiness. And should she ever feel depressed, she is to close her eyes and say "squirrels to the nuts." Upon receiving the gift and the message, Cluny runs to the train station. There, beside the train, Belinski and Cluny have what looks and sounds like their second and final psychoanalytic session. Belinski lets her speak and makes sure she hears what she is saying. Her speech is full of what I earlier referred to as Cluny's rationalizations (it's not Mr. Wilson's fault, because you see, "Men just don't marry plumbers"; she will have to stop acting foolishly, because "you can't be foolish and have a place in life"; Wilson is going to ask his mother to give her another chance, "that's very kind, isn't it?").

Belinski abstains from commenting, or comforting her. He simply lets her talk and become less and less sure about what she is saying. However, when the whistle blows to signal the imminent departure of the train, Belinski intervenes in a very direct manner. He orders Cluny to get into the train compartment, and she complies without so much as a twitch. Cluny's attitude in this scene is indeed quite strange, her passage from Wilson to Belinski takes place as if she were sleepwalking, in utter passivity, and without psychology. The movie does not attempt to suggest that Cluny has suddenly realized that, deep down, she is really in love with Belinski. She simply enters the train, sits down, and, after a while, asks "Where are we going?" And then she wakes up and gets quite excited by Belinski's answer: "General delivery." And we are already in the midst of another (love) story, following a very different logic than the previous one, and rushing forward to the film's happy ending with the speed of the speeding train.

What is this strange passivity, this *Untergang* or eclipse of the subject, Cluny's not appearing as the subject of this transition? While it could be taken as indicating a conservative view on female passivity, I think that, on the contrary, it is rather a sign of Lubitsch's revolutionary spirit.

But first, what is this transition about? It is a transition from one kind of love story to another, from one framed by the window of fantasy, to a different kind, triggered by a window of opportunity. What do we have in this other story?

It consists of three crucial elements: 1) an odd desire, related to an excessive object (plumbing); 2) a formula that sets the parameters of this desire and binds Cluny to Belinski ("squirrels to the nuts"); 3) an anonymous/general destination for this bonding formula ("general delivery," i.e. it is for everyone's enjoyment). Are not precisely these three elements also the basic elements of comedy at its best? (In this sense *Cluny Brown* is not only a comedy, but also a film about comedy, about the elementary comic structure).

We could also say that the transition from Wilson to Belinski is an instance of precisely what Lacan referred to as "traversing the fantasy." And, from this perspective, Cluny Brown's strange absentness suggests a very direct thesis: that "traversing the fantasy" is not a gradual reform in which the same subjectivity is transformed and thoroughly changed. Rather, it involves the termination of one subject and the possible emergence of another, new one (with no psychological continuity to speak of). There is a leap, a blank, not covered by any kind of subjectivity (in process of transformation). The only "sameness" in Cluny before and after she boards the train is the sameness of her unusual passion, of the object which has also caused her fantasy to fall apart; but the subject is not "the same, only transformed," and there is no continuity leading from one to another (except, that is, for the insistence of the "plumbing drive"). The second subject emerges when Cluny seizes the window of opportunity to follow the latter also subjectively, *within* the configuration of desire. (She gets subjectivized in the relation to this object, and not in the figure of desire as based on its exclusion.)

There is something involved here that we could call "Lubitschean chivalry," not to be confused with a conservative view on sexual roles and positions. In Lubitsch, men rescue women, and vice versa. But they don't rescue them from physical danger. They don't rescue them from being dishonored or disgraced. The only danger that men can rescue women from (and vice versa) is the danger of giving up on their desire, to use the famous Lacanian formula (*ne pas céder sur son désir*). It is not that women lack the courage or strength. According to Lubitsch (and comedy generally) to not give up on your desire is always-already an "objective" configuration, it is not simply a personal (subjective) matter.

So let us briefly stop at this Lacanian ethical formula, which he proposes in his reading of Antigone: *ne pas céder sur son désir*. In his later work Lacan more or less abandoned this formula and its heroic overtones, going so far as to suggest that what is at stake in this configuration is actually the "supreme narcissism of a lost cause." I would maintain, however, that there nevertheless remains something valid and valuable in the formula, and that this something comes to light when we move from tragedy to comedy—for what changes in this passage is precisely (the nature of) the configuration of desire at stake.

In conclusion, let me try to sketch out very briefly what this change or difference is all about. In its tragic paradigm "to not give up on your desire" is a subjective and *solitary* business. It is an heroic enterprise of fidelity ("to a lost cause"), carried out by a subject in the unbroken continuity of her will and determination. This fidelity manifests itself in the fact that nothing comes close to the lost thing, which functions only as a firm criterion of elimination, leading us to conclude of each and every particular thing that "This is not IT."

In comedy, on the other hand, it is clear that to "not give up on your desire" is something more objective than subjective. It involves an interruption of the subject, her "absentness" triggered precisely by an unexpected emergence of this "IT" (as the impossible object). At the same time, and precisely because of this interruption, this discontinuity of the subject, it cannot be a solitary business, something that a subject can carry out all by herself. We could say: to not give up on your desire takes (at least) two. We need a little help with this—from, for instance, someone who helps us get on the train at the right moment. Had there been no Mr. Belinski at the train station, Cluny might have ended up under the train, and so would have her unorthodox desire. This would perhaps have been more "realistic." But the mission of comedy is not about this kind of realism; it is not about saving or not saving Cluny Brown, it is about not giving up on this surplus object, which not only drives the comedy, but is also the key to our objective, (un)human "standing in the world." And if this entails saving Cluny Brown, so be it! If tragedy ultimately sacrifices the subject to save this precious object, this thing in the subject (worth) more than the subject,[4] then comedy is not something that simply reverses the order of values here (to suggest that we are in fact worth more than this thing). It rather suggests that this (inhuman) thing is precisely what makes us worth saving. Here we come across the radical comical edge: Cluny's survival is, so to speak, the collateral damage that comes with saving "her" object. And this is precisely where the anti-humanism of the Lubitschean comedy hits the nerve of what it means to be human, or a human being.

---

4   Recall the famous Lacanian rendering of this structure: "I love you, but, because inexplicably I love in you something more than you—the *objet petit a*—I mutilate you." Jacques Lacan, *The Four Fundamental Concepts of Psychoanalysis*, trans. Alan Sheridan (New York: W.W. Norton & Co., 1981), 268.

SLAVOJ ŽIŽEK

Lubitsch, The Poet of Cynical Wisdom?

Needing a short break from his dull Messianic work of preaching and performing miracles, Jesus decided to go for a round of golf with one of his disciples on the shore of the Galilean sea. Faced with a particularly difficult shot, Jesus botched it and the ball ended up in the sea. Undeterred, he walked across the water (his standard trick) to where the ball had dropped, reached down and picked it up. As he teed up to try again, the disciple warned him that it was a very tricky shot that only someone like Tiger Woods could hope to pull off. Jesus replied, "What the hell, I'm the son of God, I can do anything a miserable mortal like Woods can do!," and took another strike. Again, the ball ended up in the sea, and again Jesus took to walking on the water to retrieve it. At this point, a group of American tourists passing by turned to the disciple and said, "My God, who does that guy think he is? Jesus Christ?" To which the disciple replied, "No, he thinks he's Tiger Woods." This, then, is how fantasmatic identification works: no one, not even God himself, is directly what he is—even God needs an external decentered point of identification in some minimal fantasy scenario.

The filmmaker whose opus consists of multiple variations on this kind of decentering is Ernst Lubitsch. The theme of a decentered fantasy sustaining a sexual relationship takes a weird turn in his *Broken Lullaby* (1932—the film's original title, *The Man I Killed*, was initially changed to *The Fifth Commandment* to avoid creating "wrong impressions in the minds of the public about the character of the story," before ultimately being released as *Broken Lullaby*). Here is an outline of the story: French musician Paul Renard is haunted by the memory

Improbable family happiness in *Broken Lullaby*.

of Walter Holderlin, a German soldier he killed during World War I. A priest encourages him to visit the dead man's grave and family in Germany. Mindful of the anti-French sentiment that continues to permeate Germany, Dr. Holderlin initially refuses to welcome Paul in his home. At that moment, Walter's fiancée Elsa recognizes Paul as the man leaving flowers on Walter's grave. Rather than reveal the real connection between them, Paul tells the Holderlins that he was a friend of Walter's from their days studying at the same musical conservatory (he learned about Walter's violin in the letter which he found on his body). Although the hostile townspeople and local gossips disapprove, the Holderlins befriend Paul, who duly falls in love with Elsa. However, when she shows Paul her former fiancé's bedroom, he becomes distraught and tells her the truth. She convinces him not to confess to Walter's parents, who have embraced him as their second son, and Paul agrees to forego easing his conscience and stay with his adopted family. Dr. Holderlin presents him with Walter's violin which, in the film's final scene, Paul plays while Elsa accompanies him on the piano, both observed by the loving gazes of the parental couple… No wonder that Pauline Kael dismissed the film, claiming that Lubitsch "mistook drab, sentimental hokum for ironic, poetic tragedy."[1]

There is something disturbing in the film, a weird oscillation between poetic melodrama and obscene humor. The couple (of the girl and the killer of her

---

[1]   Pauline Kael, *5001 Nights at the Movies* (New York: Macmillan, 1991), 107.

fiancé) are happily united under the protective gaze of the fiancé's parents—it is this gaze that provides the fantasy frame for their relationship, and the obvious question is: are they really doing it just for the sake of the parents, or is this gaze an excuse for them to engage in sex? This obvious question is, of course, a false one, because it doesn't matter which of the alternatives is true: even if the parents' gaze is just an excuse for sex, it is still a necessary excuse.

This same decentering sustains one of the most efficient jokes in Lubitsch's absolute masterpiece *To Be or Not to Be* (1942). The Polish actor Joseph Tura impersonates Colonel Ehrhardt of the Gestapo in conversation with a high-level Polish collaborator. In (what we take as) a ridiculously exaggerated way, he comments on rumors about himself—"So they call me Concentration-Camp-Ehrhardt?"—accompanying his words with a vulgar laughter. A little later, Tura has to escape and the real Ehrhardt arrives; when the conversation again touches on the rumors about him, the real Ehrhardt reacts in exactly the same ridiculously exaggerated way as did his impersonator. The message is clear: even Ehrhardt himself is not immediately himself, he also imitates his own copy or, more precisely, the ridiculous idea of himself. While Tura acts him, Ehrhardt acts himself.

The Shop Around the Corner (1940) deals with this decentering in the guise of overlapping fantasies. Set in a Budapest store, it tells the story of co-workers Klara Novak and Alfred Kralik who, though they dislike each other intensely, are maintaining an anonymous letter-writing relationship with each other, neither of them realizing who their pen-pal is. They duly fall in love via their correspondence, while being hostile and peevish towards one another in real life. (The more recent Hollywood hit *You've Got Mail* (1998) was a remake of *The Shop Around the Corner* for the email era. One might also mention here a curious incident which took place a couple of years ago in—of all places—Sarajevo: a husband and wife were both involved in an intense email love affair with an anonymous partner; only when they decided to meet in the flesh did they discover that they had been flirting with each other all along... Was the final outcome then a happy rejuvenated marriage, now they had discovered that they were each other's dream partner? Probably not—such a realization of one's dreams as a rule turns into a nightmare.)

The lesson of such decentering is simply that, in a love relationship, we are never alone with our partner: we are always playing a role for a foreign gaze, imagined or real. It is in this direction that we should re-read Lacan's text on logical time, where he provides a brilliant interpretation of the logical puzzle of the three prisoners.[2] What is not so well-known is that the original form of this puzzle comes from the era of eighteenth-century French libertinage, with its mixture of sex and cold logic (which culminates in Sade).[3] In this sexualized version, the governor of a woman's prison has decided that he will give an amnesty to one of the three prisoners; the winner will be decided by a test of her intelligence. The three women will be placed in a triangle around a large circular table, each naked from the waist down and leaning forward on the table to enable penetration *a tergo*. Each woman will then be penetrated from behind by either a black man or a white man, so she will only be able to see the color of the men who are penetrating the other two women. All that she will know is that there are only five men available to the governor for this experiment, three white and two black. Given these constraints, the winner will be the first woman to establish the skin color of the man fucking her, pushing him away and leaving the room. There are three possible scenarios here, of increasing complexity:

In the first scenario, there are two black men and one white man fucking the women. Since the woman being fucked by a white man knows that there are only two black men in the pool, she can immediately rise and leave the room.

In the second scenario, one black man and two white men are doing the fucking. The two women fucked by the white men can thus see one white man and one black man. The woman fucked by a black man can see two white men, but—since there are three white men in the pool—she also cannot immediately rise. The only way for a winner to emerge in this case is if one of the two women being fucked by a white man reasons as follows: "I can see one white man and one black man, so the guy fucking me might be white or black. However, if my fucker was black, the woman in front of me being fucked by a white man would see two black men and immediately conclude that her fucker was white—she would have stood up and moved immediately. But she hasn't done this, so my fucker must be white."

In the third scenario, each of the three women is being fucked by a white man, so that each of them sees two other white men. Each can accordingly reason in the same mode as the winner in case 2, in the following way: "I can see two white men, so the man fucking me may be white or black. But if mine was black,

2   See Jacques Lacan, "Logical Time and the Assertion of Anticipated Certainty," in *Écrits* (New York: W. W. Norton, 2006), 161–75.
3   Since we live in times increasingly bereft of even an elementary sense of irony, I feel obliged to add that this sexualized version is in fact my own invention.

either of the two others could reason (as the winner in case 2 does): 'I can see a black man and a white man. So if my fucker was black, the woman fucked by a white man would see two black men and immediately conclude that her fucker was white and leave. But she hasn't done this. So my fucker must be white? But since neither of the other two has stood up, my fucker must not be black, but white too."

But here enters the logical time proper. If all three women were of equal intelligence and indeed arose at the same time, this would cast each of them into a radical uncertainty about who is fucking them—why? Because each woman could not know whether the other two women have stood up as a result of going through the same reasoning process she has gone through, since she was being fucked by a white man; or whether each had reasoned as the winner in the second scenario had, because she was being fucked by a black man. The winner will be the first woman to interpret this indecision correctly and jump to the conclusion that it indicates that all three are being fucked by white men.

The consolation prize for the other two women is that at least they will be fucked to the end, a fact that becomes significant the moment one takes note of the political overdetermination surrounding the choice of this particular group of men: among upper-class ladies in mid-eighteenth-century France, black men were, of course, socially unacceptable as sexual partners, but were nonetheless coveted as secret lovers because of their alleged higher potency and extra-large penises. Consequently, being fucked by a white man entails socially acceptable but ultimately unsatisfying sex, while being fucked by a black man entails socially inadmissible but much more satisfying sex. This choice is, however, more complex than it may appear, since, in sexual activity, *the fantasy gaze observing us is always there*. The message of the logical puzzle thus becomes more ambiguous: what the three women observing each other while having sex have to establish is not simply "Who is fucking me, a black guy or a white guy?" but rather, "What am I for the Other's gaze while I am being fucked?," as if their very identity is established through this gaze. And this brings us back to *Broken Lullaby*, where the implicit question raised by the couple at the film's end is precisely: "What are we for the parents' gaze while we are fucking?"

This *decentering* is, of course, not enough to circumscribe the so-called Lubitsch touch—what one must add is a feature most clearly discernible in his *Design for Living* (1933), based on a play by Noël Coward. "Trouble in Paradise," the title of a film made by Lubitsch a year earlier, is actually a much better fit for the story of

Design for Living: Commercial artist Gilda Farrell works for advertising executive Max Plunkett, who tries in vain to seduce her. On a train to Paris, she meets artist George Curtis and playwright Thomas Chambers, fellow Americans who share an apartment there; they both fall in love with her. Unable to choose between the two, Gilda proposes to live with them as a friend, muse, and critic—on the understanding they will not have sex. However, when Tom goes to London to oversee the staging of his play, Gilda and George become involved romantically. After his return to Paris, Tom discovers that George is in Nice painting a portrait, and uses the opportunity to seduce Gilda himself. When the three meet again, Gilda orders both men out and decides to end their rivalry by marrying Max in New York; but when she receives potted plants as a wedding gift from Tom and George she is so upset that she fails to consummate the marriage. When Max hosts a party for his advertising clients in New York, Tom and George crash the event and hide in Gilda's bedroom. Max finds the three of them laughing on the bed and orders the men out. In the ensuing brawl, Gilda announces that she is leaving her husband, and she, Tom, and George decide to return to Paris and their previous *ménage à trois*.

What then is the trouble that occurs in the paradise of the happy *ménage à trois*? Is it the monogamous marriage, which introduces the dimension of the Fall, of Law and its transgression, into the happy prelapsarian promiscuity, or is it the competitive jealousy of the two men, which disturbs the peace and forces Gilda to escape into marriage? Is the film's conclusion then "better a little trouble in paradise than happiness in the hell of marriage"? Whichever is the answer, the ending stages a return to paradise, so that the overall result can be paraphrased in G. K. Chesterton's terms: marriage itself is the most sensational of departures and the most romantic of rebellions. When the couple proclaim their marriage vows, alone and somewhat fatuously fearless amid the multiple temptations to promiscuous pleasure, it certainly does serve to remind us that marriage is the original and poetic figure, while cheaters and participants in orgies are merely placid old cosmic conservatives, happy in the immemorial respectability of promiscuous apes and wolves. The marriage vow is based on the fact that marriage is the most dark and daring of conspiracies.[4]

In 1916, when Lenin's (at that point ex-) mistress Inessa Armand wrote him that even a fleeting passion was more poetic and cleaner than kisses without love between man and woman, he replied: "Kisses without love between vulgar spouses

---

4   Cf. G. K. Chesterton, "A Defense of Detective Stories," in H. Haycraft (ed.), *The Art of the Mystery Story* (New York: The Universal Library, 1946), 6.

are filthy. I agree. These need to be contrasted … with what? … It would seem: kisses with love. But you contrast 'a fleeting (why a fleeting) passion (why not love?)'—and it comes out logically as if kisses without love (fleeting) are contrasted to marital kisses without love … This is odd."[5] Lenin's reply is usually dismissed as proof of his personal petit-bourgeois sexual constraints, sustained by his bitter memory of the past affair; but there is more to it than this: namely, the insight that the marital "kisses without love" and the extramarital "fleeting affair" are two sides of the same coin—both shirk from *combining* the Real of an unconditional passionate attachment with the form of symbolic proclamation. The implicit presupposition (or, rather, injunction) of the standard ideology of marriage is that, precisely, there should be no love in it: one gets married in order to cure oneself of the excessive passionate attachment, to replace it with boring daily custom (and if one cannot resist passion's temptation, there are extra-marital affairs…).

From the very beginning of his career, Lubitsch was well aware of these complications pertaining to the formula "trouble in paradise." In his first masterpiece, *The Doll* (*Die Puppe*, 1919), the Baron of Chanterelle demands that his nephew Lancelot get married to preserve the family line. A skittish and effeminate fellow, Lancelot does not wish to marry, so when his uncle presents him with 40 enthusiastic brides, he hides out with a group of monks. The gluttonous monks learn about Lancelot's potential cash reward for his nuptials, so they cook up a plan: since Lancelot does not want to marry a real "dirty" woman, he can marry a doll. However, after the toymaker Hilarius finishes making the doll, her arms are accidentally broken; in order not to lose the reward, the monks convince Ossi, Hilarius's daughter, to take the place of the doll and pretend to be artificial. The wedding ceremony is a success, Ossi plays her role well, Lancelot gets the promised money from the Baron and returns with his bride to the monastery where he falls asleep in his cell and dreams that Ossi is alive, not a doll. When he awakens, Ossi tells him that she really is alive, but Lancelot only believes her when she cries out in fear upon seeing a mouse. They both promptly escape from the monastery and enter a forest, where they embrace and kiss passionately. In the meantime, his hair having gone grey from worry, Hilarius is desperately looking for his daughter; when he finally locates the couple, they show him their marriage certificate— they are properly married, this time as real persons. When Hilarius sees this his worries are over and his hair goes dark again… Surprisingly, we can discern here

---

5   Quoted from Robert Service, *Lenin* (London: Macmillan, 2000), 232.

the motif of remarriage which characterizes later Hollywood screwball comedies: the first marriage is without true love, an opportunistic marriage with a doll; only the second marriage is the true one.

At the film's beginning, we see Lubitsch himself behind a miniature of the film's set: he begins by unpacking a toy box, first placing its wedge-shaped landscape atop a table, then attaching a cabin, trees, a white background and a small bench to the base. After placing a pair of wooden dolls in the house, Lubitsch cuts for the first time to a full-size facsimile of the toy set with the two human figures stepping out of the cabin. This artificiality characterizes the film's entire set design and costuming: paper trees, a cut-out moon, a horse replaced with two people under a black sheet, etc. Lubitsch thus directly presents the film as a product of his manipulation, reducing the film's human subjects to inanimate objects (dolls) and positing himself as the puppet master of his actors-marionettes. Here, however, one has to avoid the trap of a simple humanist reading that would oppose woman as a mere doll (mechanically obeying male whims) to a "real" living woman. What does a puppet (more precisely: a marionette) stand for as a subjective stance? We can turn here to Heinrich von Kleist's essay *Über das Marionettentheater* from 1810,[6] which is crucial with regard to his relationship to Kant's philosophy (we know that reading Kant threw Kleist into a shattering spiritual crisis—this reading was *the* traumatic encounter of his life). Where, in Kant, do we find the term "Marionette"? In a mysterious subchapter of his *Critique of Practical Reason* entitled "Of the Wise Adaptation of Man's Cognitive Faculties to His Practical Vocation," in which he endeavors to answer the question of what would happen to us were we to gain access to the noumenal domain, to the *Ding an sich*:

> instead of the conflict which now the moral disposition has to wage with inclinations and in which, after some defeats, moral strength of mind may be gradually won, God and eternity in their awful majesty would stand unceasingly before our eyes ... Thus most actions conforming to the law would be done from fear, few would be done from hope, none from duty. The moral worth of actions, on which alone the worth of the person and even of the world depends in the eyes of supreme wisdom, would not exist at all. The conduct of man, so long as his nature remained as it is now, would be changed into mere mechanism, where, as in a puppet show, everything would gesticulate well but no life would be found in the figures.[7]

---

6   Reprinted in Vol. 5 of *Heinrich von Kleist. dtv Gesamtausgabe* (München: dtv, 1969).
7   Immanuel Kant, *Critique of Practical Reason* (New York: Macmillan, 1956), 152–3.

More than a woman: the doll (Ossi Oswalda), with her timid "master" Lancelot (Hermann Thimig).
Die Puppe

So, for Kant, direct access to the noumenal domain would deprive us of the very "spontaneity" which forms the kernel of transcendental freedom: it would turn us into lifeless automata, or, to contemporary terms, into "thinking machines."— What Kleist does is to present the *obverse* of this horror: the bliss and grace of marionettes, of those creatures who have direct access to the noumenal divine dimension, who are *directly* guided by it. For Kleist, marionettes display the perfection of spontaneous, unconscious movements: they have only one center of gravity, their movements are controlled from only one point. The puppeteer has control only of this point, and as he moves it in a simple straight line, the limbs of the marionette follow inevitably and naturally because the figure of the marionette is completely coordinated. Marionettes thus symbolize beings of an innocent, pristine nature: they respond naturally and gracefully to divine guidance, in contrast to ordinary humans who have to struggle constantly with their ineradicable propensity to Evil, which is the price they have to pay for their freedom. This grace of the marionettes is underscored by their apparent weightlessness: they hardly touch the ground—they are not bound to the earth, for they are held up from above. They represent a state of grace, a paradise lost to man whose willful "free" self-assertions make him self-conscious. The dancer exemplifies this fallen state of man: he is not upheld from above, but feels himself bound to the earth, and yet must appear weightless in order to perform his feats with apparent ease. He must try consciously to attain grace, which is why the effect of his dance is affectation rather than grace. Therein resides the paradox of man: he is neither an animal wholly immersed in his earthly surroundings, nor an angelic marionette floating gracefully in the air, but a free being who, thanks to his very freedom, feels the unbearable pressure that attracts and ties him to the earth where, ultimately, he does *not* belong. It is in terms of this tragic split that we should read figures like Kaetchen von Heilbronn from Kleist's play of the same name, this fairy-tale figure of a woman who wanders through life with angelic equanimity: like a marionette, she is guided from above and fulfils her glorious destiny merely by following the spontaneous assertions of her heart.—Against this background then, new light can be thrown upon the Lubitsch motif of "trouble in paradise":

What is the nature of the Lubitschean comic object? One hint may be discerned from an aphorism by Emil Cioran: "I ponder C., for whom drinking in a café was the sole reason to exist. One day when I was eloquently vaunting Buddhism to him, he replied, 'Well, yes, nirvana, all right, but not without a café.'" For Cioran's colleague, the café is the "troublesome object" which both disturbs the peacefulness of paradise and, through this very disturbance, renders it bearable. One could reiterate, "Well, yes, paradise is wonderful, but only on one condition: the odd detail that messes it up." This would also seem to be Lubitsch's underlying message, that the trouble *in* paradise is also the trouble *with* paradise: imbalance and disharmony are the very soul of desire, so that the object of desire is what embodies this turbulence rather than putting a "happy end" to it.[8]

One should nonetheless add to this general point (about the odd detail that disturbs the harmonious order as the cause of desire) a more specific turn of the screw: the true trouble in paradise is the very fall from the state of grace (that characterizes the doll) to the ordinary human life of mortal passions. In other words, the move from doll to real woman is a fall, not a growth towards maturity. The point is thus not that women should stop playing stupid sexy dolls for the sake of men and act like real women—the detour through the doll figure is a necessary one, as it is only against the background of such a figure, i.e., as a fall from it, that the "real" woman can emerge.

No wonder *Die Puppe* echoes "The Sandman," one of the best known of Hoffmann's tales about a poet falling in love with a beauty who turns out to be a doll: the three most famous tales (brought together in Offenbach's opera) render precisely the three principal modes of the failure of a sexual relationship—the woman either turns out to be a mechanical doll (Olympia), or she prefers her vocation to love and dies singing (Antonia), or she is simply a promiscuous cheater (Giulietta). (And, as Offenbach's opera makes it clear, all three adventures are fantasies of Hoffmann, ways to postpone or avoid the encounter with his actual love.) This brings us back to *Trouble in Paradise*, Lubitsch's first *absolute* masterpiece and, one should never forget, the first part of his *political* trilogy:

> If *Ninotchka* is a film about communism and *To Be or Not to Be* about fascism, *Trouble in Paradise* is a comic treatment of the worst economic crisis the world has seen, the Great Depression. These three films, the most socially conscious in Lubitsch's oeuvre, form a kind of trilogy which deals with the crisis of capitalism and its two historic solutions: fascism and communism.[9]

---

8   Aaron Schuster, "Comedy in Times of Austerity," in this volume, 27–8.
9   Ibid., 29.

The lyrics of the song heard during the opening credits offer a definition of the "trouble" alluded to (as does the image that accompanies the song: first we see the words "Trouble in," then beneath these words a large double bed appears, and then, over the bed in large letters, "Paradise"). So "paradise" is the paradise of a full sexual relationship: "That's paradise / while arms entwine and lips are kissing / but if there's something missing / that signifies / trouble in paradise." To put it in a brutally direct way, "trouble in paradise" is thus Lubitsch's name for the fact that *il n'y a pas de rapport sexuel*. Perhaps this brings us to what the Lubitsch touch represents at its most elementary—an ingenious way of making this failure work. That is to say, instead of reading the fact that there is no sexual relationship as a traumatic obstacle on account of which every love affair has to end in some kind of tragic failure, this very obstacle can be turned into a comic resource, can function as something to be circumvented, alluded to, played with, exploited, manipulated, made fun of ... in short, sexualized. Sexuality is here an exploit which thrives on its own ultimate failure.

So where is the trouble in paradise in *Trouble in Paradise*? As has been noted by perspicuous critics, there is a fundamental (and irreducible) ambiguity surrounding this key point, an ambiguity which echoes that in *Design for Living*. The first answer that imposes itself is that although Gaston loves Lily as well as Mariette, the true "paradisiacal" sexual relationship would have been the one with Mariette, which is why it is this relationship that has to remain impossible/unfulfilled. This unfulfilment confers a touch of melancholy on the film's ending: all the laughter and boisterousness, all the merry display of partnership between Gaston and Lily as they exchange their stolen goods, only fills in the void of this melancholy. Does Lubitsch not point in this direction with the repeated shot of the big empty double bed in Mariette's house, a shot which recalls the empty bed of the film's opening credits? What about the poignant romantic exchange between Gaston and Mariette when he leaves her—"It could have been glorious." "Lovely." "Divine..."? It is all too easy to read the excessive romantic sentimentality of this parting scene as a parody, as a case of the characters directly acting as actors, reciting the lines they have learned. Undoubtedly there is an ironic distance in this scene, but it is a properly Mozartean irony: it is not the excessive romantic passion which conceals the ironic distance, it is the appearance of ironic distance itself, the ridicule of the sentimental scene, which conceals the utter seriousness of the situation. In short, the two (prospective) lovers are play-acting in order to obfuscate the Real of their passion.

There is, however, also the possibility of the exact opposite reading:

> Could it be that paradise is actually the scandalous love affair of Gaston and Lily, two chic thieves fending for themselves, and trouble is the sublimely statuesque Mariette? That, in a tantalizing irony, Mariette is the snake luring Gaston from his blissfully sinful Garden of Eden? … Paradise, the good life, is the life of crime full of glamour and risks, and evil temptation comes in the form of Madame Colet, whose wealth holds the promise of an easy-going *dolce vita* without real criminal daring or subterfuge, only the humdrum hypocrisy of the respectable classes.[10]

The beauty of this reading is that paradisiacal innocence is located in the glamorous and dynamic life of crime, so that the Garden of Eden is equated with that life while the call of high society respectability is equated with the snake's temptation. However, this paradoxical reversal is easily explained by Gaston's sincere and raw outburst, enacted with no elegance or ironic distance, the first and only one in the film, after Mariette refuses to call the police when he tells her that the chairman of the board of her company has for years been systematically stealing millions from her. Gaston's reproach is that, while Mariette was immediately ready to call the police when an ordinary burglar like him steals from her a comparatively small amount of wealth, she is ready to turn a blind eye when a member of her own respectable class steals millions. Is Gaston here not paraphrasing Brecht's famous question "What is the robbing of a bank compared to the founding of a bank"? What are direct robberies like those of Gaston and Lily compared to the theft of millions through obscure financial operations?

There is, however, another aspect which has to be noted here: is Gaston's and Lily's life of crime really so "full of glamour and risks"? Beneath all the surface glamour and risk, are they not

> a quintessential bourgeois couple, conscientious professional types with expensive tastes— yuppies before their time. Gaston and Mariette, on the other hand, are the really romantic pair, the adventurous and risk-taking lovers. In returning to Lily and lawlessness, Gaston is doing the sensible thing—returning to his "station," as it were, opting for the mundane life he knows. And he does so with full regret, apparent in his lingering final exchange with Mariette, full of rue and stylish ardor on both sides.[11]

---

10   In this volume, 28, 34.
11   James Harvey, *Romantic Comedy in Hollywood from Lubitsch to Sturges* (New York: Da Capo Press, 1998), 56.

This brings us back to Chesterton, and the already-mentioned passage from his famous "Defense of Detective Stories" in which he notes how the detective story in some sense keeps before the mind the fact that civilization itself is the most sensational of departures and the most romantic of rebellions:

> When the detective in a police romance stands alone, and somewhat fatuously fearless amid the knives and fists of a thief's kitchen, it does certainly serve to make us remember that it is the agent of social justice who is the original and poetic figure, while the burglars and foot-pads are merely placid old cosmic conservatives, happy in the immemorial respectability of apes and wolves... [The police romance is thus] based on the fact that morality is the most dark and daring of conspiracies.[12]

Does this not also offer the best description of Gaston and Lily? Are these two burglars not "placid old cosmic conservatives, happy in the immemorial respectability of apes and wolves," i.e., living in their paradise before the fall into ethical passion? What is crucial here is the parallel between crime (theft) and sexual promiscuity: what if, in our postmodern world of ordained transgression, in which marital commitment is perceived as ridiculously anachronistic, those who cling to it are the true subversives? What if, today, straight marriage is "the most dark and daring of all transgressions"? As we have already seen, this is exactly the underlying premise of Lubitsch's *Design for Living*: a woman leads a calm and satisfied life with two men; as a dangerous experiment she tries single marriage; the attempt fails miserably and she returns to the safety of living with the two men—the participants in this *ménage à trois* are "placid old cosmic conservatives, happy in the immemorial respectability of apes and wolves." Exactly the same thing happens in *Trouble in Paradise*, wherein the true temptation is the respectful marriage of Gaston and Mariette.[13]

---

12 Chesterton, "A Defense of Detective Stories," 6.

13 Aaron Schuster has pointed out the Hitchcockian object in *Trouble in Paradise*: Mariette's expensive purse which circulates between the principal figures (Mariette, Gaston, Lily), embodying their intersubjective tension and imbalance, similarly to Poe's purloined letter (in this volume, 37). However, in contrast to Poe and Hitchcock in whose work the letter does reach its destination (returns to its proper place)—say, at the very end of *Strangers on a Train* (1951), Guy gets back his cigarette lighter—in *Trouble in Paradise* the object does *not* get back to its rightful owner (it is again stolen by Lily). It would be all too easy to take this as proof of Lubitsch's subversive dimension, as an indication that he rejects narrative closure (established when the object returns to its proper place); we should rather risk a move which may appear naive and instead read the fact that the purse does not return to its proper place as a melancholic reminder and remainder of a loss which persists in the merry atmosphere of the film's ending.

But, again, there is a further complication here. We should always bear in mind that first impressions do not deceive, in spite of the numerous proverbs and wisdoms that try to convince us otherwise (in the style of "I fell in love at first sight—what should I do?" "Take another look!"). It is the first impression which, as a rule, provides the encounter with the object in the freshness of the Real, and it is the function of second impressions to obfuscate and domesticate this encounter. What cannot but strike us on a first encounter with the finale of *Trouble in Paradise* is the sudden, "psychologically unconvincing and unfounded" reversal of the subjective position of Gaston and Lily: after the ultra-romantic sad farewell between Gaston and Mariette, we are all of a sudden thrown into the screwball universe of Gaston and Lily, a couple of thieves exchanging witty repartees, lovingly making fun of each other, mischievously penetrating each other's clothes, and clearly fully enjoying each other's presence. How to account for the thorough emotional dissonance between these two closing scenes? How come the preceding sad farewell leaves no bitter aftertaste? The easy explanation would be that the sad farewell scene is a fake, a cynical performance which should not be taken seriously. Such a reading, however, would flatten the emotional dissonance, leaving no space for obviously sincere moments like Lily's earlier expression of cynical despair or Gaston's outburst about the hypocrisy of the rich. We must therefore fully embrace the "psychologically unfounded" reversal of tone from pathos to comedy—what does it indicate?

Let us make a (perhaps unexpected) detour. At the end of Howard Hawks' classic Western *Red River* (1948), another "psychologically unfounded" twist occurs which is usually dismissed as a simple weakness in the scenario. The entire film moves towards the climactic confrontation between Dunson and Matt—a duel of almost mythic proportions, predestined by fate, as an inexorable conflict between two incompatible subjective stances. In the final scene, Dunson approaches Matt with the determinacy of a tragic hero blinded by hatred and marching towards his ruin. The brutal fist fight which ensues ends unexpectedly when Tess, who is in love with Matt, fires a gun into the air and shouts at the two men that "any fool with half a mind can see that you two love each other"—a quick reconciliation follows, with Dunson and Matt talking like buddies. This "transition of Dunson from anger incarnate, all Achilles all the time, to sweetness and light, happily yielding to Matt ... is breathtaking in its rapidity."[14] Robert Pip-

---

14   Robert Pippin, *Hollywood Western and American Myth* (New Haven: Yale University Press, 2010), 52.

pin is fully justified in detecting beneath this technical weakness in the scenario a deeper message, the same message uncovered by Alenka Zupančič in her reading of the final moments of Lubitsch's *Cluny Brown* (1946).[15] After the lively dialogue between the Professor and Cluny at the train station, the Professor simply orders her to get into the carriage with him (implying that they will get married and live together), and she obeys without a moment's hesitation. The Professor's order can be read as a case of successful psychoanalytic intervention: it brings about in the analysand (Cluny) a radical subjective transformation that cannot be accounted for in psychological terms.

Similarly, as was noted by Russell Grigg,[16] Lily's unexpected and apparently nonsensical moves towards the end of *Trouble in Paradise* display the same quality of an analytic intervention. How does Lily get Gaston back? It is again all too easy merely to oppose the romantic couple (Gaston-Mariette) to the vivacity of the risky pragmatic partnership (Gaston-Lily). To paraphrase Marx, the secret lies in the form itself, in the apparently nonsensical and repetitive circulation of money between Mariette and Lily. Lily proceeds in three moves, which effectively form a nice Hegelian triad. First, in a moment of cynical realism, she steals the 100,000 francs from Mariette's hidden safe in front of Gaston, declaring hysterically that money is the only thing that matters, that everything else is just empty sentimentality. Then—her second move—she throws the cash back on Mariette's bed, in a gesture of pride, renouncing the money out of fidelity to ethical principles: "I don't want your money, you can have my man for free, you already bought him cheaply and he deserves you!" But what makes Gaston return to her is not this "ethical turn", i.e., her renunciation of her initial cynical realism, since she then makes her third move: taking the money back and running away with it. The key here lies in the repetition of the same gesture (stealing the money), which acquires the second time a totally different, even opposite, meaning: Lily gets Gaston back by again *taking* the money, not, as one might have expected, just by throwing it back at Mariette and in this way proving her sincerity. Lily's second move resembles the so-called empty gesture, the gesture meant to be rejected: she returns the money only to take it away again. Why does the money have to be taken (stolen) twice? The first theft is a simple act of cynical despair: "OK, I've got it, you love Mariette, so let's forget the sentimentality, I will act as a cold realist."

---

15   In this volume, 177–8.
16   Ibid., 61.

The second theft, however, changes the entire terrain: it repeats the "egotist" act within the field of ethics, i.e., it suspends the ethical (sacrifice of material goods), but does not return to an immediate cynical realism/egotism—in short, it does something similar to Kierkegaard's religious suspension of the ethical. With the second theft, Lily sets Gaston free: her taking the money plays the same role as does the payment of the psychoanalyst; its message is "by accepting money I am out of the game, there are no symbolic debts between us, I renounce all moral blackmail, it's up to you now whether to choose Mariette or not." Only at this point does Gaston break down and return to Lily.

Unfortunately, Lubitsch seems not to embrace fully the consequences of this "suspension of the ethical." He sees marriage as the supreme transgression, as a daring conspiracy, but ultimately he opts for the placid old conservative *ménage à trois*. Lubitsch thus remains within the cynical position of respecting appearances while secretly transgressing them. So if Lubitsch does act as an analyst-director, the subjective position implied by his movies is close to that advocated by Jacques-Alain Miller, for whom a psychoanalyst

> occupies the position of the ironist who takes care not to intervene in the political field. He acts so that semblances remain at their places while making sure that subjects under his care do not take them for *real* … one should somehow bring oneself to remain *taken in by them* (fooled by them). Lacan could say that "those who are not taken in err": if one doesn't act as if semblances are real, if one doesn't leave their efficiency undisturbed, things take a turn for the worse. Those who think that all the signs of power are mere semblances and rely on the arbitrariness of the discourse of the master are bad boys: they are even more alienated.[17]

In the matter of politics, a psychoanalyst thus "doesn't propose projects, he cannot propose them, he can only mock the projects of others, which limits the scope of his statements. The ironist has no great design, he waits for the other to speak first and then brings about his fall as fast as possible … Let us say this is a political wisdom, nothing more."[18] The axiom of this "wisdom" is that

> one should protect the semblances of power for the good reason that one should be able to continue to *enjoy*. The point is not to attach oneself to the semblances of the existing power,

17   Nicolas Fleury, *Le réel insensé. Introduction à la pensée de Jacques-Alain Miller* (Paris: Germina, 2010), 93–4.
18   Jacques-Alain Miller, "La psychanalyse, la cité, les communautés," *La Cause freudienne* 68 (2008), 109–10.

but to consider them necessary. "This defines a cynicism in the mode of Voltaire who let it be understood that god is our invention which is necessary to maintain people in a proper decorum" (Miller). Society is held together only by semblances, "which means: there is no society without repression, without identification, and above all without routine. Routine is essential" (Miller).[19]

How can one miss here the echo of Kafka's *Trial* affirming the public Law and Order as a semblance which is not true but is nonetheless necessary? Having listened to the priest's explanation of the story about the Door of the Law, Joseph K. shakes his head and says:

> "I can't say I'm in complete agreement with this view, as if you accept it you'll have to accept that everything said by the doorkeeper is true. But you've already explained very fully that that's not possible." "No," said the priest, "you don't need to accept everything as true, you only have to accept it as necessary." "Depressing view," said K. "The lie made into the rule of the world."

Is this not also Lubitsch's basic position? Law and Order are a semblance, but we should pretend to respect them and meanwhile enjoy our small pleasures and other transgressions... Recall Heinrich Heine's well-known quip that one should value above all else "love, truth, freedom, and crab soup," "crab soup" standing here for all those small pleasures in the absence of which we become (mental, if not real) terrorists, following an abstract idea and forcing it onto reality without any consideration for the concrete circumstances. (We should note here that such a "wisdom" is precisely what Kierkegaard and Marx did *not* have in mind when they proposed their own versions of Heine's quip—"freedom, equality, property, *and Bentham*"; "officers, house maids, *and chimney sweepers*"—their message is rather the opposite one: that the principle itself, in its purity, is already stained by the particularity of the crab-soup element, i.e., the particularity sustains the very purity of the principle.)

Nowhere is this position of wisdom revealed more clearly than in *Heaven Can Wait* (1943). At the film's beginning, the old Henry van Cleve enters the opulent reception area of Hell and is personally greeted by "His Excellency" (the Devil) to whom he relates the story of his dissolute life so that his place in Hell can be

---

19 Fleury, *Le réel insensé*, 95.

determined. After hearing Henry's story, His Excellency, a charming old man, denies him entry and suggests he try "the other place," where his dead wife Martha and his good grandfather are waiting for him—there might be "a small room vacant in the annex" up there. So the Devil is nothing but God himself with a touch of wisdom, not taking prohibitions too seriously, well aware that small transgressions make us human... But if the Devil is a good and wise being, is it then God himself who is the true Evil, insofar as he lacks ironic wisdom and blindly insists on obedience to his Law?[20] Recall another nicely vulgar joke about Christ: the night before he was to be arrested and crucified, his disciples began to worry—Christ was still a virgin, so wouldn't it be nice for him to experience a little bit of pleasure before he dies? So they asked Mary Magdalene to go to the tent where Christ was resting and seduce him. Mary gladly agreed and went in, but five minutes later she ran out screaming, terrified and furious. The disciples asked her what had gone wrong, and she explained: "I slowly undressed, spread my legs and showed Christ my pussy; he took one look, said 'What a terrible wound! It should be healed!', and gently put his palm on it..." Beware, then, of people too intent on healing other people's wounds—there must be some trouble in paradise if we are to enjoy it.

Is this not the "dark and awful" secret at the very core of Christianity? In his religious thriller *The Man Who Was Thursday*, Chesterton tells the story of Gabriel Syme, a young Englishman who makes the archetypal Chestertonian discovery that order is the greatest miracle and orthodoxy the greatest of all rebellions. The focal figure of the novel, however, is not Syme himself, but the mysterious chief of a top-secret Scotland Yard unit who hires Syme. Syme's first duty is to penetrate the "Central Anarchist Council," the seven-member ruling body of a secret superpowerful organization bent on destroying our civilization. In order to preserve their anonymity, the members are known to each other only by days of the week. After some deft manipulation, Syme gets elected as "Thursday." At his first Council reunion, he meets "Sunday," the larger-than-life president of the Council, a big man of incredible authority, mocking irony, and jovial ruthlessness. In the ensuing series of adventures, Syme discovers that all the other members of the council are also secret agents, indeed members of the same secret unit as himself, hired by the same chief whose voice they've heard but whose face they've never seen.

---

20 There is a weird inconsistency in the figure of the Devil: he is evil embodied, he pushes us towards sin, but he is simultaneously the executioner of the punishment for our evil deeds, i.e., he runs Hell where we will be punished—how can the supreme criminal be the very agent of justice?

So they join forces and finally, at a lavish masked ball, confront Sunday. Here, the novel passes from mystery to metaphysical comedy, and we discover two surprising things. First, that Sunday, the president of the Anarchist Council, is the same person as the mysterious chief who has hired Syme and the others to fight the anarchists; second, that he is none other than God Himself. These discoveries, of course, trigger a series of perplexed reflections from Syme and the other agents—one of them notes, in a terse English-style remark: "It seems so silly that you should have been on both sides and fought yourself."[21] If ever there was a British Hegelianism, this is it—a literal transposition of Hegel's key thesis that, in fighting the alienated substance, the subject fights his own essence. The novel's hero, Syme, finally springs to his feet and, in a mad excitement, spells out the mystery:

> I see everything, everything that there is. Why does each thing on the earth war against each other thing? Why does each small thing in the world have to fight against the world itself? Why does a fly have to fight the whole universe? Why does a dandelion have to fight the whole universe? For the same reason that I had to be alone in the dreadful Council of the Days. So that each thing that obeys law may have the glory and isolation of the anarchist. So that each man fighting for order may be as brave and good a man as the dynamiter. So that the real lie of Satan may be flung back in the face of this blasphemer, so that by tears and torture we may earn the right to say to this man, "You lie!" No agonies can be too great to buy the right to say to this accuser, "We also have suffered."[22]

This, then, is the formula provided: "So that each thing that obeys law may have the glory and isolation of the anarchist." So that the Law is the greatest transgression, and the defender of the Law the greatest rebel. But where is the limit of this dialectic? *Does it hold also for God himself?* Is He, the embodiment of cosmic order and harmony, *also* the ultimate rebel, or is He a benign authority observing from a peaceful Above with bemused wisdom the follies and struggles of mortal men? Here is God's reply when Syme turns to him and asks "Have you ever suffered?"

> As [Syme] gazed, the great face grew to an awful size, grew larger than the colossal mask of Memnon, which had made him scream as a child. It grew larger and larger, filling the whole sky; then everything went black. Only in the blackness before it entirely destroyed his brain

---

21 G. K. Chesterton, *The Man Who Was Thursday* (Harmondsworth: Penguin, 1986), 180.
22 Ibid., 182–3.

The Devil forgives: "His Excellency" (Laird Cregar) and Henry van Cleve (Don Ameche). *Heaven Can Wait*

he seemed to hear a distant voice saying a commonplace text that he had heard somewhere, "Can ye drink of the cup that I drink of?"[23]

This final revelation—that God Himself suffers even more than us mortals—brings us to the fundamental insight of *Orthodoxy*, Chesterton's theological masterpiece (which belongs to the same period: he published it a year later than *Thursday*), not only the insight into how orthodoxy is the greatest transgression, the most rebellious and adventurous thing, but a much darker insight into the central mystery of Christianity:

> That a good man may have his back to the wall is no more than we knew already; but that God could have His back to the wall is a boast for all insurgents for ever. Christianity is the only religion on earth that has felt that omnipotence made God incomplete. Christianity alone has felt that God, to be wholly God, must have been a rebel as well as a king.[24]

Or, more precisely, that the conservative premise according to which it is better not to inquire into the origins of power (if we do, we'll find the crime of usurpation) holds also for God himself: God is also a rebel who has usurped the place of the king (and not just a king who plays at being a rebel in order to introduce some dynamism into the boring stale order of his creation). This last step into what Hegel would have called speculative identity is the one that Lubitsch was unable to take; it is what is absent from his universe. It is a limitation that can be felt in the pathetic moment in *To Be or Not to Be* when the old Jewish actor recites the famous lines from Shylock's speech in front of Hitler—the truly subversive thing would have been to imagine something like Hitler making the same speech if, by some miracle, he were to have been brought to trial at Nuremberg and accused of inhuman monstrosities: "I am a Nazi German. Hath not a Nazi eyes? Hath not a Nazi hands, organs, dimensions, senses, affections, passions? Fed with the same food, hurt with the same weapons, subject to the same diseases, healed by the same means, warmed and cooled by the same winter and summer, as a Jew is? If you prick us, do we not bleed? If you tickle us, do we not laugh? If you poison us, do we not die? And if you wrong us with your Jewish plot, shall we not revenge?" In short, the murdered Jews are just the "pound of flesh" extracted for

---

23 Ibid., 183.
24 Ibid.

all the injustices Germany has suffered in its recent history… Such a paraphrase is, of course, a disgusting obscenity—but it makes one thing clear: a general appeal to a shared humanity can cover up any particular horror; it holds as well for the victim as for his or her executioner. The truth of such an appeal would have been in its extreme form—imagine Shylock saying something like: "If we are constipated, don't we need a laxative? If we hear a dirty rumor, don't we like to spread it further just like you do? If we get a chance to steal or cheat, don't we take it just like you do?" The true defense of a Jew should not have been the appeal to a common humanity that we all share, but precisely an appeal to the specific and unique character of the Jews (it was, surprisingly, none other than Hegel who claimed that the problem with Napoleon's emancipation of Jews was not that it granted them full citizenship in spite—or irrespective of—their religion, but that it did not emancipate them on account of the special features that make them unique). It should not have been "You should accept us because, in spite of our differences, we are all human!", but "You should accept us because of what we are in our uniqueness!"

Not all of Lubitsch's work can be reduced to this position of a humanist cynical wisdom—in many of his films (*Broken Lullaby*, *To Be or Not to Be*…) there are elements which point to an uncanny dimension beyond wisdom, and his last (completed) film, *Cluny Brown*, definitely leaves wisdom behind, effecting a kind of "epistemological break" in Lubitsch's oeuvre—but this is already a topic for another analysis.[25] The question we should approach in conclusion is this: since Lubitsch's films are clearly marked by their era, what would today's version of the Lubitsch touch look like? Let us make a detour through two exemplary movies: Neil Jordan's *The Crying Game* (1992) and David Cronenberg's *M. Butterfly* (1998).

In spite of their fundamentally different character, both films tell the story of a man passionately in love with a beautiful woman who turns out to be a man dressed up as a woman (the transvestite in *The Crying Game*, the opera singer in *M. Butterfly*), and the central scenes in both films revolve around the man's traumatic confrontation with the fact that the object of his love is also a man. Why is this confrontation with the lover's body such a trauma? Not because the subject encounters something alien, but because what he confronts is the core fantasy that sustains his desire. The structure of the heterosexual love of the man is homosexual, sustained by the fantasy that the woman is a man dressed up as a

---

25   For a close reading of *Cluny Brown* see Alenka Zupančič's chapter in this volume.

woman. Here we see what it means to traverse the fantasy—it does not mean seeing through it to perceive the reality it obfuscates, but confronting the fantasy as such—once we do so, its hold over us (the subject) is suspended. Once the hero of *The Crying Game* or *M. Butterfly* confronts the fact, the game is over (with different results, of course: a happy ending in one case, a suicide in the other).

What is the solution here? How do we break out of this deadlock? We can do so by re-framing the universal dimension itself, by imposing a new universality which will encompass all the desired particularity. To conclude, let us take another example from contemporary cinema: *Strella* by Panos Koutras (2009). Having been turned down by both state funding bodies and all the major production companies, Koutras was obliged to make his film without any financial support whatsoever, and so *Strella* became a completely independent production with nearly all the roles played by non-professionals. The result was a cult movie which went on to win numerous prizes. Here is the story: Yiorgos is released from jail after 14 years for a murder he committed in his small Greek village. (He found his 17-year-old brother playing sex games with his 5-year-old son and, in a fit of rage, he killed him.) During his long stay in prison he lost contact with his son, Leonidas, whom he now tries to trace. He spends his first night out of jail in a cheap downtown hotel in Athens, where he meets Strella, a young transsexual prostitute. They spend the night together and soon fall in love. Yiorgos is accepted by the circle of Strella's tranny friends, and he admires her personification of Maria Callas. However, he soon discovers that Strella *is* his son Leonidas: she had known this all along, having followed him when he left prison and waited for him in the corridor of the hotel. At first she had just wanted to see him, but after he made a pass at her she went along with it. Traumatized, Yiorgos initially runs away and breaks down, but the couple reestablish contact and discover that, in spite of the impossibility of continuing their sexual relation, they really care for each other. Gradually they work out a modus vivendi. The final scene takes place at a New Year's celebration: Strella, her friends and Yiorgos all gather at her place, along with a small child that Strella has decided to take care of, the son of a deceased friend. The child gives body to their love *and* to the deadlock of their relationship.

Strella takes perversion to its (ridiculously sublime) end: the traumatic discovery is repeated. Early on in the film, Yiorgos discovers that the beloved/desired woman is a transvestite and accepts this without further ado: when he realizes that his partner is a man, the partner simply says "I am a tranny. Do you have a problem with that?", and they go on kissing and embracing. The truly traumatic discovery comes only later, when Yiorgos realizes that Strella is his own son and has knowingly seduced him—here, his reaction is the same as that of Fergus confronted with Dil's penis in *The Crying Game*: shattering disgust followed by escape, wandering around the city unable to cope with the revelation. The outcome is also similar to *The Crying Game*—the trauma is overcome through love, and a happy family with a small son emerges.

The production notes describe *Strella* as "the kind of story told at dinner parties, a kind of urban legend"—which means that we should not read it in the same way as *The Crying Game*. The hero's discovery that his transvestite lover is his son is not the actualization of some unconscious fantasy, his disgust is truly just a reaction to a sudden bad revelation. In other words, we should resist the temptation to mobilize the psychoanalytic apparatus in order to interpret a case of father-son incest: there is nothing to interpret here, the situation at the end of the film is *completely normal*, that of a genuinely happy family. Treated as such, the film lays down a challenge to the advocates of Christian family values: embrace *this* authentic family of Yiorgos, Strella, and their adopted child, or shut up about Christianity. The family that emerges at the film's end is a properly sacred family: something like God the father living with Christ and fucking him—the ultimate gay marriage *plus* parental incest—a triumphant re-framing of the fantasy.

This is how we should deal with Christian family values: the only way to redeem them is to redefine or reframe the family so that it includes the situation at the end of *Strella* as its exemplary case. *This* is Lubitsch for today, the repetition of his famous "touch"—even if the family of father and son violates all divine prohibitions, one can be sure that for them there will always be "a small room vacant in the annex" of Heaven.

Contributors

Elisabeth Bronfen is Professor of English and American Studies at the University of Zurich and, since 2007, Global Distinguished Professor at New York University. Her publications include: *Home in Hollywood: The Imaginary Geography of Cinema* (Columbia University Press, 2004); a cultural history of the night, *Night Passages: Literature, Philosophy, Film* (Columbia University Press, 2013); and *Specters of War: Hollywood's Engagement with Military Conflict* (Rutgers University Press, 2012).

Mladen Dolar is a Professor at the Department of Philosophy, University of Ljubljana, and the author of a dozen books in Slovene as well as numerous papers and book chapters in many languages. His main focus is on German idealism and the Lacanian psychoanalysis, and his most recent book in English is *A Voice and Nothing More* (MIT, 2006).

Russell Grigg practices psychoanalysis in Melbourne and teaches at Deakin University. A member of the École de la cause freudienne (Paris) and the Lacan Circle of Melbourne (Melbourne), he has been closely involved in the translation of Lacan into English, having translated Lacan's *Seminar III: The Psychoses* and *Seminar XVII: The Other Side of Psychoanalysis* and collaborated with Bruce Fink on the translation of *Écrits*. He has published on questions of logic, language, and ethics, as well as on clinical issues concerning psychosis and neurosis. His *Lacan, Language and Philosophy* is published by SUNY Press (2008).

Tatjana Jukić is Professor of English Literature at the University of Zagreb. She is the author of two books, *Revolution and Melancholia: Limits of Literary Memory* (*Revolucija i melankolija. Granice pamćenja hrvatske književnosti*, Naklada Ljevak, 2011), and *Liking, Dislike, Supervision: Literature and the Visual in Victorian Britain* (*Zazor, nadzor, sviđanje. Dodiri književnog i vizualnog u britanskom devetnaestom stoljeću*, Zavod za znanost o književnosti FF sveučilišta, 2002). She has also written several articles, in English and in Croatian, on nineteenth- and twentieth-century literature, psychoanalysis, film and philosophy.

Jela Krečič is a philosopher and journalist at the cultural department of the Slovenian daily newspaper *Delo*. She is the author of several theoretical articles focused on aesthetical problems, contemporary art and film theory. She co-edited *Contemporary TV Series and Seriality*

(*Sodobna TV serija in serialnost*, Slovenska kinoteka, 2012) and the original Slovenian edition of *Lubitsch Can't Wait*.

GREGOR MODER works as a researcher at the Faculty of Arts, University of Ljubljana. He is a member of the editorial board of *Problemi*, the Slovenian journal for philosophy, psychoanalysis and culture. Recently, he researched comedy at the Jan van Eyck Academy in Maastricht and taught Philosophy of Art at the University of Ljubljana. His monograph *Hegel und Spinoza: Negativität in der gegenwärtigen Philosophie* appeared with Turia+Kant in 2013.

IVANA NOVAK is a film critic and editor. She contributes articles to Slovenian magazines, notably *KINO!*, *revija za filmsko*, and *Delo*, and frequently collaborates with the Programme and Research department of the Slovenian Cinematheque. She coedited *Contemporary TV Series and Seriality* (*Sodobna TV serija in serialnost*, Slovenska kinoteka, 2012) and the original Slovenian edition of *Lubitsch Can't Wait*.

ROBERT PFALLER is Professor of Philosophy at the University of Applied Arts in Vienna and a founding member of the Viennese psychoanalytic research group "stuzzicadenti". In 2007 he was awarded "The Missing Link" prize for connecting psychoanalysis with other scientific disciplines, by Psychoanalytisches Seminar Zurich. His most recent publications include *The Pleasure Principle in Culture: Illusions without Owners* (Verso, 2013) and *Zweite Welten und andere Lebenselixiere* (Fischer, 2012).

AARON SCHUSTER teaches on the Theory Program at the Sandberg Institute, Amsterdam, and is a fellow at the Institute for Cultural Inquiry, Berlin. He is an editor-at-large at *Cabinet* magazine, to which he frequently contributes. His book *The Trouble With Pleasure: Deleuze and Psychoanalysis* is forthcoming from MIT Press in 2014.

ALENKA ZUPANČIČ is a research adviser at the Institute of Philosophy of the Slovenian Academy of Sciences and Arts and visiting professor at the European Graduate School. She is the author of numerous articles and books, including *The Shortest Shadow: Nietzsche's Philosophy of the Two* (MIT Press, 2003), *The Odd One In: On Comedy* (MIT Press, 2008), and *Ethics of the Real: Kant and Lacan* (Verso, 2012).

SLAVOJ ŽIŽEK is a senior researcher in the Institute for Sociology and Philosophy at the University of Ljubljana, international director of the Birkbeck Institute for the Humanities, and a professor of philosophy and psychoanalysis at the European Graduate School. His recent titles include *Living in the End Times* (Verso, 2011), and *Less Than Nothing: Hegel And The Shadow Of Dialectical Materialism* (Verso, 2012).

Index

Ernst Lubitsch abbreviated as E.L.

Allen, Woody **69**, **168**n
Als ich tot war (E.L.) **ix**
Althusser, Louis **122**n**18**
Anna Christie (Clarence Brown) **96**
Anna Karenina (Clarence Brown) **106**
Arendt, Hannah **98**, **100**
Aristotle **54**, **57**, **111**
Armand, Inessa **186**
Arsenic and Old Lace (Frank Capra) **51**
Assange, Julian **68**
Assmann, Jan **73**
Atkinson, Rowan **51**
Atwill, Lionel **138**
Aurelius, Marcus **74**
Austerlitz, Saul **43**
Awful Truth, The (Leo McCarey) **69**, **79**

Bandits (Barry Levinson) **66**
Barnes, Peter **120**
Baron Cohen, Sacha **166**
Barthes, Roland **91**
Beast of Berlin (Sherman Scott) **134**
Being There (Hal Ashby) **163**n
Benjamin, Walter **88**
Benny, Jack **99**, **121**, **124**, **127**–**8**, **138**–**9**, **146**, **149**
Bergson, Henri **3**n, **162**n**10**
Blanchett, Cate **66**
Bluebeard's Eighth Wife (E.L.) **40**–**1**

Bodenheimer, Aron Ronald **121**–**3**
Bogdanovich, Peter **44**
Bonello, Bertrand **68**
Borat: Cultural Learnings of America for Make Benefit Glorious Nation of Kazakhstan (Larry Charles) **166**
Boyer, Charles **170**
Brackett, Charles **42**
Brecht, Bertolt **10**, **193**
Breillat, Catherine **68**
Bressart, Felix **134**, **139**, **142**–**3**, **146**–**8**
Breuer, Josef **92**
Brief Encounter (David Lean) **48**, **62**
Broken Lullaby (E.L.) **182**
Bronfen, Elisabeth **3**, **6**
Brüno (Larry Charles) **166**
Buffon, Comte de **25**, **27**
Buñuel, Luis **114**n

Callas, Maria **204**
Casablanca (Michael Curtiz) **140**
Cavell, Stanley **51**, **68**, **91**–**9**, **109**–**10**, **140**
Chaplin, Charlie **vii**, **12**, **17**, **72**, **114**, **118**, **126**, **154**, **159**
Chéreau, Patrice **68**
Chesterton, G.K. **186**, **194**, **199**, **202**
Chevalier, Maurice **3**, **45**
Cioran, Emil **27**–**8**, **190**
City Lights (Charlie Chaplin) **126**
Clair, René **114**n
Claire, Ina **84**

Claudel, Paul **165**
Cluny Brown (E.L.) **17**, **22**, **80**, **107**, **165–79**
Colbert, Claudette **40**
Conway, Jack **66**
Cooper, Gary **40**
Coward, Noël **185**
Cronenberg, David **203**
Crying Game, The (Neil Jordan) **203–5**
Cukor, George **94**

Deleuze, Gilles **24**, **92**, **98–9**, **103–4**, **106–10**
Derrida, Jacques **122**, **155–6**, **158**
Descartes, René **122n18**
Design for Living (E.L.) **7**, **65–7**, **73**, **76–8**, **80**,
   185–6, **192**, **194**
Dessuant, Pierre **73n15**
Dolar, Mladen **3**, **9**, **152n**
Double Wedding (Richard Thorpe) **66**
Douglas, Melvyn **84**, **95**, **104**, **109**
Dugan, Tom **134**
Durgnat, Raymond **20**

Easton, Dossie **78**
Emerson, R.W. **93**
Engels, Friedrich **81**, **86**, **128**

Faller, Greg S. **43**
Fénelon, François **24**
Fonda, Henry **110**
Fonteyne, Frédéric **68**
Ford, John **78**
Foucault, Michel **74n21**, **86**, **88**, **101**, **108–9**
Francis, Kay **22**, **35**, **42**, **45**, **58**, **63**, **79**,
   102n40
Freud, Sigmund **14**, **24–5**, **52**, **74n18**, **76**,
   81, **90n10**, **92**, **103**, **108–9**, **122n17**, **131**,
   *Group Psychology and the Analysis of the
   Ego* **54**, **78**, *Jokes and Their Relation to*
   the Unconscious **28**, **42**, **48**, **50**, **72**, and
   melancholia **88–9**, **91**, **94–5**, *Three Essays
   on the Theory of Sexuality* **73**
Fristoe, Roger **43**, **75**
Fuller, Samuel **131**
Fussell, Paul **131**

Garbo, Greta **83–4**, **86–8**, **90–6**, **98**, **102**, **104**,
   106–7, **109–10**, and laughter **12**, **14**, **87–8**,
   95–6
Genet, Jean **157**, **160n**
Giraudoux, Jean **125**
Good Neighbor Sam (David Swift) **66**
Graduate, The (Mike Nichols) **81**
Granach, Alexander **91**
Grant, Cary **46**, **51**, **110**
Great Dictator, The (Charlie Chaplin) **72**,
   114, **118–9**, **154**, **156**, **159–60**
Grigg, Russell **5**, **196**
Grunberger, Béla **73n15**
Guédiguian, Robert **68**

Halton, Charles **134**
Hardy, Janet W. **78**
Harlow, Jean **66**, **79**
Harvey, James **35–6**, **83**, **95**, **104n42**, **118–9**
Hawks, Howard **94**, **195**
Heaven Can Wait (E.L.) **vii**, **198**
Hegel, G.W.F. **viii**, **111**, **115**, **122n18**, **128**, **200**,
   202–3
Heidegger, Martin **122n18**, **176**
Heine, Heinrich **198**
Hepburn, Audrey **91**
Hepburn, Katharine **110**
Hergé (Georges Remi) **52**
His Girl Friday (Howard Hawks) **79**, **94**, **110**
Hitchcock, Alfred **vii**, **4**, **27**, **37**, **46**, **97**, **112**,
   114, **140n**, **194**

Hitler, Adolf 113, 170, in Lubitsch's cinema
    9, 67, 70, 99n34, 100, 107, 119, 126–7,
    133–6, 141–6, 152–3, 157, 159n, 202
Hoffmann, E.T.A. 191
Hopkins, Miriam 22, 40, 43–4, 79, 102n40
Horton, Edward Everett 51
Houellebecq, Michel 68

I Love You Again (W.S. Van Dyke) 66
Ice Storm, The (Ang Lee) 68
Ich möchte kein Mann sein (E.L.) 7
Intimité (Patrice Chéreau) 68

Jankélévitch, Vladimir 41
Jones, Jennifer 168
Jordan, Neil 203
Jukić, Tatjana 12, 14, 90
Jules et Jim (François Truffaut) 68

Kachelmann, Jörg 68
Kael, Pauline 39n, 182
Kafka, Franz 161, 198
Kanin, Garson 66
Kant, Immanuel 122n18, 188, 190
Katz, Ephraim 43
Kierkegaard, Søren 197–8
Kinsey, Alfred 81
Kiss Me Again (E.L.) 66
Kiss Me, Stupid (Billy Wilder) 66
Kleist, Heinrich von 125, 188, 190
Koutras, Panos 204

Lacan, Jacques 1, 15, 23n, 25, 27, 50, 122n18,
    125, 197, and comedy 157–8, 160n, 166–7,
    and desire 178, and law 98, 100, 108–9,
    and love 41, 79, 183, and style 25–7
Lady Eve, The (Preston Sturges) 94, 110
Lanchester, John 29

Lee, Ang 68
Lejeune, C. A. 105
Lenin, Vladimir Ilyich 186–7
Leone, Sergio 27
Levinson, Barry 66
Lewis, Michael 29
Liaison pornographique, Une (Frédéric
    Fonteyne) 68
Libeled Lady (Jack Conway) 66, 79–80
Lifeboat (Alfred Hitchcock) 114
Lombard, Carole 67, 99, 132, 135, 138–9,
    140n
Love Parade, The (E.L.) 66
Loy, Myrna 66
Lubitsch touch 1, 5, 19–20, 23n, 24–5, 27, 38,
    42–4, 47, 60, 65, 99, 128, 152, 185, 192,
    203, 205
Lugosi, Bela 86–7, 89–90, 98, 100, 106
Lynch, David 122

M. Butterfly (David Cronenberg) 203–4
Macdonald, Dwight 39, 48
Mannoni, Octave 71
Marie-Jo et ses deux amours (Robert
    Guédiguian) 68
Marks, Scott 43
Marriage Circle, The (E.L.) 66
Marshall, Herbert 22, 40, 42, 44–6, 63, 79,
    102n40
Marx, Karl 11, 86, 128, 196, 198
Mast, Gerald 20
Mayer, Edwin Justus 113
McCarey, Leo 69
Miller, Jacques-Alain 197–8
Millet, Cathérine 68
Moder, Gregor 6
Modern Times (Charlie Chaplin) 12
Molière 125

Monsieur Verdoux (Charlie Chaplin) **126**

Monte Carlo (E.L.) **2, 7**

Mozart, Wolfgang Amadeus **48, 192**

Mr. and Mrs. Smith (Alfred Hitchcock) **140n**

Mussolini, Benito **113**

My Favorite Wife (Garson Kanin) **66**

My Man Godfrey (Gregory La Cava) **132**

Napoleon **203**

Napoleon III **128**

Nichols, Mike **81**

Ninotchka (E.L.) **9, 12, 14, 16, 29, 83–110, 166, 191**

Niven, David **83**

North by Northwest (Alfred Hitchcock) **98**

Nothing Sacred (William A. Wellman) **132**

Offenbach, Jacques **191**

One Hour With You (E.L.) **3**

Parmenides **22**

Party, The (Blake Edwards) **163n**

Parvulescu, Anca **161**

Pascal, Blaise **67, 126**

Paul, William **36**

Perkins, Anthony **171**

Pfaller, Robert **4, 6, 125, 152–3, 164**

Philadelphia Story, The (George Cukor) **94, 110**

Phillips, Adam **65**

Pickford, Mary **20, 36**

Pink Panther, The (Blake Edwards) **163n**

Pippin, Robert **195**

Plato **22**

Plautus *Amphitruo, Maenechmi* **125**, *Miles Gloriousus* **166**

Poague, Leland **43**

Poe, Edgar Allan **194n13**

Pornographe, Le (Bertrand Bonello) **68**

Powell, Dilys **115**

Powell, William **66, 79**

Preminger, Otto **6**

Psycho (Alfred Hitchcock) **171**

Puppe, Die (E.L.) **187, 191**

Raphaelson, Samson **20, 44**

Red River (Howard Hawks) **195**

Reinhardt, Max **44, 119**

Ridges, Stanley **140**

Riefenstahl, Leni **114n**

Romance XXX (Catherine Breillat) **68**

Ruggles, Charles **51**

Ruman, Sig **145**

Russell, Rosalind **110**

Sacher-Masoch, Leopold von **103**

Sade, Marquis de **184**

Sallitt, Dan **45, 48**

Sandler, Adam **51**

Sartre, Jean-Paul **45**

Schiller, Friedrich **78**

Schuster, Aaron **1, 5, 8, 10, 194n**

Scoop (Woody Allen) **69**

Scorsese, Martin **27**

Scott, Sherman **134**

Seeßlen, Georg **67, 112n, 115n, 118–9n**

Sellers, Peter **163n**

Sennett, Richard **80–1**

Shakespeare, William **51, 124, 135–6, 141–3, 145–6, 148–9**, *The Comedy of Errors* **125**, *Hamlet* **100, 107–8n, 113, 120–1, 123–4, 127, 132–3, 136, 138, 141–3**, *The Merchant of Venice* **87, 108n, 113, 132, 138, 143**, Shylock **113, 142–9, 202–3**

Shop Around the Corner, The (E.L.) **16, 106n45, 107, 183**

Socrates 22, 122n18
Some Like It Hot (Billy Wilder) 69, 74
Spinoza, Baruch 122n18
Stack, Robert 138
Stagecoach (John Ford) 78
Stanwyck, Barbara 110
Stiller, Ben 51
Strangers on a Train (Alfred Hitchcock) 194n13
Strauss-Kahn, Dominique 68
Strella (Panos Koutras) 204–5
Sturges, Preston 94, 102n39
Sullivan's Travels (Preston Sturges) 102n39
Sundermeier, Theo 73
Swift, David 66

Tarkovsky, Andrei 27
That Uncertain Feeling (E.L.) 16, 24, 66
Thornton, Billy Bob 66
Thorpe, Richard 66
To Be or Not to Be (E.L.) 6, 9, 16, 19, 26, 29, 65, 67, 69–71, 76, 99–100, 106n45, 107, 111–5, 126, 132–4, 136, 140, 144, 148, 151, 154–5, 157, 159–60, 183, 202–3, Hamlet's monologue 120–4, 127, 138
To Catch a Thief (Alfred Hitchcock) 46
Tolstoy, Lev Nikolayevich 106
Trevor, Claire 78
Triumph des Willens (Leni Riefenstahl) 114n
Trouble in Paradise (E.L.) 5, 9–10, 12, 16, 20, 23–5, 32, 35, 38–9, 42–64, 76, 79–80, 102n40, 103, 105, 185, 191–2, 194–6
Truffaut, François 19, 23n, 38, 68

Van Dyke, W.S. 66
Villiers de L'Isle-Adam, Auguste 41n
Virgil 89
Voltaire 198

Wallace, Richard 43
Watzlawick, Paul 75n22, 98
Wayne, John 78
Weinberg, Herman G. 44
Welles, Orson 112
Wilder, Billy 6, 39–40, 42–3, 66, 120
Willis, Bruce 66
Woods, Tiger 181

You've Got Mail (Nora Ephron) 183

Zupančič, Alenka 14n, 15, 17, 75n23, 98n31, 108, 157n, 162–3, 196

Žižek, Slavoj 8, 119

LIST OF ILLUSTRATIONS

Portrait of Ernst Lubitsch by Alexander Binder, 1920 (PD): **vi**

The following archives provided the illustrations appearing on the pages indicated:

Slovenian Cinematheque Archive: **13, 85**

Collection Austrian Film Museum: **33, 49, 55, 77, 105, 117, 137**

The Royal Belgian Filmarchive: **169, 175**

Deutsche Kinemathek Photo Archive: **189**

All other illustrations, mostly appearing in small format, were captured from film.